Mermaid

Mermaid

A memoir of resilience   **EILEEN CRONIN**

W. W. Norton & Company | *New York · London*

For information about permission to reproduce selections from this book,
write to Permissions, W. W. Norton & Company, Inc.,
500 Fifth Avenue, New York, NY 10110

For information about special discounts for bulk purchases, please contact
W. W. Norton Special Sales at specialsales@wwnorton.com or 800-233-4830

Manufacturing by RR Donnelley, Harrisonburg
Book design by Chris Welch
Production manager: Devon Zahn

Library of Congress Cataloging-in-Publication Data

Cronin, Mary Eileen.
Mermaid : a memoir of resilience / Eileen Cronin. — First edition.
pages cm
ISBN 978-0-393-08901-1 (hardcover)
1. Cronin, Mary Eileen. 2. People with disabilities—United States—Biography.
3. Women with disabilities—United States—Biography. I. Title.
HV3013.C76A3 2014
362.4'3092—dc23
[B]
                    2013036717

W. W. Norton & Company, Inc.
500 Fifth Avenue, New York, N.Y. 10110
www.wwnorton.com

W. W. Norton & Company Ltd.
Castle House, 75/76 Wells Street, London W1T 3QT

1 2 3 4 5 6 7 8 9 0

For my parents, who showed me how to love and persevere, and for Andy and Ania Sophia, who make both very easy to do.

Contents

Author's Note

The events in this story are told as I remember them, except that I have changed names and minor details relating to individuals and establishments in order to respect their privacy. Where dialogue appears, I strived to re-create the essence of conversations, in both content and delivery, since it was not possible to recall the precise words.

Mermaid

A long the oceanfront at dusk, my friends drag me past the fern bars and wet T-shirt contests to catch up to the aerobic pulse from the disco ahead, which we call "flashback" because its flashing lights leave you with a psychedelic impression of dancing dots when you come back onto the street. We enter when the bar is as black as the inside of a pocket. White light blinds us before a series of colors flicker.

I rush ahead to join Heidi and Jennifer, who have earned our pledge class's reputation as the prettiest girls on campus (although I may be responsible for our "partyest girls" reputation). Because of Heidi and Jennifer, we are quickly greeted by a couple of football players from Notre Dame. Standing beside these two girls from my sorority, I could pass as their biological sister. We have tanned faces, copper-feathered hair and golden highlights—Farrah Fawcett–style—along with upturned noses and pointed chins, though typically I do not carry mine as high as the others. Back in Cincinnati, I am "that girl who was born without legs." Yet here on spring break in Fort Lauderdale I become a beautiful girl with a limp.

The place is crowded and smells of stale beer. A sandy-blond guy with Donny Osmond teeth makes eye contact with me. I'm handed a daiquiri with a parasol and a cherry on a spear. Half of the drink is down before it freezes my brain. Over the rim of my hurricane glass I see the sandy-blond crossing the dance floor. I jam the cherry into my mouth, and when he taps my shoulder I swallow it whole. Speakers coo "How Deep Is Your Love?" I glance up and this guy is grinning at me. His lashes are longer than mine.

See, I say to myself, if not for the legs I could be another Heidi or Jennifer. I've been telling myself this line all year, only now I've got this sandy-blond guy to prove it. He is the most handsome man in the bar, this boy from where? Vanderbilt.

He wants to know about me, so I tell him I'm the highest-seeded tennis player on our varsity team—a freshman, at that.

My friends stop flirting with their fan club. Twin Farrahs turn to face me.

I'm terrified and exhilarated all at once, heart ricocheting against the walls of my chest.

This button-down boy is with me, though. He's riding the roller-coaster grandeur of a wounded tennis star. He grabs a chair and he's nodding his head; yes, he can see that, the bit about my athletic prowess. He squeezes my biceps. Only a tennis player could have arms like those, he says. Heidi and Jennifer bite down on a snort. I blush, and my sunburned cheeks break into a sweat. I do not explain that biceps like these come from lifting the dead weight of my entire being every time I get out of a chair. Instead I say I tripped on a tennis ball that got under my feet, don't know how it happened, both ankles twisted, and here I am: a limping tennis star.

Heidi's hazel eyes expand to impossible proportions. In the morning we'll have mimosas, poolside, where we'll laugh about taking our mothers' schoolgirl pranks to a new level. (My mom used to spy from Heidi's mother's front porch on my dad, while he was being stood up on her own doorstep across the street.) I have three older sisters, and I could write a book: *The Art of Coquetry*. But honestly, because of my legs, my allegiance is with the jilted party.

Tonight, however, I take the opportunity to run with the pack of popular girls. Maybe I could break a heart?

The sandy-blond guy says he could see something like this clumsy, tennis-ball stuff happening, stuff like that happens to him all the time, but what the hell? Should we dance? Could we dance with the limp and all?

I shake my head no but he's already standing with his hand out, the silver-studded disco ball dangling over him with its million tiny mirrors reminding me that I'm a one-in-a-million girl—and that right now I want to be one of the other 999,999. I stand up and my knee (the only one I have) begins to wobble. Colored light beams snap and scatter from the rotating ball. As soon as I accept his hand my knee steadies itself.

On our way to the dance floor he says, you sure screwed up those ankles, and I think, I'm just glad they're attached to my feet. I don't tell him I once stepped out of my car to find that the foot with which I'd been driving was still on the floorboard.

Mobs of couples jam onto the dance floor. My man in pink cotton takes me in his arms for this slow dance. I look up at his smile and feel a pang of concern: the lie.

And yet it is so intoxicating, this lie. I want to keep it going. I can't believe he's picked me. Or maybe this is how it should always be. Why not? The song ends before I'm ready to let it go and we are hurled into "Stayin' Alive."

I clap for my partner, mesmerized by his John Travolta hips. No man in Cincinnati moves his pelvis like that. He takes my hands in his and gives me an easy twirl. I'm light as a spirit, ready to soar.

He sees that and now he's grinning; he has plans for us. In an instant he's grasping my waist and lifting me up. Am I spinning?

We gain momentum, and I'm reminded of my legs just as the left one comes loose. No, I scream, as he twirls me at top speed.

The left leg launches from my lemon-yellow corduroys, the penny loafer guiding the missile into the mob.

"NOW! Put me down NOW!"

He finally hears me and puts me down. I crumple to the floor, a one-legged Raggedy Ann, in the midst of a throbbing disco. My partner is still dancing, not realizing what's happened. His face earnest, sincere, he's reaching for the ghost-partner in front of him.

But which one of us is more naïve? He only asked for a dance. What was I expecting? Was it selfish of me to want to be beautiful just this once without disclaimers, riders, or caveats? I'm eighteen. Am I not entitled to a few delusions of grandeur? Right now I'd settle for being just another face in the crowd because here on the floor I'm about to be trampled while above me the lyrics taunt: *Ah ha ha . . .*

I have to get that leg. The crowd is drunk, and a wooden leg would make a nice fraternity souvenir. One last time I glance back at the sandy blond in his pink oxford shirt, still dancing. He doesn't even notice me, the girl who now wriggles away on her elbows. And if he does, he doesn't follow.

CHAPTER I

Tracing the Blue Light

I was almost four when it first occurred to me that no one else was missing legs. Flooded by questions without words to articulate them, I connected images with explanations. Those first confusing moments unravel in my mind like an old film. It begins with me being nudged awake by a waxy moon spilling silver-white light through the window as I sucked my thumb. But it wasn't my window. I grabbed the bars to pull myself up and thought, "Where am I?"

I held my breath and searched for clues. Below was a driveway. My parents' Volkswagens were not in it. I found instead a pearl-blue station wagon with pointed tailfins. A scary tree shook its fists at the moon, and I drew back. My bedroom was square and yellow and brand-new; this one was an attic with a gray-blue wall curling into its ceiling.

Quickly I grabbed my Gaga Bobo, stuffed a corner under my nose, shoved my thumb back into my mouth. In this aqua blanket with its frayed edges I smelled home: warm laundry, bacon frying, coffee and cigarettes.

Then I saw the black-and-white portrait of a baby crowned by a golden hula hoop: my cousin's baby Jesus. I whipped my head to the opposite wall and saw on the nightstand a pair of cat's-eye glasses. In the bed, I found blond hair awash in moonlight: my cousin Sally. Her hair was lighter than mine, but we shared the same bowl-shaped haircut.

I tottered backward onto the mattress. How did I get here?

Sally was a year younger than me but she had a real bed, and I still had a crib. The assignment of beds—who had a real bed and who didn't—puzzled me.

I did not remember rolling off my parents' bed when I was six months old and breaking my femur, the only bone in my right leg. There was something bigger than a bed troubling me, though, and I wondered if it had to do with legs. Sally had two legs and a bunch of toes, whereas mine ended at the knee, one above and one below it. I wasn't concerned about the missing fingers on my left hand, which had been "webbed" until a surgeon reconstructed it. My sisters Rosa and Liz called it "the claw," lovingly at times, and at other times I was not so sure.

Right now I was focused on legs, and I wondered if grown-up beds were only for people with two whole legs. When would I get some? What if they didn't grow in? These mysteries mounted until I hurled myself against the bars of the crib and found my voice, a wrathful screech, bold and steady. My chest pressed into the foot of the crib, arms outstretched through bars, I wailed at an open door to an empty staircase.

Soon Aunt Gert climbed those stairs and scooped me up. I relaxed. "Oh, oh, oh," she whispered, her voice soothing in that it matched my mother's, then agitating because it wasn't Mom's. Gert's arms were sturdier than my mother's, and she sang "Goodnight, My Someone." Every year she starred in Saint Vivian's variety show: a bulky woman best known for roller skating in a clown suit while singing "I'm the Greatest Star" and playing a violin. Right now I wanted Mom's meager voice and made-up lyrics to songs no one sings anymore: *Whaddaya know, Joe Joe from Kokomo?*

Before my aunt had children, she was a psychiatric nurse at the state mental hospital. Since then, she'd become every child's mother and every adult's best friend. I looked into her eyes and she explained that my family was on vacation. They would be back for me. Soon.

This was a soothing thought until I made the connection: my family had chosen to go on vacation without me. There were eight of us kids by then. Why was I the one they left behind?

I screamed loud and long, hoping to reach my parents wherever they had gone.

While I bellowed from my aunt's Tudor home on a street lined with buckeye and oak trees in Cincinnati, my family was apparently trekking north to a lakeshore cottage in Michigan along with a caravan of other Catholic families. Our father owned a Volkswagen dealership. He had brought home a sleek new camper with a kitchenette, polished wooden cabinets, and foldout beds. My brother Frankie and I had built forts in it all week. *Frankie couldn't have known they would leave without me.*

Exhausted, I fell asleep.

Over the next week I basked in the attention of my aunt. At home I competed with seven siblings by wrapping myself around Mom's ankles to bend her to my will. Here, Aunt Gert doted on my cousin and me. She lulled us with her violin. In her cramped kitchen she mashed pork fat with oatmeal and sculpted a loaf, which she fried up in patties. Geotta! Sally ate it with maple syrup; at home we ate the store-bought kind with ketchup. Out back my aunt pinned up the wet clothes while we hid in the sheets. On my hands and knees, I "squiddled," which was the word my sister Rosa gave to my idea of walking: a cross between crawling and running on my knees. Sally didn't note the difference; she just chased me around on her knees.

Twenty-five years later, Aunt Gert would remind me of that day under the canopy of drying sheets when I picked up my cousin's shoe and tried to put it on my own leg. Of course it didn't fit. I'd forgotten about the incident with the shoe, though I never forgot that moment in the crib when I began to see that I was different. I'm not sure why my parents didn't include me in the vacation. Maybe they assumed I'd have more fun with Sally, but in my four-year-old mind I believed my legs were to blame.

The week with my aunt gave me time to ease into the idea of being different. I doubt that my placement with Aunt Gert was planned for this purpose, and yet I couldn't have found myself in more comforting arms for such an event. No one in my family would have imagined that I might connect my family's trip to my legs and abandonment. Until I grew to adulthood I would not fully realize the crucial role that Aunt Gert had played in my life, nor would I notice the similarities between my closest high school friend and Aunt Gert. Each exuded warmth, stability, intelligence, and a sense of humor, all qualities valued by the women in my home, although at home sense of humor topped the list, with intelligence next but only in the service of a sharp wit. Otherwise, according to Mom, intelligence could handicap a woman. As for stability and warmth? Both were considered excellent qualities to have *in a friend*.

If Gert had been everyone's mother and best friend, her sister Joy, our mother, was everyone's muse: part Blanche DuBois, part circus trainer, and mostly a pregnant Lucille Ball. While Aunt Gert skated her way to stardom in the Saint Vivian's variety show, Mom was placed front and center in the opening act of a chorus belting out something about the greatest show on earth. It was the yellow evening gown with the bejeweled neckline and the slit revealing her tanned calf that won Mom the spotlight, although the chorus might have been better served by placing Mom in the back row, or at least requiring her to simply mouth the words because she affected an Ethel Merman posture, outstretched arms casting a shadow over the faces of the others while she crooned in a voice closer to marmot than Merman. She didn't mind it a bit when we heckled her the next morning. Mom just tossed her head back, eyes turned heavenward as if she knew something about herself that no one else could possibly understand, and grinned.

Our house on the hill—a bull's-eye in the farmland shifting to suburb—was the house where the neighborhood gathered to play. When a child went missing, their parents' first move was to call the Cronins. My sisters opened a beauty parlor in their bedroom, curling hair with crisscrossed bobby pins and calling it a perm. My brothers ran a basketball league from the patio court. Our parents poured cocktails for friends and family on our screened-in porch.

If my legs made me a nuisance, I vowed to become less of one. And I kept to that promise—until Christmas.

We spent the holiday at another family's house across town. We knew several Irish families with at least a half-dozen children. I was always the one in dresses, partly because I had nothing to put into long pants, but also because Mom and I liked the pink and frilly effect of Polly Flinders, which we bought at their warehouse downtown. I must have looked like a broken doll in that dress, with my silky hair around a heart-shaped face with wide brown eyes shifting from mischievous to doleful.

In the basement where the small children played, I wiped the foam of a red pop from the smocking of my dress while Frankie opened his third orange soda and watched it spill over the top. Frank was five years old and not a bulky, in-your-face boy. He had skinny legs and bloated ribs fanning from his torso like an accordion strapped to his chest. Surrounding those chocolate-almond eyes was the creamiest skin in the world. The women in my family often rubbed their palms against his cheek, though it was his eyes that made him so beautiful. Our parents both had almond eyes, almost Asian-looking, and yet our ancestry was Irish and German. Frankie inherited the most exaggerated version of their features. With his black hair and eyes, he could as easily have been pedaling a bike on the streets of Hong Kong as wielding a baseball glove on a grassy field in Ohio. Some of the more unsavory boys from the neighborhood called him "chink." Perhaps because we both stood out in our homogenous town, Frank protected me.

He lived for sports, and every neighborhood boy with athletic potential was drawn into his network. Our backyard had a baseball diamond and a "Pickle" path worn into the lawn because of Frankie. Our father seeded the lawn every spring, and a gang of Frankie's friends would tear it up by June. His friends tossed balls through our windows, pilfered golf clubs from our garage, and dripped sweating Popsicles on the garage floor so that it was stained not by motor oil but by purple, orange, and lime-green Popsicle juice. When it came time to divide teams for basketball, Frank always picked me. His friend Stilts, who would go on to local basketball fame, often balked and said, "I quit," to which Frank gritted his crooked teeth in defiance. He knew his best friend, Chief Taylor, would stand by him and that Stilts would have to capitulate. Soon Stilts would be stepping his spidery legs over me to face off with Frank.

After dinner, we crammed into the family room for home movies. I climbed onto Dad's lap in a reclining chair, his belly round and hard as a gibbous moon tucked into a red cardigan. We sat opposite the Christmas tree, fourteen or so kids fanned around us.

My mother leaned into the archway while resting Ted on her hip, and let out a sigh of exhaustion. Her hair was a black-lacquered crown and she looked to me like a queen after another long night at the ball—olive skin on high cheekbones with tarnished eyes. Ted tugged at the brass buttons of her red, wool-crepe dress. She looked too exhausted to stop him.

The other family's father fiddled with the projector and called, "Lights!" Someone pulled a plug and the Christmas tree went from multicolored speckles to a black haze in the corner.

The first movie at every holiday was usually my oldest brother's sixth birthday party. Mom sparked to life because this was her favorite film. Michael was now a proud thirteen-year-old carrying his head as if guided by his chin, while onscreen a six-year-old girl pecked his cheek and, as she did every year, my mother laughed the loudest. Next, the screen darkened until a glowing cake with six candles floated down a long table toward the young Michael. I imagined myself in the illumination of that candlelight. I could feel the heat of melting wax at my nose as I blew into this crowded family room, while onscreen my brother blew out the candles. Usually Mom would doze off at this point, opening an eye to catch only what she found pertinent.

I opened my eyes as the screen brightened with waves of sparkling water.

"Michigan," someone said.

This family was on that vacation, too? Was everyone in the world there but me? I leaned hard into Dad's belly, pressing my elbow into his gut, shoving away all memory of that desperate moment in the crib at Aunt Gert's house. "Hey, there," Dad whispered, "not so hard."

I jammed my thumb into my mouth and almost choked on it while the screen lit up with sunny skies on a gleaming lake. My oldest sister, Bridget, water-skied in a two-piece bathing suit, her long brown hair lifted off a noble neck. She batted her blue eyes at the camera; they were like diamond studs over a silver platter lake.

"Is that a two-piece?" said Mom, squinting at the screen, and Bridget blushed from her place on the floor.

The camera shifted toward the beach and zeroed in on the faces of children, while the kids from the floor, one by one, shrieked, "That's me!" Liz, Kevin, and Rosa: each a flash onscreen, the middle children, barely present in the film and yet, when I saw Liz in this movie without me, my eyes welled with tears. Two years older than me, Liz was more often in the company of Rosa, who was now almost in high school. Together, Liz and Rosa made a brilliant pair of comediennes, and—I couldn't be sure because of the quick sweep of the camera—it looked as if Rosa had just pushed her nose up while Liz pretended to swing a strand of pearls. At not quite seven, and under the twelve-year-old Rosa's direction, Liz could mime "Second Hand Rose" with such mastery that even Barbra Streisand would have had to laugh.

And now the inside jokes began. Ted, the toddler, appeared onscreen in a black bathing suit with white polka dots. Someone shouted, "Black-eyed monster!" This was where he got that nickname? Why was the baby in Michigan when I was not? In the archway Mom was half asleep with Ted in her arms. Onscreen, he shoved his jaw out, jutted his hips, and sneered at the camera.

Dad laughed out loud, his belly quaking underneath me. "He looks like a miniature Anthony Quinn," said the other father. That quickened the bounce of Dad's belly until I tipped from his lap. I clambered back to my place and turned to the screen to find that *Frankie* was now the star. To my horror, he was romping with a girl on a white beach, a scrim of sand dusting her tan skin.

I had no idea that Frankie had a girlfriend. He called me Lear Dear and, except when he was at school, Frankie and I were inseparable. Now the camera zoomed in on the rollicking bundle. I knew all about the sports and the boys, but the last thing I ever thought

I'd have to share Frankie with was another *girl*. Every belief I held about Frankie was dashed.

This girl, with her white-blond hair and tan legs, had won the hearts of everyone here: sandy-faced, wrinkling her nose, a few teeth missing, adorable. She and Frankie kissed onscreen. Every kid in the room roared while, on the floor below Dad and me, Frankie's shoulders formed a turtle shell to hide his blushing face.

Frankie in love? The grief of losing Frankie to this trip so overwhelmed me that I let out one long screech.

I was still screaming five minutes later, only by then Dad was rushing me to the car, the other father chasing us with our coats, apologizing: "We didn't know she felt this way . . ."

Outside, Dad set me in the passenger seat of our Microbus, and I heard the tinny echo of the slammed door. From my cocoon I held onto the other father's apology amidst the chaos of a scattering crowd. I imagined myself protected from the mob of angry siblings now cutting across the lawn toward me.

Within seconds they tore open the door. Silence gave way to sorrow that flickered to panic, and then I had about ten seconds of a peculiar ecstasy—floating on a cloud of glee. For some years afterward I recalled that instant with shame, and still later with pride. I would not be left behind. Even as I felt that first kid thump the back of my head, I thought, "Got 'em back." Sadly, that moment turned into, "Am I so awful that they should have abandoned me?"

I looked up at the other family's house, at their father crossing the damp lawn, still apologizing. It had just stopped raining. Water splashed from their slate roof onto the driveway and flooded gutters as it pushed its way down the street, while my family finished squeezing into two Volkswagens.

Behind us, my oldest sister took the baby from Mom, who was left holding car keys in one hand and a cigarette in the other. Mom drew deeply on her cigarette, fingers shaking on the exhale. "Dick!" she called to my father. "I'm a nervous wreck." She said this a lot.

And he shook his head. "I can only drive one car at a time, Joy."

With sangfroid, Mom snuffed out her cigarette with the toe of her high heel.

In her youth, Mom had been an aspiring artist specializing in pen-and-ink fashion drawings like those in the ads for Giddings Jenny or Henry Harris, the toniest stores in town. Now she was a suburban housewife in a camel-hair coat, which she wore like a movie star wore a mink; she was angular, from her lean calves locked onto feet that seemed rooted in the concrete, to her head tilted just so above the collared coat. She was an unlikely mother of eight. Her brown-velvet eyes often soothed me, although her eyebrows added to her every demand: "I mean business!" At the wheel she always swiped a hand over her hair, checked her lipstick, and then attended to the business of driving.

As Dad took the driver's seat of the Microbus, I shifted toward the passenger door because he tended to muffle his rage so that he moved like a gorilla in a restraining jacket. Yet my next thought, being only four, was, "At least I get the front seat." My brothers and sisters in the back seat formed an a cappella choir chanting an enraged "Eileen!" along with one weak note from Frankie, who asked, "Lear?"

It could have been that the others were angry about the front seat, or the aborted party, or about something I didn't understand, but I felt their fury hurled at me and clamped my hands over my ears.

"Hush," said Dad, and the back seat went silent. He hadn't started in on me yet. I wondered if he felt as bad as the other father. With his body poised at the wheel, Dad became the tight end in an endless fourth quarter, score tied. *Overtime. Overtime. Always overtime.*

He started the engine, and I looked again at the house. Through a front window I saw the blue light of the running projector, making silhouettes of the children. I focused on the light, as if by watching the film I could become a part of their vacation.

Just then the father of the other family stepped closer to our car to wave goodbye, and in doing so he blocked the blue light. He shrugged and kicked at the lawn. As we pulled away, he turned back to meet his wife at the front door. She rubbed the shoulders of their daughter, the one my age, who was now crying.

The blue light came back.

Dad gripped the wheel, his jaw set. He was already putting distance between himself and this memory. My gaze followed the blue light, watching it grow dimmer with distance.

CHAPTER 2

Rosa's Game

As a teenager I would scoff at Mom's volubility whereas Dad said only what was necessary and took no questions. For a while I felt certain that his silence was part of an elaborate scheme to keep us guessing, thereby distracting us from some covert mission he and Mom had cooked up. Perhaps I read too much into the incongruity of tension on the face of a man of so few words. Maybe he was merely trying to stay afloat. What about my mother and her singsong language? She made "silly" an art form. While I was studying Dad's brooding silence, I might have taken Mom's simplicity too literally. *Joe Joe from Kokomo* . . . Was this some sort of code?

The first of my mother's secrets was revealed in the summer before I turned five, on a morning when Aunt Gert stopped by, envelope in hand, on her way to play tennis. Gert was two years older than Mom, and although Mom shook a disapproving head at Gert's lackluster fashion sense, it was clear which one was the big sister. Gert and her friends dominated the tennis courts at our swim club every summer, some in tennis dresses and ankle bracelets, though Gert favored sun-bleached golf shirts and baggy shorts. While my aunt teed off or chased down a wicked serve, Mom played bridge or shopped. The one time Gert coaxed Mom to play the fourth in a golf game Mom picked up the ball after a few holes and chucked it, not toward the hole but out of sheer frustration. Afterward in our kitchen, Mom said, as if making a pronouncement, "I'm stickin' to bridge!" Gert clamped her chipmunk cheeks tight in an effort not to laugh in Mom's serious face.

Despite their different sensibilities, Mom called her sister daily while still in her nightgown, newspaper tucked under an arm, to say, "Mornin', Gert. Didja read the bridge column yet? No? Well, go get it . . . I'll wait."

Frequently Gert popped in for a cup of coffee on her way to the A&P, but on this day Mom was shopping. I spotted the envelope in my aunt's hand and looked around to find the oldest child in the kitchen. Rosa stepped forward; my heart plunged.

Out of some hope that Aunt Gert would give those photos to me, I stood on my chair at the kitchen table and reached out. Rosa stepped between us. "I'll take those," she said.

I slumped down in my seat while Aunt Gert considered Rosa's offer. She kept the photos in her right hand, folded her arms, and said, "I'll just wait for your mom." Then she settled against the copper-and-gold-flecked Formica countertop to wait.

There were about five of us eating cereal at the table, many in the swimsuits we lived in from June through August. Mine was faded pink and worn at the bottom. I had liked it better two years before when it belonged to Liz. Everything looked better on Liz, who shared Mom's looks and tastes. On that day Liz was wearing the swim team's red-white-and-blue-striped tank suit. The suit itself was a reminder of what I could never possess—membership on the swim team.

Since Frankie was often playing baseball in the summer while others were at swim practice, this left me in the company, and care, of Rosa. The third child of eight siblings, Rosa had to compete with Bridget and Michael for authority. The two eldest siblings viewed themselves as the residents in this town that we knew as family, and they tolerated us younger children as townies might accept that their economic power came from tourists, even if the tourists did clog Main Street and gum up the village green with taffy. Rosa craved Michael and Bridget's "townie" status, and for us middle children she ran the show. She even wrote and directed plays, which we performed for the Jesuits and Girl Scouts.

Later she would direct a play in which I provided the "commercial break" by squiddling onstage to eat a bowl of Corn Flakes before exiting stage right. Kevin, behind the curtain, lifted me into my wooden legs before I re-entered stage left and said, "Tall up with Kellogg's Corn Flakes!" This was among the better roles Rosa assigned to me. Typically I played the naïve hausfrau to Liz's cosmopolitan woman. My lines always fell flat while the audience roared with every impatient roll of Liz's eyes. Afterward I would chide myself for agreeing to play these roles, while Rosa was handed flowers at the curtain call.

Now, at the counter, Rosa and Aunt Gert exchanged notes on their favorite soap opera. During the school year Mom and I were to be found in front of the television set, where she chain-smoked, bouncing a baby on her knee or folding laundry, while we watched the soaps. This was crucial bonding time. Mom's eyebrows were always screwed into a knot of puzzlement, and she would stop bouncing to ask me, "Now, why would Erica say such a thing to her mother?"

And I would think to myself, "Because she's Erica Kane, of course!"

"Erica is the devil!" she'd say. "I just love Erica."

When summer came, Rosa and Bridget horned in on our routine and talked as if only *they* understood Erica's evil charms. Now, as Rosa and Aunt Gert chatted, I wanted to join in so I jumped up again. Rosa shot me a look that said, "What do *you* want?"

I wanted to talk, but if I did, Rosa would smirk at Aunt Gert, and they would both go silent. "Nothing," I said, skidding down again—time to mind my own business, or *try* to mind it, but then I caught Rosa's eyes flickering to the envelope and back.

Everyone finished breakfast. The crowd thinned as kids rushed off to swim practice or a friend's house. I stuck around. So did Rosa. Aunt Gert saw the clock on the oven and said, "Uh oh." She grabbed her cigarettes. "My court time's in ten minutes."

She started for the door, stopped, and gave Rosa a measured look. "These are for your mom," she said, handing Rosa the envelope.

"I'll make sure she gets them," said Rosa, sober-faced under a bubble perm, adolescent thighs fighting the seams of her cutoffs.

As soon as Aunt Gert's Keds hit the back porch, Rosa ripped into the envelope and shrieked, "What!" I scrambled over to the chair at the head of the table, stood up crookedly, and, because of the differing lengths of my legs, leaned into Rosa's forearm, which she yanked away. I stumbled and grabbed one of the little horse heads on the back of the chair to regain my balance.

Mom had chosen this kitchen set at the suggestion of the father in another Irish Catholic, larg*ish* (only six kids) family, the Keatings. While our parents clucked their tongues at our neighbors' Lincoln Continentals and chauffeured limousine, Mom carefully studied Mrs. Keating's clothes. After Mass Mom would say, "She didn't buy that dress here. Not even at Giddings. I'll bet Mary Elaine bought that dress in New York. Heck! I'll bet she went to *Paris*." This would have been after the eleven o'clock, a Mass we always attended because of what some in our town called "The Mary Elaine Keating Show." When Mom was really impressed she'd put Rosa or Liz up to spying: Get the lowdown. Were the Keatings in Paris?

"Why? Are we going to Paris?" Rosa would say.

And I'd be thinking, "Why do the Keatings live *here*? Why haven't they joined the 'filthy-rich' families in Indian Hill?"

Mom waved it off when the *nouveaux riches* bought planes or toured Europe. We were above all of that. And yet it was hard not to see that Mom was fixated on Mrs. Keating. I suppose this obsession dated back to when they were girls.

They were ten-year-olds at Fort Scott Camp when my mother first took note of Mary Elaine. Mom would have been at the camp on money that her mother had squeezed from a meager "budget." Mom would also have been trying to hide her first period, which she believed was the result of riding too roughly on a horse. She hadn't had the birds and bees talk yet. Mary Elaine would have stepped onto the porch of the opposing cabin wearing spanking-white shorts with a matching sailor top. Mom even guessed at the amount of starch in that collar, for she respected a stiff collar.

As for this kitchen set, it was one of at least three suggestions made by Charlie Keating to my mother. The first was his teen-age daughters' swim camp, which took place in the Olympic-size pool in their backyard. Mom enrolled Ted and me in the camp. I learned to swim there, but not until after another girl toppled my raft and climbed onto it, trapping me underneath. The second suggestion was this table and chairs with little horse heads shaped like knights on a chessboard. Charlie explained that his kitchen table's ends could be extended and more horse-head chairs could be added as the family grew. This was the smartest thing Charlie Keating ever said, according to Mom, and she rushed out to buy a kitchen table just like theirs. I wouldn't learn about the third suggestion until years later; it concerned a class action lawsuit over a drug called thalidomide. Mom dismissed it because she said she'd never taken thalidomide.

Now steady on my knees, I peered past Rosa's elbow to the sepia-tinted photos. "Can I see, too?"

"These are for Mom," said Rosa, curling her shoulder to block my view. "Now, squiddle on." To make her point she poked me hard in the ribs, but I was tenacious and caught glimpses of some of the photos while she riffled through the stack.

Rosa's hands were one clue to her nascent beauty. She had clean nails on tanned, shapely fingers. Often, at my urging, she manipulated her hands into silhouettes of darting serpent heads using a flashlight in a darkened room, and—because the serpents lunged to an ever-approaching hissing noise she made—I always begged her to stop. From there her hands became shackles around my wrists to go with her favorite made-up song: *You can fight; you can pinch; you can do anything, but you'll never, you'll never be free . . .*

Now she might just squeeze out the full story of Mom's past.

Except for some stock lines about growing up in the Depression, Mom had only told us that her mother could barely feed the six kids crammed into their tiny house. Yet, here were photos of a mansion with stained-glass windows, chandeliers, and sculpted gardens. This wasn't the modest house Mom had pointed out to us in the middle-class neighborhood in Pleasant Ridge. Rosa spread these photos like a croupier showcasing a deck of cards, before collecting them in a neat stack. She rubbed an index finger down one side and slipped them back into the envelope.

Our actions needed to remain clandestine; we knew that. What we didn't know was why.

Photos safely tucked away, we parted without a word, both of us already plotting how to get the real story. I squiddled into the family room, but I kept my eyes fixed on the kitchen, waiting for Mom. Rosa marked her territory there by doing a load of dishes.

Finally Mom came through the back door, two stuffed bags in her arms. Rosa took them from her, unloaded the car, and even stocked the shelves with all ten bags of groceries.

Mom's pregnant belly was just beginning to show through her white blouse and red skirt. Her tan came from walking to and from her car, and she took pride in the fact that she rarely set foot in the swim club, where we spent our summers in the care of older siblings. But she was one day shy of her Friday morning ritual at the beautician's, so her hair had gone from its lacquered state to a matted one. Her eyes had a dull sheen against brows crumpled to fight off a frown.

Based on our mother's hair, I could see that Rosa's job would be a cinch. Mom would brew a pot of coffee and plant herself at the table with a sigh. Rosa would merely nudge the envelope toward her.

When that happened, I couldn't see Mom's reaction to the photos because her back was to me. On my elbows I slinked past her chair and under the kitchen table. This was easy to do without drawing attention to myself because everyone was used to having me underfoot. Besides, Mom often boasted that she survived by "tuning kids out." Some days I listened to her chat with Aunt Gert for hours, and Mom never called me on it. I couldn't say if she didn't see me or if she did, but I didn't count. Maybe she didn't mind that I eavesdropped.

In fact, I was there to spy. If I didn't get this news firsthand, I'd have to rely on Rosa. She'd sit me on her lap and divulge family history as if she had been present for all of it. As young as I was, I could tell the difference between a bedtime story and the truth, and I was greedy for the truth. I wanted to know what happened when I came into the world without legs. Rosa always told the story as if she had been in the delivery room at my birth. "You just slipped out like a piece of raw meat," she'd say. "Out of what?" I'd ask, and she would plant a sloppy kiss on my cheek.

I would press her even when she said things like "Eileen did nothing but scream as a baby," a story that Mom would back up, adding, "All day and all night," while lolling her head as if she were on an endless bus ride, although Mom would grant that my grumpiness came from the body cast I wore for the second half of my first year. "That dickens," Mom would say, her birdlike voice trailing off, "who knew she could already roll off the bed? But I guess without legs . . ."

Rosa was now seated at the head of the table, the captain's-chair arms snuggling her waist, horse heads flanking her shoulders. She faced my direction as I came in, but was too busy with the pictures to notice when I slipped under the dark-stained oak table into my foxhole, where I rested my chin in the cradle of its crossed legs. Below me were Rosa's feet with their fingerlike toes, which she often used to pinch, then twist, the tender flesh under my arms, bringing me to tears before she'd say, "See what I mean? Always crying." Right now her feet were dormant.

Mom's legs, to my side, were crossed with one foot rocking. She pointed at the photos and reminded Rosa that her widowed mother, Ida Bruehl Fanger, the saint, would be canonized when the Pope got around to it. I was dying to climb up and see Ida. I loved the "visitation from Mary" story. But if I joined them at the table the conversation would end.

Rosa ignored the saint routine. "I thought you said you were poor," she said.

"I *was* poor," Mom said, as if she were recalling her old life for the first time in years. She said the mansion was in East Walnut Hills, which in the twenties was the poshest neighborhood in Cincinnati. My ears perked up. I loved that part of town, with its intricate architecture. Now, in the sixties, it was one mansion-turned-tenement after another. I fantasized about its grand entrances and even its trash. In later years I would imagine Frankie and myself as inner-city orphans roaming its streets, while he sported a James Dean slicked-back hairdo and a leather jacket. In reality we lived in a place that included a lot of empty squares, a few crowned with brick-and-siding colonials and the rest ironed flat—a landscape that threatened the city's claim to seven hills supposedly reminiscent of Rome. The city had been named for Cincinnatus, a Roman farmer who rose to dictator status as a fierce opponent of the power-hungry forces known as the plebeians.

Above me, Rosa and Mom studied a photo of children dressed in white linen and lace, my aunts and uncles at the bottom of a grand staircase in a foyer with a vaulted ceiling. "That's you," said Rosa, probably pointing to a baby with a gold bracelet in a baptismal gown. Mom was the youngest. But Mom said no, the baby in the picture was Matthew, who died of leukemia before she was born.

How sad for Mom, I thought, not registering that she wouldn't have known him.

"So what's this?" said Rosa. She lifted her hand. I heard a swish; she must have pulled a photo out to show Mom. "Oh, that," said Mom. She would have been looking at the mansion's façade: a cascade of half-moon stairs flanked by tall windows, one of which contained a stained-glass cameo of Mom's father as a baby.

In a studied tone, Mom said, "This is my Grandpa Fanger's house. We lived with Grandpa until he died. Then we moved to the other place."

"Why did you live with your grandpa?"

"Look at the house, Rosa." Mom shifted her crossed legs, the opposite foot now wagging under the table, where Rosa couldn't see it though I had to move from its path. "Wouldn't *you* want to live there?" Mom did not explain that her father had abandoned his large family, leaving them dependent on her grandfather. Rosa spotted the omission and said, "Okay. But why didn't your *dad* own that house?"

The foot froze. "Mmm," said Mom.

"Hmm," said Rosa.

Then silence.

Mom's voice perked up. She told Rosa about her grandfather's store, emphasizing its location on the riverfront and its success. She said it was a fashionable shoe emporium for elegant ladies.

Underneath the table, I inhaled cigarette smoke, a smell I loved. The floor was squeaky clean. Mom would not abide a dirty kitchen. She didn't do all of the cleaning by herself because Candy came in twice a week to clean, usually clamping between her teeth a filterless Camel—lit or, depending on her finances, unlit. Having been born black in turn-of-the-century Mississippi, Candy had never been granted a birth certificate or an education. She called me "Owleen," which made me wonder for a time if she'd never been taught to say "I." Her nurturing was selfless; during the year I had mononucleosis she carried me to the sofa every time she found me asleep on the floor by a heater. Because she brought us a bag of gumdrops every week, I thought of her as "Candy." I couldn't understand why Mom cried when she drove up to the bus stop each week and saw her holding a fresh bag. "Oh, I wish she wouldn't waste her money on you kids," Mom would say with a sniffle.

Now because of the summer heat, the table seemed sticky, as if the wood itself sweated. No matter how hot the weather or how pregnant she was, Mom wore nylons. By late fall she would deliver her ninth baby, and despite her legs' shapeliness, varicose veins ruptured their surface in a few spots. Rosa's knees were rounder but also golden brown.

Rosa asked her, "Well, what about your dad? Where was he?"

Mom just drew on her cigarette. I heard the crackle of the ember; she held the smoke and said, "My daddy was good-looking." She exhaled forcefully. "He liked nice clothes. But he gambled. He was sick. That's what Louise always says about Daddy." She stamped out her cigarette.

I sucked my thumb and thought of Aunt Louise, my godmother. Mom told me once that Louise was the prettiest of her sisters when they were young. We rarely saw Louise, who was now skeletally thin and had a slight tremor. Her pale blue eyes bulged from their sockets as if she were seeing a ghost. Unlike my other aunts, she never came by for coffee because she had no time for idle chitchat. She was a widow in a rundown neighborhood not far from East Walnut Hills, and she supported her large family by working as an aide in a nursing home.

Mom was lost in thought. Again I heard her knock a Kent from its package, then the seductive strike of a match. I tried to imagine a young and glamorous Louise but couldn't see it. Instead, I could imagine Mom's squint as she held the match to her cigarette, and the way she clasped the Kent between her lips while she inhaled. I smelled the burning tobacco. Sedated, I rested my cheek in the cross of the cradle supporting the table. The gummy varnish stuck to my face.

Mom's foot went still, her voice doleful, almost weepy. "Louise always says we should forgive Daddy. He was sick. That's all. Just sick." She started to cry, and her foot dropped to the floor as if to pin her to the ground; her free hand went up, maybe to her face, and through tears she said, "It's not your fault if you're sick." She said this like she knew what it meant to be sick. Maybe because of the Depression, Mom could cry over things like the amount of sugar we poured on our cereal, but I'd never heard her cry like this before.

I wanted to come out and climb into her lap. Instead, I reached for her ankle to stroke it but stopped just shy of that when Rosa said, "Whaddaya mean sick? You mean crazy?"

I sat up. My head narrowly missed the frame rimming the underside of the tabletop. My face was inches from Mom's hip. Rosa had a magnetic control over Mom. Even I could tell that Mom would be wise to quit right here. Mom stopped crying and ground her foot into the floor. I thought she might spring up and call an end to this talk. Instead she barked, "I already told you he gambled."

Maybe here Mom would walk out. No. Rosa leaned forward. "Why would he gamble?" Was this a gentler voice, or was it a setup?

Mom's waist bent in Rosa's direction. I couldn't see their heads, but Mom had to be right in Rosa's face. If I poked my head out, I'd see everything, but I'd be right between them and that was not the place to be. Anyone who is one of eight children knows that you get out of the way when the force between dueling family members closes in.

"I don't know," said Mom in an affected, throaty voice before she switched to a rhythm like a rock skipping over the water: "I-real-ly-did-not-know-him, ROSE. I-guess-he-drank-too-much." Rosa backed away and her head dipped backward so that I could see her face. I wondered if she saw me, if this was all a show. They were locked in position: Rosa arching her back, smiling in Mom's face, and Mom right over her, ready to pounce. There was no sound at all.

I almost gasped. I'd seen this before. They'd look ready to kill each other, and yet Rosa would be smiling.

Finally, Mom settled back in her seat. I heard her take another drag on her cigarette. I saw the tremors in her free hand resting on her thigh before she gripped the saddle of her chair.

I was relieved it was over. I'd had enough. We'd all had enough. I began to regret that I'd sneaked under the table because I knew too much and this bordered on treachery.

Rosa now leaned forward and said, "How could you not know your dad?"

At this I was ready to spring out from under the table and throw my hand to Mom's lips and say, "Stop!"

Curiosity kept me there, though. Our maternal grandfather cast a new light on how we viewed our mother.

Mom sighed, exhausted. Her father's splintered image was now spilled across the table with these photographs. She kept trying to explain him but the harder she tried, the more he slipped through her fingers. "He didn't live with us, Rosa."

"Why not?"

"My mother kicked him out."

"What?" Rosa sneered.

"You heard me."

"Did she *divorce* him? That's a sin."

"My mother was a saint!" The volume rose, but Mom's tone stabilized in a warning. "That is no joke, Rose. Ida Fanger was a Martyr. Mary was right there at her bedside when she died."

"Mary who?"

"Mary who?" Mom held out her arms. "Are you kidding? The Virgin Mother, that's who!"

"Huh?"

"Look," said Mom, slapping her right hand on the tabletop as if it were the Bible. "It's true. I know because the room got cold and suddenly it smelled like roses. Roses, right when my mother died. That's a sign from Mary, you know? Roses and a cool breeze, that's how Mary visits people."

"Oh?" Rosa's voice teetered on the edge of a giggle.

Mom was just getting started, though. "After Mother died, the room got really warm and the smell of roses vanished. Now explain that."

For a moment there was silence, as if Rosa were convinced. Every time I'd heard the story of Ida's visitation, I imagined my grandmother's hospital room like a refrigerator full of roses, but that day the kitchen was as warm as melted butter and I smelled only the daily grind of coffee and the smoke of cigarettes. Then Rosa asked what I was dying to hear but would never dare ask: "So what happened to your dad?"

"Well," Mom said in an aloof tone, "he ended up on the streets."

I didn't buy her detachment. Neither did Rosa, who prodded, "The streets? You mean he was a hobo?"

Hobo: the word hit me as harshly as if someone had spit in my face. I went numb and felt only the sensation of drifting away without really leaving. Mom and I had seen hoboes downtown while coming from Pogue's department store on our way to Shillito's. We'd come out the door that faced Fountain Square, and there underneath the awning we'd brush past men holding tin cups and asking for money.

Earlier that same year—before I was fitted for artificial legs—we saw a man on his knees.

How odd, I had thought, but from Mom's arms I looked hard at him and saw that he had no legs. I pulled the hem of my Polly Flinders dress over my exposed knee. After that I went numb. As we approached him, I saw for the first time the image that most people associate with the word "amputee"—a beggar. What happened next was something I couldn't understand at the time but in years to come I would see it this way, beginning with me asking myself, "Is that what I look like?" I'd never seen anyone else without legs. As we passed, I could not look at him. Maybe it was because I saw something of myself in him; or perhaps it was because I had to look down to see him, a grown man, which seemed wrong. The shame I felt for this man, then myself, so overwhelmed me that I actually felt myself turn light as a balloon and drift from Mom's arms, as if something crucial had been wrenched from my body and set loose for an instant. I don't know how long the feeling lasted, but I do know what made me come back to myself: Mom. She had me right there in her arms, the legless man now behind us, and while she toted me the few blocks to Shillito's I studied her face. I traced the lines on her forehead, the ones on either side of her mouth. The prettiest girl in Cincinnati, that's what people always said about Mom, but I could only see her lines.

As I studied her I wondered, "How does she look at me? Does she go numb all over? Is she ashamed of me?" On the next block, when she shifted me to her other hip, I felt the sudden return of my own weight. Now, from under the table, I began to wonder if Mom felt shame about things that didn't even concern me, shame about her own childhood.

In years to come, I would pick up stories of my grandfather, John Fanger, mostly through Rosa. The family historian, she was the only one who would speak of things considered taboo, my birth and Mom's father topping the list. She would tell me that our grandfather stalked Mom when she was a teenager. Maybe he was just curious to see how his baby daughter was turning out, or maybe he was attracted to Mom's sultry black curls and model's figure. He would approach her on the street in front of her friends. Mom would be mortified because he might be dirty, unshaven, wearing tattered clothes, and reeking of alcohol. Other times, he would hunt Mom down, wearing a brand-new suit and driving a car. He'd invite her to ride over to his new office. She would hop in, hopeful, thrilled to find her father redeemed. Inevitably, she'd uncover a ruse: borrowed suit, car, job, office. She'd have to pretend to go along with it because he was her father.

Much later, I heard someone ask Mom, "What was the happiest day of your life?" I expected her to say her wedding day, because she always said she loved our father more than anyone else. Instead she said, "The happiest day of my life? My First Communion. I wanted my daddy to show up for it, and he did."

I never found out whether John Fanger died in a warm bed or on the streets. In any case, it was Mom's grandfather's death that would affect her daily life more than her father's. He died in the early thirties, and Mom's brother had to take over the shoe store. While the Depression had undermined the store's success, it was the flood of '37 that devastated it. The river came up so high that my uncle had to paddle a rowboat to the store and climb in through a second-floor window to save whatever shoes were left.

There was hope that the sale of the mansion in East Walnut Hills and the antiques in it would raise enough money for Ida and her children to live comfortably. Unfortunately, Mom's father undermined the plan. He held an auction and sold the antiques. Ida moved the family to a smaller house in the suburbs. In the meantime, he sold the mansion to a funeral home and gambled all of the proceeds away. The one piece Ida took from the mansion was a Victorian clock, which now resided on Aunt Gert's mantel.

All of that seemed worlds away from where Mom sat on this day. In the fall, she would be thirty-seven and a mother of nine. And yet she seemed a girl, her voice so high-pitched that when I answered the phone even Aunt Gert would ask, "Joy?"

Just as I thought their conversation had ended, Rosa slid her chair back, scraping the linoleum, and pointed at the stack of photos. "Your *dad* was a hobo," she said.

I touched Mom at the same time that she flinched. My hand came to rest on the chiseled bone of her ankle. I rubbed my thumb over its knob, her nylons between our two skins.

Maybe she was too deflated to comment. Her devastation was so palpable that even Rosa let it go when Mom said in a coarse whisper, "It *was* the Depression, Rose. A lot of people lived on the streets."

CHAPTER 3

Open Spaces

Our father came home from work every night at exactly 6:15. He was as predictable as a clock and yet a mystery to us kids. Everything about Dad told us that he had a lot on his mind: the way he rocked back on his heels, lock-kneed, shuffling the change in his pocket. When he walked in the door, he always headed straight for a beer.

At exactly 6:30, every night, we choked down Mom's beef, dry as cotton, without complaint, except from Ted, who called Mom's stews "witch hazel" because she served them from an iron cauldron.

"Did that kid just complain?" Mom would call over her shoulder from the stove, so that Ted was met with Dad's grimace, which made Ted laugh. I was a quiet offender, usually choking on the meat, then sobbing at Dad's scowl. Laughter or tears inevitably triggered Dad to signal Michael, who dragged us up to our rooms, Ted celebrating his good fortune with arms raised in a V for victory while I clamped my hands to the saddle of my chair even as Michael's fingers bore into my armpits to break me loose.

No matter how intimidating Dad appeared to us, we savored every second we found ourselves alone with him. But he was in a never-ending quest to "finally get some peace," away from us "punk kids." To accomplish this, he had a screened-in porch built. An exposed brick wall and a Dutch door separated it from the living room. Green carpet was chosen because it reminded Dad of Astro-turf. He usually got in about two hours of peace on a Sunday—the one day his dealership was closed. By late afternoon the porch filled with Jesuits and neighbors, aunts and uncles, and Dad's parents. His mother was known as Katie to everyone except for Grandpa, who called her Katherine.

I lived for the sight of Grandpa's Ford sedan in the driveway, and I harbored resentments toward Katie, who stole him away with the same line every week: "Charles, we'll be late for Margaret's." Until then I would nestle into Grandpa's enormous lap, which erupted into volcanic laughter when Mom tried to spar with Katie, who was selectively hearing-impaired, and whose motto was "If you can't say anything nice, don't say anything at all," rendering her practically mute until she could get to her daughter's house, where I imagined her chattering away.

In the warm months before our Sunday guests would arrive, Dad stretched out on the sofa like a black bear basking in the western sun, the transistor radio broadcasting a Reds game that inevitably ended with "Joe Nuxhall rounding third and heading for home." Nuxhall's departure through the crackling radio was so intimately linked with my father in my mind that it seemed as if Dad himself was signing off, though the radio was just one of his routines.

Every Sunday he rose at nine, poached eggs and fried bacon for roughly a dozen people (depending on babies born or teens off to college), went to the 12:45 mass because the pastor was too tired to lecture by then, stopped at Duke's Pony Keg for a case of Hude-pohl, made a bologna sandwich and popped a beer before lying on the couch to tune in to a game, and rose at four to pour drinks for guests. At dusk, he grilled on the back porch and heckled the bad shots my brothers made in their endless game of basketball.

Whenever a ball veered toward Dad at the grill, he'd drop his tongs to catch it and charge the basket, his legs wrestling the gravity of his beer belly as he went for the dunk. His body in motion was comic and graceful all at once. The boys would swallow their laughter, and then their pride, as Dad sank the ball, retrieved his tongs, and taunted them from behind a cloud of smoke at the grill: "I wouldn't put a nickel on any of ya."

He didn't have time to coach the boys on form. In fact, none of us knew exactly what Dad wanted from us, although he was quick to say what he did not want: "Stop your bellyaching" or "That's just yellow-bellied talk." Those vague indictments motivated us because we were certain that Dad had achieved more at age sixteen than we could hope to do in a lifetime. We knew that at ten years old he was already riding the train alone from Chicago to Katie's parents' farm in Minnesota, where he worked every summer. By age twelve his family arrived in Cincinnati after living in at least three cities. By sixteen he'd bought a car and driven it to Chicago to visit friends.

Cincinnati is a place where everyone's grandparents went to school together. Friendships are formed with family history in mind. Since Dad's family had no history in this town, he wedged his way into the social scene via football. He was known as the guy with short, bowed legs and a keen eye for the open spaces at which George Ratterman aimed his blazing passes.

Dad favored Katie's laconic style. Grandpa was the demonstrative one, coaching me through games of gin rummy with Rosa and Liz. "Let's get 'em!" he'd say. Then he'd whisper, "Breast your cards." I never could get the poker face down. Grandpa loved an underdog. The time he said, "I love you," words not often used in our family, I slept with that cheek pressed to my pillow as if to pin the whole evening down.

Our father's nurturing came in the form of structure, a structure that was up to us to delineate. He made it his job to provide us a good education, and he would see to it that all of his children went to college, if not graduate school. His own education had been interrupted by the Second World War. He was sixteen when the US joined the Allied forces and so, to his vexation, he had to wait two years to sign up. In the meantime, his older brother left Notre Dame to become a fighter pilot. Dad wanted to follow him to flight school. Since he wasn't old enough to enlist, he spent the next two years viewing his victories on the football field as something of a national duty. And he hit on a distraction more consuming than war.

Dad met Mom at his Jesuit high school May Fête dance. She was only fourteen, dark and exuding vulnerability, a stream of dance partners in her wake. All night, Dad cut in on them. When he came home he woke Katie to say that he'd met the girl of his dreams: Joy Fanger, Gert's younger sister, who was "even prettier than Gert." Katie approved, at first. She admired Gert, a grounded girl with plans for nursing school, and she might have assumed that Mom would be as focused on school as Gert.

By all accounts, Dad was mesmerized by Mom, who was mostly focused on playing the coquette. Yet she was the heartbroken one when Dad turned eighteen and went to pilot training camp, where he faced his first big disappointment. His entire squadron came down with pneumonia, recovering only in time for the war effort to dwindle and the pilots' training to cease. Dad's wartime experience boiled down to two unremarkable years on an island in the Philippines. After the war, our disappointed father did not follow his fighter-pilot brother, along with George Ratterman, to Notre Dame. His grades were excellent but he chose to stay in town, adopted his "what's done is done" outlook on life, and played football for Xavier University.

It has been said that Dad brooded for the next two years. Then he rose from the ashes by proposing to Mom and choosing marriage over college. His mother, upon hearing the news that her son was dropping out of school to get married, locked herself in her bedroom for three days without a word of explanation. None was needed. Everyone knew that Katie had turned down three marriage proposals herself in favor of college and even some graduate education. To her, marriage was the reward that came after a good many years of school. Despite this policy, she had chosen a man with an eighth-grade education who was seven years her junior. Only Grandpa, with his height, girth, and booming laughter, had been able to coax the reluctant Katie into marriage. What Katie thought of Joy Fanger, a girl who chose pen-and-ink "caricatures" over academics, Katie would not say.

Grandpa, on the other hand, was delighted by his son's marriage. At thirteen, our grandfather had punched his abusive, alcoholic father before running away. He hated to leave his nine siblings behind. He was more inclined to take care of people. Perhaps for this reason he adored our mother, a girl in need of a father. Grandpa could have cared less about her academic choices; he'd hardly been held back by his lack of education. He'd made a success of himself, first with Firestone and later with Ford. Now, under Katie's well-researched guidance, they were touring the world. By the time I left for college I had two rows, stacked in doubles, of silver spoons from three continents.

Grandpa was glad to have Dad join the sales team at his Ford dealership. He was eager for grandchildren, and Mom soon became pregnant with the first, but she miscarried. Two years later, she gave birth to Bridget. She produced five more babies during the fifties. Grandpa cheered her on. He had nurtured a large brood of younger siblings. With such an imprint, one's heart aches for the familiar clan, even as it pines to be rid of it. (I would find this out for myself one day.)

With mounting expenses from an ever-expanding family, Dad

chose to open his own dealership, for Volkswagen. He would become a risk-taker like his father. In 1960, he and Mom flew to Germany for a Volkswagen convention, their first trip abroad together. They were not entirely free of children, though. Mom was pregnant with her seventh baby: me.

Dad had finally reached the place where his own adventures would take off. Who would have imagined this victorious trip would be a precursor to tragedy? In fact, my parents wouldn't even know to connect this trip to my birth defects. The news about thalidomide would not come out until 1962, and fifty years later I can't say whether my parents, upon hearing that news, took a moment to wonder whether Mom had somehow taken it. They had innocently flown into a place where a whole generation faced pockets of devastation so random that it would take at least two years for physicians and researchers to connect the dots.

I don't know if he was changed by my birth, but the father I knew was not a risk-taker. Instead, he was a man with a daunting sense of responsibility. Maybe this is why my favorite part of the week was Dad's two-hour window of downtime on Sundays. If you were willing to listen to a lot of sports, you could spend a Sunday afternoon with him.

In the winter, Ted and I lived behind the couch in the den, Dad's second-favorite place to spend a Sunday afternoon. Ted and I thought of this couch as our hiding place, though it was the first place everyone looked when we went missing. We'd wait for golf to come on because that's when Dad promptly began to snore, and we'd crawl out from either end of the couch to dive-bomb his belly, at which point Dad always sprang to life, growling like a lion, "Arrr!" Then he took each of us by the scruff of our necks and pretended to thrash us. He owned us, and we loved it. Finally, he'd put us to work massaging his back or scalp, or even his feet. "Don't forget the dogs," he'd say in a sleepy voice. "Not the dogs!" Ted would insist.

I was willing to do anything for Dad, so I always peeled off his musty socks. His feet were too tired to sweat, let alone stink. They seemed barely alive. I'd almost weep at the sight of them; they were as dry and pale as old pie dough. If I pinched the soles the skin flaked off; when I curled the ridge of his toes it sounded like a pretzel snapping.

"Eew," Ted would say, as he fled.

But I stayed for the payoff. That's when Dad said, "Thanks, Trix." He'd look at me with genuine appreciation and rub my "angel wings," his sign of affection for me. I'd wait all week for it.

CHAPTER 4

The Hanger

On our previous visit to Hanger, Inc., an artificial limb company, the prosthetist, whom we called the leg man, had said, "Let me take a look at that stump." I drew back and sucked my thumb. He looked at me, waiting for something, until I realized that he wanted my leg. Mom sat beside me, her elbow poking into her pregnant belly, a forgotten cigarette dangling from her hand, her head cocked sideways with an open-mouthed stare fixed on the goop in the bucket. Mom could not stomach slime. The leg man, on his knees, began to unravel a scroll of wet plaster up and down my thigh, making me gasp and wheeze. "Can you lift that up?" he said, pointing with his chin at the hem of my dress. I turned to Mom, expecting her to slap his face, but she was still locked into that vacant stare so I did as he asked and closed my eyes while he molded the plaster. When I looked down again, he was dipping his hands into the bucket of water. He flattened out the last bump and said, "Gotta work fast . . . before it dries." In about fifteen minutes, he yanked the solid mold from my thigh. That's when Mom snapped to attention, stamping out the now-remembered butt with its two-inch ash. In a flash she was up, her outstretched arms the signal for me to leap into them.

Up to this point I'd seen myself as a squiddler, which wasn't an issue in our neighborhood, a suburban hub of conservative Catholicism north of the city. Perhaps we were all there for Saint Vivian, the model grade school for our brand of faith. Living within a block of our house were the Keatings, an eight-term Republican congressman, the founder of the National Right to Life Committee, and a conservative news anchor with a dozen children. Based on my neighborhood, I assumed that Republicans lived and died to raise athletes. Swimmers, cheerleaders, baseball, football, and basketball players thrived here. I claimed squiddling as my sport. If I wanted to speed up, I'd throw my arms into it and gallop. I bragged that I could outrun Chief Taylor's dog, Topper.

Squiddling was not something people outside our neighborhood appreciated, though. I gathered that from Rosa's face when she'd say, "Ska-wid-del-a-long, I-lean," in her sideways drawl. The smug grin she added as punctuation made me worry about how others might see me. There was also the fact that I would have to walk to attend the Catholic school in our neighborhood.

In an effort to get me "on my feet," someone decided that I needed braces on my legs. No one seemed to know what the braces were for, or why I had to wear them. Maybe they were supposed to train my legs for prostheses. I kept taking them off and Mom had to keep strapping them on again. There was no guidebook for how to educate a child without legs, so this became one of many issues Mom would reluctantly take up with our pediatrician. Her opinion of Dr. Epstein was complicated by her notions about physicians, particularly "Jewish doctors." Whenever Dr. Epstein suggested that Mom try birth control, she would stomp out of his office. "What does *Isaac Epstein* know about *Joy Cronin*?" she'd say in the car.

As an adult, I would ask, "If you don't trust Jewish doctors, then why do you always pick doctors who are Jewish?" To which Mom would say, "Because they're the smartest," with an expression that announced: "Everyone knows this."

Mom had an even more puzzling relationship with her obstetrician. Dr. U. never nagged her about birth control. She used the rhythm method, and after the near-fatal delivery of her eleventh child, Dr. U would finally tell her she ovulated *twice* a month.

"Why did he wait until you had eleven kids to tell you that?" I asked as an adult. And Mom said, "The man was a genius!"

"Does Dr. U happen to be Jewish?"

"Catholic," she would say. "I think. But he was *very smart*, I-lean." Mom emphasized the first syllable of my name when she was either peeved or giving me what she considered important information. I never liked the sound of those two syllables together, especially as others mimicked her. Eventually I figured out that a bad joke had been embedded into my name. At some point I turned it around in my head and heard "I-lean" selectively, as if to silently turn the joke back on my mother. As for Mom's ideas about doctors, she wasn't worrying about the irony contained within her theories. Except on matters of birth control, Mom usually followed Dr. Epstein's advice. At his suggestion, she enrolled me in a Montessori program held in a woman's basement. There the Montessori teacher allowed me to kick off my metal braces. When Mom complained, the teacher said, "But crawling is a sign of genius!"

Mom rolled her eyes at this, although later, with a hint of pride, she repeated this "hippie" philosophy to her friends. The women from our neighborhood looked doubtful, while Mom's oldest friends nodded their approval. My parents had grown up on the more liberal east side. Their childhood friends lived on tree-lined streets with hills and older homes with "character." Eastside folks would never abdicate to the flatlands, with its checkerboard lots and homogenous homes, but as our family had expanded in size so had our parents' conservatism. Like the other mothers in our neighborhood, Mom saw preschool as something akin to a mother's greatest sin, evidence of shirking child-rearing responsibilities.

But what could she do? I'd been tackling her daily, screeching the whole time that I had to go to school, "Right now!" Mom understood that I wanted to be with my siblings, but she didn't realize that I was terrified of being turned away from school. Aside from that, I was bored.

Mom was tenacious about my prosthetics despite questionable support from the medical community. One surgeon, a family acquaintance, wanted to construct a foot to attach to my knee; if Mom had followed his advice, I would have been three and a half feet tall. She instantly discarded that idea. An orthopedic textbook I would study twenty years later stated emphatically that no one could possibly ambulate on two prostheses. "Oh, really?" I said to myself, and silently I thanked Mom for pushing me into a pair of legs.

As clients of The Hanger, we would have to pay the price in time: time for fittings, time for orthopedic consultations, and time for physical therapy. In the end it would amount to dozens of appointments, and all without any guarantee of success.

Now, we were on our way back to The Hanger, another week, another drive across town. There was a red light ahead, and Mom gunned the accelerator. "I'm a nervous wreck," she said, slamming on the brakes. "What is this? Our sixth time?" Six, seven, what did I know? I only knew that we went to a place where a man's leg was hanging in the window, which I thought was the reason it was called The Hanger. Still, sitting at the light, I wished we could be here for any reason other than the leg man. We were in the rundown part of Walnut Hills, not far from the mansion at DeSales Corner where Mom had lived until her grandfather died.

We turned into a square. The oldest parts of Cincinnati have always had squares, some bounded by fancy shops and outdoor cafés, and others like this one: cars staggered diagonally by meters at the hub of businesses that people needed but wished they didn't. Here were appliance repair shops, funeral parlors, and everything medical. Mom was edgy because she couldn't find a parking place. "Used to be you *wanted* to live in Walnut Hills," she muttered. She yanked the wheel so hard that something squealed as she circled the hub.

I looked up from my window at turrets and spires jutting from third stories, my eyes sweeping down patterned brickwork to the picture windows at street level. They showcased wheelchairs, caskets, and Alka-Seltzer. Mom glided her gold square-backed Volkswagen into a metered spot. In the rearview mirror, she checked her makeup for smudges and ran a finger over her Liz Taylor eyebrows.

Below the dangling leg in the window was a March of Dimes poster. I secretly dreamed of replacing this poster child, a boy leaning into crutches as if to struggle for every step. He wore a suit and tie, his hair slicked back. I imitated the way he set his jaw, so determined. This was a boy everyone loved. If I were the March of Dimes girl, people would love me just as much. They would stand in line for a chance to lug me around. If all I had to do was dangle my own wooden leg in that window to be discovered, then I would do it.

Mom plucked me out of the passenger seat and kicked the door closed. She steadied me on top of her pregnant belly as she struggled to find change for the meter. I slipped down and shimmied up onto her baby-belly as a kitten might cling to a basketball; below us shards of glass littered the curb.

Mom twisted and wriggled to dig through her giant purse. That's when it occurred to me that aside from getting me into legs so that I could go to school, Mom wanted to fling me from a rapidly disappearing hip so she wouldn't have to carry me anymore.

I decided to quit. I would not be a part of this experiment. Even the doctors weren't sure I would walk. Why should I try? Instead, I could sit back and let Mom lug me around for life. "I'm not doing it. I'm not going in there."

Mom wasn't in the mood for my fuss. I dug my fingers into her chest and shoved away from her. She had to lift her leg higher to keep from spilling her purse while she locked me in place. She was hopping around on one leg so we wouldn't go down in a sprawl over that broken bottle. "Stop it!" she snapped. I was enjoying it, though, as we dipped and twirled, the glass pointing back at us from this angle and that—until I lost my nerve.

We both froze.

Mom's bag slid down past her knee, almost out of reach. "Damn it, Eileen." She gripped me to her chest and at the same time shifted to catch the handle of her purse. "Don't you know I have a roast in the oven? I've got three kids to pick up after this. Baseball, pimple doctor, fat doctor. All I do is run you kids around."

"But why do we have to come *here*?" I pulled away and waited for her to blast me. Instead she leveled her handbag and held me tightly. For moments such as this, Mom summoned composure from a secret source. She looked into my eyes and said, "I honestly don't know, Eileen. We're here because it's the next step. I have no idea where it's leading, but we're going to take it."

Her eyes watered. She was pleading, and I did what I always did when I wanted to bring her back. I touched the skin on her cheek and put my own cheek to hers. It was warm and moist and we melted into one.

She went back to digging in her purse, found a nickel, and shoved it into the meter. "Got it," she said with pride. Resigned, I nestled into the place below her chin and against her neck.

Mom had to lean us both into the door to open it.

The waiting room was a hodgepodge of vinyl chairs with thin, oily cushions. Tattered magazines spilled from end tables, prayers were mounted on the walls. I couldn't read but I knew about folded hands with glowing auras over words. Mom set me down on a chair and I smelled talcum powder, sawdust, and burning metal. The sound of industrial-strength machinery blasted through walls from the back room.

Another person waited that day, a man as old as Grandpa. He had one empty pant leg, and I was wondering how he'd lost that leg. I tried not to stare. Under his cold gaze I found someone who looked as if he'd just been socked in the jaw. Our eyes met and his face softened from a wince to a pity-filled look. I curled up in my chair so I would disappear and thought, "He pities me?"

The Hanger prosthetists all seemed to be missing a limb. They were the only amputees we knew. (No one in my family ever called me an amputee, except for Rosa and Liz, who had made up an "amputee camp" called "Wa-heel-la." Around the dinner table they crooned its anthem: "Sing around the campfire; throw your wooden leg in! Sing wa-heel-la. Sing wa-heel-la. Work. Whittle. Squiddle!" Our parents could not fight the grin on that one. They'd laugh out loud, then Dad would say, "Stop it. That's awful.")

As Mom and I waited, prosthetists would stagger past, toting a leg or an arm with a hook. I drew back. Mom clutched her purse to her lap as her shield.

One redeeming feature of these visits to The Hanger was that I got to have Mom to myself. Here I could forget where we were and plant myself in her childhood—no, her teens. I could grow into someone else, someone Mom equated with pure joy, her best friend from the days when she had Dad on the run. I wanted to be a part of that life.

I would say, "I saw you and Fran at the Pogue's Arcade yesterday."

She always knew I was talking about the fourteen-year-old Joy and Fran. She'd respond, "What were we doing?"

"You each had a dish of ice cream at the counter in the coffee shop."

She'd arch her back—good posture ranking among Mom's highest values—and smile. "That sounds about right."

"You had vanilla. And it only cost a nickel." I knew this from our talks about the Depression. Everything tasted better in the Depression.

"A nickel was a lot back then. Graeter's was better, though. Back then it stuck to the roof of your mouth, it was *that rich*! For a dime you could suck on a scoop of Graeter's all afternoon."

I could taste Graeter's Mint Chocolate Chip on the roof of my mouth, but then I'd drop my chin and see grass stains on another of Liz's hand-me-down sailor collars. I was forever rolling down-hill on our front lawn because I loved the tickle of grass against my skin and the way my body fit neatly into a ball if I rolled head-first.

I looked at the old man and his empty pant leg and thought, "What did I do to deserve this?"

Mom covered her nose to avoid inhaling sawdust—dust, fat, and loose hair being among the things that Mom could not abide—and said, "Aw, heck!" She tended to say this when she was really think-ing, "We are so screwed."

I didn't belong with wounded men; I could see that in her eyes.

They called us back to a fitting room with fiber-wood paneling and a full-length mirror at the end of parallel bars that looked to be about a mile long, although they measured about ten feet. We sat in chairs at the head of the bars.

"They're gonna put you in your legs today," said Mom, "and *you* are going to walk between those bars right up to the mirror."

"Really?" I thought.

The leg man entered, clutching a wooden leg in each hand. To me they looked huge and heavy, but in fact they could have been marionette legs, except that the below-knee leg—the BK as he called it—had a leather corset to fix onto my thigh, attached by metal hinges. Those hinges would bend with my knee. But would they take a chunk of my flesh along the way? The whole contraption seemed barbaric. The above-knee leg was shiny wood from the top of the thigh to the tip of its elfin foot.

The leg man cupped the legs in his hands the way Pete Rose would grip his bat after he swiped it between his thighs. I couldn't imagine how I would lift them, let alone make them walk. In his own prosthesis, the leg man kneeled inside the parallel bars, right in front of my left leg, to attach the BK to my real body. His hands coated in dried goop from someone else's thigh, he lifted a lamb's-wool sock from the pouch on his rubber apron, shook it in my face as if holding a fancy doll, and asked, "Like that?"

I shrugged before remembering to smile.

He slid it onto my real leg, covering the part just below my knee. "How's it feel?"

"Good," I said, and strangely enough it wasn't so bad. I looked down to find his part: a chalky-white line against oiled hair flecked with sawdust and talcum. This man seemed more suited to roll under a car and poke around like a mechanic in a car dealership than to wrap his hands around my thigh. But here was my future: I would look onto the crowns of others as they kneeled before me, my princes, who would not bring glass slippers for my feet.

In her own chair Mom sat with eyes wide, not saying a word, the ash on her cigarette dangerously long. The leg man slid the artificial leg over my sock. He laced up the corset around my thigh, pulling until my leg went numb. My face in the mirror was all knitted brows and pressed lips. Next to me Mom wore a haze of cigarette smoke like a halo. I wanted to tell the leg man about the tightness, but he noted my distress. "You'll get used to that," he said. "Now stand up."

"How?" I felt stupid for asking.

"Well," Mom said flatly, before she escalated to a shriek, "just like anyone else!" Her arms unraveled into an outward thrust that said, "Isn't it obvious?" A chunk of ash broke from her cigarette, landing on a floor that I was sure had seen worse.

I looked at her in the mirror: legs crossed, arms stretched out like a saint before execution. She yelled, "Come on!" I would have bet she was playing her whole afternoon out in her head: "Baseball, pimple doctor, fat doctor, roast. And get that Eileen into a pair of legs, damn it!" To this I thought, "Over. My. Dead. Body." I pushed back into my seat and crossed my arms.

She came forward, right into my face, and whispered, "Whaddaya think you're doin'?" There was silky black down on Mom's skin. It was so fine that to me, with my fairer complexion, basset-hound eyes, and hair a mixture of elements—copper, gold, and Midwestern mud—I saw Mom's down as a mark of pedigree, a symbol of what I had yet to achieve. That is, if I ever grew up. Now, with her eyes bulging and her jaw quivering under the down, I imagined she was sprouting a beard. My mouth went sour as I gave in to tears that I'd been trying to choke off.

Mom froze momentarily.

The fists at her sides relaxed, and she broke. "Oooh, I-lean!" She slammed back into her seat and tossed her head back. "What am I gonna do with you?" She raised a fist to the ceiling. Her jaw jutted, she stressed every syllable, plus a few of her own. "Will-la I e-verrrr win with this chi-old?" And then she cried.

I slumped low in my seat, bangs hiding my face so I could peer at her without showing my tears. The leg man soothed her: "Ah, now, come on. You'll be fine."

I've done it again, I thought. Some people slow down when anxious, but Mom pushes harder—a habit I'd inherited, apparently.

Finally, I rubbed my index finger over one of the metal pincers on my new leg. They were every bit as sharp as they looked. I wanted to bang my head against the wall but instead grabbed one of the parallel bars. The pincers clamped shut as my knee straightened into a standing position.

The leg man shouted, "There you go! That's it."

I squeezed every muscle and broke out in a sweat. When I finally stood up, a girl stared back at me in the mirror. Sweat chilled on my neck when I realized it was me. I swayed up and back, tightening my grip as I tried to go for the other bar. My right side, with no leg to anchor it, now pitched forward. "Get her!" yelled Mom. She tossed her cigarette butt and jumped up, grabbing her handbag instead of me and clutching it as if watching a car swerve and miss her before it slammed into a brick wall. On his knees, the leg man threw a hand to my belly the way Johnny Bench's baseball glove goes up on a strike-out pitch. He caught me.

I was steady, although I still couldn't reach the other bar, and suddenly I felt my family's signature hug: Mom's fingernails digging into my armpits. Her purse, jammed into my back, leveled me. "See that? You're doing it," she said to the mirror.

"No, you are," I said to her image in my head.

"Now," he said, "guide her hand to the other bar. Good. She has to get used to standing alone. Okay. Let go."

"Are you crazy?" said Mom's eyebrows in the mirror.

My eyes swept down the mirror to myself standing beneath Mom. I still couldn't believe it was me and yet it was the way I'd always imagined myself: a whole girl. And, even better, I would no longer have to squiddle. I would be one who walked.

As I admired the girl in the mirror, I noticed a doughnut of flesh topping the corset. No wonder it hurt. I was not a fat kid, not even chubby, but every ounce of baby fat on that thigh was being wrenched by the corset. I imagined Mom's voice: *I'll wring your neck!* The thought brought on a quake of laughter that almost took me down.

"What's so funny?" asked Mom.

"Watch it. Don't fall," said the leg man. The muscles of my thigh tightened and cramped. This was too hard. I couldn't walk even when holding onto the bars. How would I walk without them? Once a squiddler, always a squiddler, I decided. My knee wobbled.

The leg man winced. "Sit down. I don't like how it's fitting."

I fell onto my seat, relieved, jubilant, and now that I was invested, a nervous wreck.

The leg man snatched up both legs and excused himself before I'd even tried on the second. The grass stains on my dress seemed to blot out my image in the mirror. The picture of myself as a whole girl receded with every clang of machinery from the workshop: buzzing, hammering, and a noise that took me to the place where questions endlessly thudded against the walls of my skull: "What if these legs don't work? What sin have I committed?"

Sitting in The Hanger with my hopes pinned to a life of hauling my weight on wood with leather corsets and metal pincers, versus a life of squiddling, I realized something like "I am so screwed." In a burst of agitation, I asked, "Why was I born without legs?"

Mom probably felt this question coming. She swallowed, as if nauseous, before she answered, in a strangely even tone, "When you were born, Dr. U. handed you to me and said, 'Joy, your baby doesn't have any legs.' But I hugged you and said, 'Eileen is my four-leaf clover.'"

I shook my head. That didn't sound right to me.

Mom read my face and sighed. "Oh, Eileen . . . if I could just give you mine . . ." And for a moment I believed she would do that. Could a doctor put a set of legs on another body? I was giddy at the prospect. My brothers and sisters would never go for that, though. It dawned on me that there was nothing I could do to change this situation. I twisted restlessly in my seat.

"Now, that's enough!" Mom whispered, as she dug through her purse for another cigarette. I stood on my knee, eyes level with Mom, and demanded answers. "Why? But *why* was I born without legs? What happened to *me*?" I wanted to dump this problem on someone else. And that, to Mom, was abhorrent: shirking responsibility was the lowest of crimes.

She stopped digging, and I steadied myself for the backlash.

My mother's face shifted to the sure smile of a Bible salesman. As she opened her mouth, I squeezed my eyes shut. Why had I asked her again?

"You don't have legs," she said, "because baby Jesus chose *you* to carry the cross!"

I opened my eyes and saw the picture with the folded hands above her head. A salty taste built up in the back of my throat. I swallowed, fighting tears until my mind went numb.

CHAPTER 5

Digging to China

Finally I had legs. But who needed legs when my friend Penny and I were digging to China? Behind a bush we dug an escape tunnel with Frankie and Ted and the Taylor brothers, who kept yelling, "Faster, faster. The Russians are gonna drop the A-bomb!"

Several days a week I was learning to walk. In a pressed white uniform and a nurse's cap, my therapist, Miss Connor, coaxed a champion out of me. Her eyes danced over a patient smile. Six months later, I was ready for kindergarten. But which school? Saint Vivian did not begin until second grade, and I was told I would not be attending the kindergarten in our neighborhood. Possibly Mom or the school district chose to keep me off of the regular school bus, and Mom had her own transportation policy: she would not drive a child to school.

In the end, Mom chose a kindergarten program at the high school she had attended because the nuns agreed to drive across town to pick me up. Briefly, and possibly experimentally, the school ran a kindergarten staffed by nuns who had fled war-torn countries. If this kindergarten in a high school was an odd combination, Mom didn't question it.

My worries about walking in a pair of flesh-chewing baseball bats quickly faded in contrast to nuns who had escaped war. Two nuns came for me each morning. They demanded that I greet them in their native tongues, French and German. Otherwise they refused to budge, in which case Mom would scream, "I do not drive kids to school!"

"Bonjour" and *"Guten morgen, Schwester"* might as well have been an epic poem. I could never memorize it.

On this morning I sprawled on the kitchen floor right next to Mom, who fried bacon and eggs while kids weaved past her in blue-and-green plaid uniforms. Several ate at the table, Bridget the mini-Mom made sandwiches at the counter, and Ted traversed the cabinets monkey-style. Baby Matthew gurgled in his high chair, hands outstretched like miniature stars webbed with pureed peaches.

From the floor I gripped Mom's ankle and bellowed, "What are the lines?"

"For the play?"

"For the NUNS!"

"Get it right!" Mom screamed back with a stomp of the foot. She had all these kids to feed. "Not driving, no sir."

In my head *"Schwester"* turned into Uncle Fester from *The Addams Family.* I howled in panic. Mom shook me off as she flipped the bacon and screamed, "Dick!" until Dad heard her from their bathroom upstairs. "Dick! She's pitching a fit!"

Dad moved at his own pace. He came downstairs from his morning ritual smelling of aftershave, wearing a crisp white shirt, a tie that cut like a noose into his aging football neck, and one of his "Dutch" suits. Mom called anything that she considered cheap "Dutch." She preferred tailored wools and linens, whereas Dad went for any suit that fit, and if it happened to come in a polyester plaid, so be it.

As Dad presented himself in the kitchen, Mom winced at his attire and the rest of us twitched from fear. He'd entered wearing his don't-mess-with-me look. His black hair was now graying, but still thick. "What's the problem?" he asked. All activity came to a halt, except the sizzling of bacon. Even Ted stopped swinging from cabinets.

"She doesn't remember the lines," said Mom. "What is it? *Guten*-what?"

"How long's she been at that school? I tell you every morning. It's *bonjour* and *Guten morgen*."

"Uncle Fester?" I asked.

"What?"

"That's not all of it. There's something else," I moaned. "They won't drive me if I don't get it right!"

"Not doing it," Mom muttered under her breath.

Dad looked at me without emotion and said, "Get up." He knew that this voice got every kid in the house moving, so the sandwich-maker went into overdrive, the breakfast-eaters downed their eggs, and Dad headed toward the den, calling Michael to fetch me and Kevin to find my legs, which might be anywhere: under Frankie's bed, in the toy closet, or down in the basement. Kevin always got the impossible tasks, while Michael was often asked to present the prize on a silver platter. Michael snatched me up and carried me football-style, under his arm, to deposit me at Dad's feet.

The den had a wall of bookshelves with a fireplace and a brick hearth, a stereo inside a buffet table, and a sea of toys spread over its electric-blue carpet. Often the toys got under Dad's feet, causing him to mutter curses. On this carpet we held nightly flying con-tests. Rosa and Michael would flip and toss us on their feet until one of us little ones would fly into the brick hearth, barely missing a lively fire. Then Dad would call from the kitchen, "Kevin, if I have to tell you to cut that out again."

Now, I looked up at Dad and bolted, but he grabbed me by one arm and lifted me onto the sofa. "Settle down," he said, and called impatiently to Kevin, who was probably on his fourth bedroom upstairs, empty-handed and frantic. Finally Kevin rushed in and dropped the legs next to us. "About time," said Dad.

Meanwhile, the French nun came to the back door, and someone yelled from the kitchen, "They're here!"

"Stall 'em," Dad yelled back.

He knelt down with a sock in one hand and a leg in another, mumbling, "Damned if I know." He said this every day, and I'd wonder: *Know what?*

We both stared at the metal hinges on each side of my knee as he fixed the leg over chewed-up flesh. He tightened the laces around my thigh, gritting his teeth until he turned red as fire. "That oughta do it," he said.

My thigh throbbed, and I stood up which made the whole leg go numb. The left one burned since Dad had wrapped an Ace bandage around it and yanked the end of the bandage from a valve at the bottom, sucking me in as if I were being swallowed by a mongoose. "That tight enough?" he asked.

I nodded and my eyes watered, but Dad said, "Oh no you don't. Now, get going." He patted my shoulder and stood up.

Wobbling like the Bride of Frankenstein, I took off for my hiding place behind the couch. Michael stood in my path.

Finally Dad carried me to the back porch, where we faced the dogwoods, which I thought of as our palace guards. In the driveway, the idling station wagon was spray-painted off-white over a dark unidentifiable color. Dad set me in the backseat and nearly slammed the door before plodding back up to the house. Pressed against the torn plastic seat cover, I saw only black cloth in the front seat, the German nun at the wheel. Both nuns waited in bitter silence until I said, "*Bonjour,* Uncle Fester."

"No," said the German nun from inside a shaking wimple, "no, no, no."

The French nun turned to her, eyes stressed in a silent plea.

My anxiety escalated with the thought of another tardy slip from my teacher, a nun who had escaped from a Chinese concentration camp. Mom would always say, "I loooove Sister China," and I would nod, even though "Sister China" marched from aisle to aisle slapping a yardstick on random desktops and calling out problems in accented English: "How many pennies in knicker? How many knickers in dime?" I was terrified of her yardstick.

Briefly, the French nun turned and smiled, while the other kept her hands locked on the wheel, mouth clamped. Then the sympathetic nun turned to her window and prayed. Up at the house the screen door slammed and Kevin, on his way to school, came through the evergreens that flanked the basketball court. He spotted my pleading face, shrugged, and headed back into the house. Seconds later, Mom's voice escalated from inside, "I will not . . . !" and before she finished I heard the screen door again, then Dad stepped out of the dogwoods, face tight. My panic escalated until he stuck his head in the window and said, "Morning, Sisters!" The nuns nodded, and the French nun started to say "*Bonj*—" but the driver nudged her.

Dad's face was right in front of me. He bit his lower lip, trying to hold back from a scolding or trying to remember the lines himself. He was not solidly on my side, but this was the best I would get. He was out there, maybe only because Mom had shoved him, but he was there. "Honey, I just told you. It's *Bonj* . . . ."

And the line seemed to fall from the sky. I cut him off. "*Bonjour* and *Guten morgen, Schwester.*"

Silence filled the car. Dad's eyes narrowed, then he fussed with my hair. "Have a good day, Trix." The engine started. Exhausted, I fell into the seat. This was the easy part; awaiting me at the school across town was the yardstick-tapping Sister China. As we left the driveway, I tugged at the nylon laces of the corset on my thigh. It might take a while to break out of it, but by 3:30 I would be digging to China, having stepped from this ancient chariot and kicked myself free of my bindings.

CHAPTER 6

Under This Chair

Late in the summer during Mom's tenth pregnancy, Dad hosted a reception at his new showroom. He was moving from the shadows of the Procter & Gamble smokestacks to the commercial strip north of the city. For the big event, Mom bought a misty-green chiffon dress and scheduled an extra trip to Ken's Beauty Shoppe for a fancy up-do.

In the salon I waited for Mom under a broken hair dryer and checked my own Joan-of-Arc haircut in the mirror. It had a gap in the front where I'd lopped off my bangs in an attempt to look like my sisters, who all wore their hair long and parted off-center. I smiled: more gaps where there had once been teeth. Humbled, I watched the owner wash Mom's hair, coat it in goop, and wind it into tight curls, leaving pinwheels at her ears. She came out of the hair dryer talking: "As if the nuns weren't enough, Ken, I tell you, it's those priests . . ." The hairdresser ratted Mom's hair while she addressed him in the mirror, black frizzle shooting up from her scalp, the pin curls like quotation marks on either side of her mouth.

At the time I didn't realize that Mom did not distinguish between hairdressers and confidants. I just assumed that everyone was her best friend. Ken was a middle-aged man buttoned into a barber's tunic. His wife, Josie, worked at the next station, wearing her hair in a turban with a spray of curls poking out. Both hairdressers listened to Mom drone on about the Church. I'm not sure they were even Catholic, but they listened as if tuning in to their favorite sitcom.

"Those Jesuits are a bunch of damn liberals nowadays," she said to Ken. "We send our boys to the Jesuits because they're supposed to be the smartest, and they come home with a list of questions about God. I'll be dipped! At least the Franciscans don't *think* so much. They certainly don't question God. That's not what Catholics do. Question. No. Not my kind, anyway. Is that what we're paying all this tuition for? Questions? If those Jesuits are so smart, why don't they have answers?"

By the conclusion of her hour-long monologue, Mom's hair had been swept into a ring of curls forming a crown. Her hair became her shield, which she would tap whenever she felt under attack. Rosa told me a few years later that secretly Mom sobbed in our laundry room about being pregnant again. I don't know how many pregnancies Mom had cried over, but if one were to ask her how she felt, Mom would have said, "Fantastic!" Then she would have tapped her hair and muttered under her breath, "I shoulda been a nun."

During this reception of Dad's, Mom was confronted by a man she barely knew who took her hand, looked down at her pregnant stomach, and said, "Joy, don't tell me you made *that* mistake again."

The next day, on our screened-in porch, she recounted the story to Grandpa and Katie: "Mistake?" she told that man. "That's right. The same one your mother made!" After a tap, she finished with a smile that showed off teeth that were a tad too large. Grandpa was dazzled by her gumption. (He had once showed up at the Russian Tea Room in a cowboy hat, pretending to be an oil-rich millionaire in order to get a table.)

With each baby came another eighteen years of servitude. Mom fought to hide her gloom over her tenth two-decade commitment, but couldn't. The burden became so great that it meddled with even the tiniest of her promises. I learned then that once a person is in over her head, it is true that the small stuff is what takes her down. In Mom's case, it was a movie.

Back in July, Mom had promised to take Liz, Frank, Ted, and me to see *The Sound of Music*. She was tense, trying to do forty things at once. Mom hadn't been to a movie theater in years. She loved to watch oldies on television, chain-smoking and calling out the well-worn lines, but she disliked movie theaters, imagining them to be full of greasy popcorn, stray hairs, and filth. This movie took on such importance to her, though, that she would tough out her misgivings. How could she not go to a film involving a nun—one played by Julie Andrews—and Nazis? Mom loved a movie with Nazis.

That morning she tried to cram in a quick trip to the A&P. The temperature, which was well into the nineties, made the parking lot sizzle, and four of us crammed half our bodies through the car windows to gasp for air. We didn't realize that we were blocking oxygen from the toddler, Matthew, who passed out in the backseat. I think it was Liz who glanced back and screamed, "Matthew!" Frank ran for Mom, who almost fainted when she found her baby unconscious. She zipped us over to our Aunt Margaret's house, where Shirley, the level-headed babysitter who cared for us when our mothers had babies and had fifteen children of her own, was in charge that day. Carefully lowering Matthew into a bath of cool water, she revived him. Once Matthew was breathing regularly, Shirley calmed Mom down. We returned home and even though we missed the movie, we knew not to complain. In fact, we didn't speak of that day afterward. To do so would have seemed like a betrayal.

In September, I entered first grade at the public school where, I was led to believe by my Catholic family, chaos ruled. Frankie was now going to Saint Vivian. I was lonely, and for company I turned to our mother, who was praying rosaries nightly and attending Mass every morning at six.

In the darkened living room, by an upholstered chair under a crucifix, I'd lean on my one knee beside Mom, who knelt with her elbows pressed into the prayer chair and launched into *Ho-lee-Mar-ee-motherofGod*. Her words whirred like the static on Dad's transistor during a thunderstorm. This prayer was taking Mom somewhere else, and I wanted to go there with her. If she wanted to be a nun, I would be one also. Holy Mary, Mother of God, would lift us up and fly us away. From the power of our faith, Mom and I might coast on devotion alone.

If only prayer were more than a string of syllables to me. I knew syllables. I was learning phonics. And these were just sounds, a buzzing blur. I'd look at Mom clutching the rosary to her lips, kissing it every time she said "Mary." She'd cradle her head in her arms, the rosary spilling from her crown, beads jiggling. I didn't get it. Sometimes I would touch her cheek to see if she was crying.

Later in my bed I'd run through my list of mothers to call upon in times of distress. Every one of them could fly: Mary Poppins, a "housewitch," a genie, and a nun in an aerodynamic wimple. They would rescue Mom, whom I envisioned lumbering down to the main road, where she would step into P & G commuter traffic just before a flying nun plucked her from death.

The next night we'd be back at the prayer chair, Mom on her knees and me in my nightgown. Hovering over our right shoulders would be Jesus on his crucifix. *Our father, who art in Heaven . . .*

There was a six-inch skirt around the bottom of our prayer chair, and I was able to fit my entire body—lying flat—underneath it and stay perfectly hidden beneath its pleats. I'd been practicing doing this since Rosa told me about Hitler. She said he'd put me in a shack with all the other crippled kids and blow it up. After that I would silently say to myself, "Under this chair is where I'll be when the Nazis come for me."

This was also the chair where my older sisters' dates had to wait after they came through the front door. One night, as we finished the rosary, the doorbell rang. Mom answered it while I squiddled to the front hall to spy. I perched on the bottom step, staring at Bridget's boyfriend standing in the foyer. He was all blue eyes and Irish features. I started for the landing and stopped because I was squiddling. This was one of the side effects of walking on legs—I became ashamed of squiddling.

As I tugged at the hem of my nightie, I wondered when someone would come to call on me. Mom ushered the boyfriend into the prayer chair and turned on the lamp, which required her to bend over him in her nightgown, and yelled right in his ear, "Dick! We have company." Then she took off.

I squiddled to the top of the stairs and clamped my hands on the wrought-iron railing, where I could only see the boy's shadow over the crucifix on the wall adjacent to him. Bridget opened her bedroom door and whispered to me, "That him?"

I loved being the go-to girl for my oldest sister. It made me feel like I actually knew something.

"What's happening down there?" she asked.

"Mom's getting Dad."

"Oh, no!" She ripped at her curlers. Coiled brown ribbons fell. Her blue eyes were ablaze and her cheeks flushed because she was so easily embarrassed. I couldn't wait to be a teenager. I figured it was all just like Patty Duke running in circles with a head full of curlers in a pair of tight pants. Meanwhile, Dad would be reluctantly setting his newspaper aside at the kitchen table. Seconds later he was in the living room, where we both knew that he would square off to the boyfriend in the opposing chair. The boy would have nowhere to turn to escape Dad's fisheye except to that crucifix. I couldn't wait for the day when Dad would stare down my dates.

In a year Bridget would leave for college. Someone else would launch just about every year after that. In the meantime, I still slept in a crib, which was lately in Frankie and Kevin's room. My crib had been shifted from room to room as more babies arrived. I liked it here best, because Frankie was coaching me on how to survive the playground. In the dark we focused on how to kick or otherwise beat up a boy at school named Trent, who followed me everywhere and screamed, "Walkie-talkie legs, walkie-talkie legs!" It felt as if everyone on the playground knew this about Trent and me, and I worried that I'd have Trent stalking me until one of us drew our last breath. If that had to be the case, I was determined to have the last breath.

Sadly, my kick was not powerful enough to take Trent down. It was like leaning into one stilt while slapping an opponent with another stilt, and it was probably more dangerous to me than to Trent. I'd made it through fall by pacing the edges of the playground while Trent hounded me. Any other girl would have run away, but I was trapped. There was nowhere to hide on that stretch of asphalt, around which the school formed a horseshoe.

To cut down on the amount of time I spent dodging Trent, I took long lunches with my new Maxwell Smart lunchbox. I'd begged Mom for it and this was one of the few things I owned that none of my older siblings had handed down to me.

One winter day, I spotted Trent waiting for me in the snow with his black hat, straps hanging loose at his chin, a faux-fur flap over menacing eyes. He was walking in circles, a madman, as far as I could tell.

The recess teacher, Mrs. Jarvis, was holding hands with two girls at a time while a crowd of girls waited their turn. Since I was too late to hold her hand, I tried to draw out my lunch, perspiring in my coat, but a lunch lady said, "You have to have recess. *Everyone* needs exercise. Now go on!"

Outside, I stepped onto a sheet of ice packed hard by children racing and skidding. The perspiration on my back chilled when it met the cold air. Trent's eyes flashed as he started toward me. I'd never get Mrs. Jarvis's attention, so I edged slowly toward the perimeter of the courtyard, into the shadows, clutching Maxwell Smart while Trent chanted at my back, "Walkie-talkie, walkie-talkie." Suddenly, I found myself at the opening of the horseshoe, and without thinking, I hobbled—although I saw myself as making a mad dash—around the corner of the brick building, away from everyone and into an area that was off-limits. There, in the alley, I leaned against the doors, which remained locked until Mrs. Jarvis blew the whistle for lineup.

Just as I relaxed, Trent came whizzing around the corner and pinned me to the door. "Walkie-talkie, walkie-talkie, walkie-talkie!" Automatically my hand rose and fell as I clutched my lunchbox. Kaboom! I clocked Trent with Maxwell Smart, tin to nose, with an apple inside for leverage.

His nose bled into his gnashing teeth. I hadn't meant to do *that*. I reached out but he took off, wailing as he rounded the corner headed right for Mrs. Jarvis, a trail of bloody snow in his wake. I lagged behind, fully expecting Mrs. Jarvis to give me a gold star for protecting myself. Instead, she took one look at Trent and dropped the girls' hands, hustling to meet him. Trent sniffled. The loose straps from his hat rippled at his chin. He clapped a palm to his bloody nose and pointed back at me, while I limped fast toward her, weapon in hand.

Mrs. Jarvis looked up from Trent's face. I could see from her narrowed eyes that she had no gold star for me. Stopping, I looked down at Maxwell Smart, my smoking gun.

In the principal's office, Mrs. Jarvis did most of the talking. My lunchbox was confiscated. Maxwell Smart gone, "forever," said the principal, dropping it into her trashcan.

The secretary called my home, and Candy tried to tell her that Mom was out and that she herself could not drive to pick me up. The secretary handed me the phone. "I don't know what this colored woman is saying." When I heard Candy's wheezing breath I started bawling. She hummed in my ear, which calmed me down. Finally the receptionist yanked the receiver away. "Okay, go have a seat."

Mom arrived at the office three hours later. She apologized to the principal on my behalf. In the car I said, "I didn't mean to hurt him. I was just trying to get away."

"I know that, Eileen," said Mom, backing onto Winton, a four-lane road. I'd never seen anyone back onto this bustling road. A car swerved and a bunch of other cars honked. I was more concerned about Maxwell Smart. Why had Mom let the principal take my lunchbox? I was sorry that I'd bloodied someone's nose but, then again, not entirely. I still could not see any other way out.

That night, Frank and I went over the situation. Our focus in the past had been clocking Trent. We needed a new plan. Still, I loved that Frankie had tried. Primal instincts now off the table, Frankie came up with loftier plans: miracles.

Whether we liked it or not, Frankie and I were both serious candidates for the clergy. Any respectable Catholic family was expected to pony up one kid to the cloth. Logically it followed that with almost ten children, half girls and half boys, we should offer up at least one priest and one nun.

Frankie seemed content to become a priest, although he'd rather have been a professional basketball player. His athletic goals were sketchy at best. He could sink a ball from anywhere on the court—that was *if* he got his hands on it—but he was scrawny and not aggressive. Later, coaches would *bribe* Ted to join their teams; he would be Dad's best hope for a football star, although his heart was buried in books. Frankie would have given his right eye for a fraction of Ted's strength, but for all his coaching on how to beat up Trent, Frank was not himself a fighter.

As for me, no one would say the words but I suspected that there would be no boy waiting in the prayer chair for me, and that could only mean that I was headed for the convent.

Secretly, I longed to become a ballerina. I'd dreamed of being one since Aunt Gert's costar danced in a gold-sequined pantsuit at Saint Vivian's variety show. When people asked me what I wanted to be when I grew up, I would say, "Ballerina," until I learned to read faces. Once I saw my grandmother's impenetrable face go slack, I added, "Or a missionary nun in Africa."

The aspect of Catholicism which obsessed me was miracle stories. Frankie nurtured that hope by parting with his baseball books temporarily and choosing instead books on saints from Saint Vivian's library. At night, under the tent of his plaid bedspread, he'd read to me about stoning, starvation, degradation, and burning at the stake. When Frankie saw a picture of the shrine at Lourdes, he pointed excitedly. "That's where we're going. If you drink water from the well, you'll get a pair of legs." We imagined the miracle to come: a sky opening up to a magnificent light and wonder-filled faces surrounding me as my legs transformed. There were three things I would do immediately: I would run; I would ride a bicycle; and I would leap in a series of grand jetés. The only problem was how to get to Lourdes.

When Lent arrived that year, our neighbor, a Girl Scout leader, said she was taking her daughter and Liz to the shrine in Mount Adams on Good Friday. They went every year. Frank decided that the shrine in Mount Adams might be a reasonable substitute for Lourdes. We begged to be included, and our neighbor agreed to take us. At the shrine, you were expected to say a rosary while climbing an enormous staircase to its plaza. The idea was that you said a Hail Mary on each step and an Our Father on every tenth step. At the top, you were to kiss the feet of Christ, and we thought this would be Jesus himself.

From my bed in the crib, I imagined my lips pressed to a suffering man's flesh. "I can't do that," I said.

"You want legs?" Frankie asked.

Did I want them that much?

On the morning of Good Friday we eyed the stone church on the hill. The tip of a life-sized crucifix hovered above a mob in its courtyard. I cringed with every step. Momentarily I forgot why we were there, and I marveled at the hills dotted by shotgun houses. Rosaries lacing their hands, a string of Catholics formed a line several blocks long. "He's really up there?" I asked Frank.

"You don't believe, do you?"

"So it'll work?"

"Lear." He shook his head. His expression told me, "We've gone over this."

I was getting angry now. To think that Mom and Dad had let me go on this long without legs when all it took was a drive across town on Good Friday, a few prayers, and a kiss? "Why didn't we do this before?"

He shrugged.

I bit my lip. My faith was weak. If Frankie were the one without legs, he would surely be the one awarded a miracle.

When we reached the top, I had to shield my eyes against the sun to get a good look at the crucifix. I halfway hoped Jesus wasn't alive and suffering, even if that meant I couldn't have legs. "It's not him," I said to Frank.

"Go on, Eileen," said our neighbor, and she nudged the back of my neck. "It's your turn." I closed my eyes, and Frankie gave me a gentle shove. I kneeled to kiss the feet, but they were only cold porcelain. Nothing changed. Frank finally led me away.

"Maybe it takes a while," he said, on the drive home.

"Shut up," I told him. Staring out the window, I was looking for someone with whom I could lodge my complaint.

CHAPTER 7

An Education

Second grade, the year of great expectations: I could finally go to Saint Vivian. In the spring I would make my First Holy Communion. Simultaneously I was shifted from Frankie's bedroom into Liz's, where I now had a real bed and a sister to share my nighttime stories. Mom was pregnant with her eleventh baby. The tenth baby was a boy, Tim, and so were the eighth and ninth children, Ted and Matthew. As I saw it, we were *owed* a baby girl.

New obstacles threatened my expectations, though. Transportation to school posed the first. Since the bus for Saint Vivian did not come by our house, Mom signed me up for a county van that shuttled mentally retarded adults to a sheltered workshop. A woman with Down Syndrome would ask me daily, "Eileen, are you retarded?" I would blush and say, "I don't think so." I always kept my cheek pressed to the window while chiding myself for thinking I was better than her. At the same time I would be praying to slip from the van unnoticed. Inevitably, as we pulled into Saint Vivian's parking lot some kid would yell, "Retarded bus!"

Coming off of the "retarded bus" was bad PR at any school.

People would tell me that no one saw me any differently, but I knew that only *some* people saw me as the same. My job would be to find those people. At school I would learn precisely how far my

69

neighborhood friends' loyalties stretched: they would choose me *not last* for a team sport but second-to-last, which left me feeling both grateful and betrayed.

Saint Vivian was a machine for churning out athletes. The parents here valued three things in an education, in this order: athleticism, devotion to the Church, arithmetic. Even as young as the second grade, the girls shortened their pleated skirts by rolling the waistband. They tied their blazers over the bulge so the nuns wouldn't notice; their knee socks were scrunched down to anklets so they'd be ready to kick ass; and they wore a look in their eyes that said, "Wanna bet?" They played kickball and softball in the rain, in the snow, and possibly in their sleep. Often I ended up playing hopscotch with the other girls who'd been picked last because no one noticed when we abandoned the outfield.

Now that I was in a twin bed in Liz's room, I'd lost Frankie's coaching and the drone of his RBI calculations at night. I couldn't sleep, and Liz wasn't a talker. She was the quintessential Saint Vivian girl: athlete, cheerleader. And I was on the retarded bus. I worried that she was embarrassed by me. I was embarrassed by me.

The tension between us wasn't helped by this new arrangement of bedrooms. Liz was eager for Bridget to go to college so she could move in with Rosa, but that was a year away. In the meantime she was stuck with me. Already I had awakened with the flu one morning and threw up on her brand-new turntable, so Mom stuck the turntable in its case in the bathtub to wash it. "See, it's all better," she'd said to Liz, who narrowed her eyes at me before turning away in disgust.

Then came the winter morning when we awakened to the news that Mom was in the hospital. She had slipped on the icy staircase after six o'clock Mass and broken her leg. It seemed as if she would never come home. When she arrived finally, I latched back onto her, sobbing inconsolably on the nights Dad took her out to dinner.

Within weeks Mom was gone again. This time she delivered a girl, Nina, who came with a shock of black hair and smelled like the peach pie that Shirley baked. Shirley, who had revived Matthew when he almost suffocated in the car, was now staying with us. Her stay had been extended since the doctors had kept Mom in the hospital after some complications. Strangely enough, the baby came home with Dad. I missed Mom but I was so in love with our baby girl that I hardly noticed. "Now, don't lick her cheeks," Shirley would say. "Give that child space to breathe."

Finally news trickled down to us younger children that our mother wasn't bouncing back this time. When she came home from the hospital, Mom peered out from her white coverlet like a grounded bird who'd forgotten how to fly. She stayed in bed by day and paced at night. Her hair flat and skin yellow, she reeked of cigarette smoke and a stale odor that I came to know as a smell worked up from the mere effort to stay alive.

At night, Shirley went home to her own huge family as soon as Dad stepped through the back door. To help out, Candy came more often to clean. Since the oldest children became parent substitutes, Rosa was assigned to bath duty. Each night Frankie, Ted, and I went to bed with the notion that by emptying the tub we'd drowned an imaginary boy, Jimmy Quigsley, who, according to Rosa, lived in the drain. Meanwhile our mother prayed and paced outside our doors. I'd call to Frankie from my new bed in Liz's room, but he'd have fallen asleep. I'd turn to Liz who, without opening her eyes, would say, "I'm asleep."

One morning, Bridget stood in my doorway. "Mom's in the hospital again," she said. "You'll have to put your own legs on today."

"Where's Dad?" I asked, but Bridget was already gone. I turned to Liz. Her bed was already vacated.

Somehow we children had slept through the previous night while our mother was taken by ambulance, against her will, to the hospital. I picked up on what had happened by listening from under the kitchen table to adult conversations. Eventually I would hear Mom's account, and I would see for myself what she was like during a later episode. Based on everything I heard about my mother's mental state on that night and based on what I would learn about psychosis and mania, I imagine the night unfolding this way:

Days after she has the baby, Joy is still only able to doze in brief spurts. One night she wakes panicked, feeling as if her body will forget how to breathe if she gives in to sleep. It's an early summer night. Her pale pink nightgown is pasted to her back and chest with sweat. Everything is musty; her skin is oily. She throws off her sheet. If she could throw off her flesh, she would do it.

Everyone's in bed, except Dick, who's still reading his Time *magazine downstairs. Instead of pacing with her rosary, Joy goes to the window that overlooks the neighbors' backyards. The yard to the left used to be a nursery. Because it has a deep pond and a swimming pool, it is fenced off. Right now it seems like a sanctuary. A weeping willow dips into the pond; pines darken most of the land.*

In the breeze at the window, Joy peels her nightgown away from her skin. Her breath is short. She draws in a deeper breath, but it all feels labored.

Then she hears God's voice. She's never heard Him before, and she can't quite trust that it's real. But if Mary has visited Joy's mother, why shouldn't God visit Joy?

Or maybe this is the Devil?

God senses that she doesn't believe Him. He tells her that she has to prove her devotion by going next door and jumping in the pond. But she can't swim. She tells Him that, and he says that it is because she can't swim that she has to try. She has to prove her devotion to Him.

Really?

Or is this the Devil talking?

Now God wants to know why she questions Him. Doesn't she know that He's always protected her?

Yes, she does know that. But He doesn't believe her, and if she wants Him to believe her she has to go to the pond.

She wrestles with this voice until she's so confused she can't think. It looks cool by the pond. She dashes from her room and down the hall, then the stairs, bare feet slapping the slate in the front hall, silk fluttering as she passes Dick in the kitchen.

"Why are you up?" asks Dick, glancing over his magazine. From across the kitchen he smells her musty odor. She hasn't slept because of her praying. He'd assumed this would pass, but she's not the same this time. "Joy?"

She doesn't answer him.

"Joy!"

She passes him, racing toward the back door. He jerks up from his chair, and it scrapes the floor. "Stop!" He chases after her, reaches out and catches only her nightgown, but the damp silk ripples through his fingers. She tugs free. Her hand is on the doorknob, and she's talking gibberish in something like Latin. Her mouth is working so furiously that it's foaming. Her free arm is batting him away, flapping like a crow, while he's trying to hold her. In between the gibberish, she's saying, "I can't swim . . . I believe you. I do!" Then she's crying, saying, "All right. All right. I'll go. I'm going. But will you save me?"

"Be still, Joy! Save you from what?"

She pulls open the door and pushes the screen door next.

"Where do you think you're going?"

"I told you I would do it. I'm going. I'm going to the pond."

He starts to ask why, but he knows she'll drown if he lets her go. He has no choice but to tackle her; she fights him as if he were trying to strangle her. He's dragged her back to just inside the door, and now he has to sit on her to keep her down. She's pushing into his chest. She says she can't breathe, and he almost gets up but then she hisses, "Ssstop it, you devil! Get off of me!"

"That's not right," he says. "What's gotten into you? Joy?" He needs to drag her to the phone so he can call for help. Jack Campbell is across the street. No, Gert. No one else should see this.

But the phone's all the way over by the door to the den, and she's slapping his face so that he has to pull back. He doesn't want his kids to hear this, so he whispers, "Hush, Joy! It's me. It's Dick." When he sees her wince in pain from his weight, he knows that he's gone too far. Now, with his guard down, she's squirming free, twisting her hips to break away. He has to tighten his grip.

"Devil! I can't breathe."

And that's when Gert comes through the screen door. "Dick?"

"Gert!"

Gert couldn't sleep, so she was driving to the A&P to pick up a few things. On the way she saw the light on in Joy's kitchen, so she turned around because she's been worried about Joy. Gert can't believe what she's seeing. She's known Dick since they were teenagers. She liked him so much she introduced him to her baby sister. "Dick! What are you doing?" He looks up at Gert like he's never before seen this woman beneath him. "What do you know about this, Gert?" His eyes are brimming with tears.

"Gert, please!" cries Joy. "He's killing me!"

"She wants to jump in the pond."

Gert knows that would be suicide.

"Devil!" says Joy to Dick.

Gert flinches. Joy's mouth is foaming. Her body is quivering underneath Dick like someone with an unyielding chill, but she's perspiring. "Oh, Joy," says Gert. She closes her eyes, squeezes them shut, and her life as a nurse in the state mental hospital comes back to her. She knows these faces—twisted faces, yellow. Opening her eyes, she says, "I'll get help."

"What do you mean?" Dick asks, as if he knows what she's going to suggest and he's not sure he should agree to it.

Gert mouths the word "hospital."

"Oh no you don't!" screams Joy. "I'm not crazy. Don't say that, Gert. Don't you gang up on me! Let me go, Dick!"

Dick looks as if he's considering what he should do, and he asks Gert, "How?"

"I'll get help," says Gert. She keeps her back to Joy as she dials the operator, takes the receiver into the den, and whispers that she needs an ambulance.

"I can't believe this is happening," says Gert, yet somehow she was almost expecting it.

"Don't, Gert! Don't gang up on me," cries Joy in the voice of a small child, the same voice she used when she overheard the news that her grandfather, the man Joy thought of as her own father, had just died. Now she's all alone in her room and begging, "Come back . . . Gertie? . . . Please!"

CHAPTER 8

A Communion

I waited for Mom's return with a fear that eclipsed even the anticipation of my First Holy Communion. On that day I'd wear a new
white dress with a veil and maybe have a portrait taken, posing with
a miniature Bible in gloved hands. I was afraid to hope for Mom's
attendance at the ceremony, afraid to ask and afraid that it could
become the first of many events without Mom.

Each night Dad returned with eyes swollen and an emotion I'd
never seen on his face. Our aunts had taken the three babies. Dad
barked orders at the oldest kids. When he saw us middle kids running to him, he threw up his hands and we pulled back. No one
asked him to sign school papers; Shirley signed and our teachers
accepted them.

Instead of going to Dad for help with math, I jotted random
numbers down on pages of loose-leaf stained by crumbs from the
kitchen table. The whole neighborhood knew our situation. My
teacher was a friend of Aunt Gert's. Mom had pushed to get me into
her class. If it weren't for this second-grade teacher, I'm not sure
I would have passed that year. She frequently told me I was smart,
when inside I felt as dull as a slug.

Aside from school, I was learning some of life's hardest lessons.
At night I would sneak under the kitchen table to learn about the

straitjacket, the shock treatments, and that Mom had believed she was talking to God. Now she thought she was Jesus. There was no way she would be home in time to see me make my First Communion.

On the Sunday morning of the ceremony, we awakened to Dad's voice from the bottom of the staircase. "I want every one of you to get up and clean this house. Right now!"

"What's the big deal?" said some sleepy voice.

"Your mother's coming home, that's what. Now get to work."

Downstairs Dad explained, "It's just for today, so we're not going to mess it up, right?"

Within minutes everyone was vacuuming, dusting, or making a bed. A few of us scrambled to clear out the debris in the den. While I chucked a xylophone into the toy closet, Rosa marched in, already dressed for church. The xylophone made a sour crash as she dragged me by the elbow to the stairs in the front hall and said, "Sit down." By now Rosa was a slender teen in a miniskirt. Her hair was parted dramatically off-center so that it rippled over one shoulder, giving her a smoldering movie-star look.

"Don't," she said, tapping my nose so that I blinked. "Don't you dare throw one of your fits while Mom's home." Her lips shimmered pearl-pink. "If you start crying, Mom will get sicker and we'll never see her again. Do you hear me?"

There was no way I would get this right. I followed that finger and heard every word, every pause. I had to agree that I was needier than the others and could never let go of Mom easily. Usually someone had to rip me from her ankles, and my parents would call on Rosa to do that. I was terrified of Rosa, so I always screamed louder, never understanding why it couldn't have been Kevin or Bridget coming for me instead.

Now after Rosa stormed off, Bridget found me on the staircase. "Eileen," she said, shaking my shoulder, "aren't you dressed? Come on." Up in my room, she pulled Liz's white organza Communion dress from Liz's closet. "You're wearing this one, right?"

I nodded my acceptance as it occurred to me that there was no other choice. Until now I had believed that someone would surprise me with a new Polly Flinders dress. That disappointment was quickly swallowed by the more upsetting news that Mom would not make it to Mass, which Dad explained on our way into the church. My eyes filled with tears and he said, "Now don't do that. She'll make it to the party."

Instead of attending the afternoon ceremony with my class, I made my First Communion at the 11:30 Mass. I worried that all the fanfare would be taken away from me, but Dad held a small gathering afterward.

By early afternoon I was wearing seven new necklaces and carried in one hand a miniature Bible while clutching in the other a brown paper bag in which I had dumped my greeting cards and gift money: eight dollars and some change. Like other soon-to-be communicants I'd been calculating the gifts I would receive, remembering when Liz had fingered a necklace sent to her by her godfather George Ratterman and boasted that he was a pro football legend. I favored the necklace from my godmother, Aunt Louise: a gold cross with a miniature pearl in the center. She shouldn't be spending money on me, I thought. Mom always said that Louise's tremors came from "working her fingers to the bone." Her gift left me with a bittersweet feeling that would change forever my appreciation of gifts.

Earlier that day, my aunts had filed into the den to drop off the babies. We argued over who would get to hold Nina. Her black hair was pulled up like Pebbles Flintstone. She gave a big smile, all gums, and we started grabbing for her at once.

Soon Dad showed up with Mom on his arm. A few of us gasped

when we saw her standing at the threshold between the kitchen and den. More than anything else, I remember Mom's face that day. Melancholia does in fact color the skin. Mom's flesh was so wan that against her white dress her face was yellowish-green. I wondered if the shock treatments had sucked the light from her eyes, which had gone from their velvety luster to lead-brown. The image was so odd in contrast to my memories of Mom in that smart dress, which Dad had brought to her. Usually Mom wore the dress with pearls and spectator pumps. Now she wore it with clunky shoes, no makeup, and flat hair. She could have been a nun dressed in Mom's clothes.

We took turns hugging her. Dad guarded Mom closely, nudging her away when we held on to her too long. I was just beginning to adjust to seeing her when Dad led her into the living room. That room was off-limits unless we were invited.

By afternoon the neighbors had arrived, along with a few priests, and Katie and Grandpa. The adults were ushered out to the screened-in porch while Herb Alpert and the Tijuana Brass played "Bittersweet Samba" on the turntable. Rosa had talked me into buying the album as a Christmas present for Mom and Dad. I had balked at the cover: a photo of a naked woman immersed in whipped cream. Mom loved it. She played this album every Sunday during the cocktail hour. Today it seemed all wrong, but Barbra Streisand, another of Mom's favorites, would have been a wistful reminder of better days.

Eventually we middle children snuck into the living room and peered over the bottom half of the Dutch door. Mom sat at the wrought-iron table between Dad and one of the priests. I was still in my First Communion dress, although I had taken off my veil. Frankie had to hold me up so that my chin rested on the door. I glanced back and saw Frankie watching Mom with his tongue hanging out in a plaintive daze. Liz was biting her tongue, looking tentative. Ted shimmied up and hefted his belly over the rim. Shirley's delicious comfort food had made a doughboy of him, while I'd been refusing to eat.

Once the other kids realized that we were not invited to the adults' party, they scurried off to play a game of Pickle outside, but I wasn't ready to give up on Mom. I waited in the living room. Eventually Bridget and Rosa paraded the babies out to the porch, and I followed. As I stood just inside the door, I watched Nina's delight with the crowd. She was weeks old and didn't yet notice the difference between Mom and one of my sisters. The baby boys were less content. They were old enough to know their real mother, and at the first glimpse of her they began to whine. Dad sensed trouble. He jerked his head at my oldest sisters—his code for "Take them away now." The babies were whisked back to the den, which made them cry, although we heard their cries hushed by the teenagers' cooing and coddling.

Out on the porch, Mom's empty hands trembled. Dad put his palm on her back. She wasn't talking. I'd never known Mom to be silent, particularly in a crowd.

Finally, Dad moved over to the makeshift bar that he'd set up on a built-in cabinet. This was my chance since Mrs. Campbell, who lived across the street, called to me. I trudged past Dad at the bar when Grandpa joined him and said, "Joy probably shouldn't have alcohol. Let's just give her a little crème de menthe instead."

In her pink Jackie Kennedy suit and heavenly perfume, Mrs. Campbell patted her lap. "Come sit with me, Eileen." I tried to shimmy over her knees without slicing her legs or ripping her nylons. Mom's favorite shopping buddy, Mrs. Campbell wore her blond hair in a French twist. Her gold bracelets clinked along with the ice cubes in her highball glass, kissed by pink lipstick. She looped a finger through my stringy hair, as my sisters described it, but Mrs. Campbell said, "What silky hair you have. We could have so much fun with this hair." I relaxed into her bosom. "Oh, I wish

I had a girl!" she said. "Four boys. I got four boys! Wanna come live with me?" I wasn't so sure I wanted to live with her four boys, but I would have loved to have Mrs. Campbell dote on me. I wondered if I should go upstairs and pack a bag but nothing more was said, and I realized she was only trying to make me feel good.

After a while I turned back to Mom, who sipped an inky drink from a Waterford glass. Her lips and tongue had turned forest green, making her the Wicked Witch of the West. Her dark features frightened me: those green lips, that ashen skin, and those burnt-out sockets for eyes. I had to get closer, to touch her face and see that she was still Mom. Dad was back at the bar with Grandpa again, so I hopped down from Mrs. Campbell's lap and darted for Mom.

I smelled the minty alcohol before I reached her, and she probably heard the creak of my legs because she held out her arms and said, "Come here, Eileen." For a minute she slipped into her old self, lifting me by the armpits and adjusting my position on her lap so the pincers were away from her. She held me this way with my back to her chest. I stretched my arms and curled my spine to make a human body shield between my mother and the others. No one seemed to notice. They were in a heated discussion about long hair. Not the boys' hair—in our neighborhood boys still wore buzz cuts while the rest of the country had gone to ponytails. These adults were talking about the long hair that *girls* wore, straight and parted defiantly down the middle. Always in their eyes, they said, hunks of greasy hair. And those miniskirts!

Before I knew it, Dad's hand was on my shoulder. I firmed up my body to stay put, and it dawned on me that this was only a visit. Soon Mom would have to leave; I would have to let go. She would be locked up again and jolted with electricity or tied into a jacket that made her stand up straight. And I might never see her again.

I twisted around and the priest next to us blinked at the rude kick my leg gave him as I swiveled. Mom was so numb that she didn't complain when I faced her and pulled her neck so that our cheeks touched. Over her shoulder I saw Dad's face tighten. I looked instead into Mom's eyes, which now seemed too dull to belong to her. "Hello," I whispered, and she smiled timidly. "I'm here," I said, lifting the necklaces out from my collar. "I made my First Communion today." Her eyes misted over.

Eventually people began to clear out. Soon we were down to the Campbells and the priests, who would be driven back to the rectory by Dad. "Mom has to go now," Dad said sternly. He started to lift me by my upper arm from Mom's lap. I grabbed the pleats of her dress, burrowing into her chest where I sobbed. Mom stayed rigid. Why wouldn't she fight for me? She'd stopped hugging me back, but she wasn't pushing me away. Dad tried to pry me away without making a scene in front of the others. Mrs. Campbell tried bribing me with her bracelet. I would not let go.

When I peered out from Mom's dress, Dad's lips had turned white. He called for Rosa. I had gone too far. Yet I stiffened in place, tenuous as it might be. By the time Rosa peered over the Dutch door, I began to shriek. Dad shook his head in frustration. Then, as if remembering himself, he ushered the priests and the Campbells toward the kitchen while Rosa worked to pry me from Mom's lap. I tugged harder on Mom's dress. Mom was trying to talk, instead she cried. Rosa yanked me away by the hips, but I switched my grip from Mom's dress to her neck. Rosa loosened my one attached hand and pulled. I grabbed with the other at Mom's belt and all the way down her body as Rosa kept pulling. I made my last swipe for Mom's ankle, but Rosa blocked it with her foot.

Dad was coming back to the porch for Mom at the same time Rosa was rushing me through the living room toward the front hall, yanking me by the arm. I heard Mom's quivering voice as Dad led her to the kitchen. By then Rosa and I were facing the bottom of the hallway staircase. I lunged to catch Mom before she left, but

Rosa heaved me over her right shoulder. I screamed one long, shrill cry of pain and humiliation as it occurred to me that my behavior had sent Mom back to the hospital for good and that Mrs. Campbell was not about to take me in after such a scene. With every step Rosa took, my ribs came down hard on her shoulder. I kicked, and the metal pincers on my left leg threatened to bite into her arm. "Get those things off of me," she snapped.

Upstairs she dropped me on my bed and slapped me before she told me that this was for taking our mom away. She started for the door, but stopped and pointed at me for the second time that day. "And if you think you're coming downstairs again, think twice."

The door slammed and all that was left was the rhythm of pounding feet on stairs against the thumping of a distant basketball from outside, and the fading voices of a thinning crowd now gathered in the kitchen. They were saying goodbye. Mom was still in the house, and I couldn't be with her.

Because I hadn't been able to rein myself in, I had only that horrific scene to remember as my goodbye. I hated myself for what I had done. I would pay in the nights ahead, my siblings' blame leveled at me. Opening the door, I listened from my bed to a tangle of voices, none of which was Mom's. I was sure that Mom had already forgotten me while the others talked about baseball—a ploy, no doubt, to distract her from the pain of saying goodbye to her children. Soon the voices moved out to the back porch, so that I was hearing them from the direction of Frankie's room, which overlooked the basketball court. The kids from the Pickle game ran to the basketball court. "Goodbye! Goodbye!" Their voices were gloomy but somehow noble. Why couldn't I have done that?

I heard car doors open; the Campbells said goodbye. Pulling the lavender-upholstered chair to the window, I watched them descend the slope of our front yard to cross the street. Mr. Campbell had his arm at his wife's waist. She fell into his shoulder momentarily, then righted herself. Next to the Campbells' was the congressman's house, and in the distant space between the two houses I could see Frankie's friend Stilts playing basketball on his court with his sister, Scooter, a girl my age who was the best athlete in our class.

I heard the Campbells call goodbye from their front door, as Dad and Mom and the priests descended our driveway. I knew the car's trajectory, having taken that drive so many times to the leg man and doctors' appointments. The car would head down Winton Road, the main line out of our neighborhood, connecting to Clifton and over to Vine, which was the dividing line between east and west in our city. Vine would lead them uphill just shy of Walnut Hills, where Mom had grown up. It was as if she would go back in time to merge again with her roots, and it would be like she'd never had a life here.

I heard all of that happening, although I couldn't see anything. Pulling the chair closer, I pressed my nose to the window screen and pushed against it to catch a glimpse of the car rolling backward onto the street, gears shifting, steering wheel rotating, before its launch forward. If I could just see it rocking back before that lurching motion . . .

Once I heard the motor fade away, I went to my bed.

I was there forever, or maybe just a minute, before the thump of Stilts's basketball died. It happened just after the ball hit the rim. I jerked my head toward his backyard court. His sister Scooter clamped a hand to her nose while the ball rolled away and Stilts raced toward her. The ball must have come down hard on her face. I couldn't imagine her getting hit because Scooter was brilliant at handling the ball in any game. She made only the trace of a shrill cry. Maybe because she'd been playing so long with boys, she'd learned to stifle her pain. It was one of the loneliest sounds I'd ever heard.

I turned my attention back to my room, to its stillness, and the separation between sunlight and shadows. Dust filled that strip of light in the window, making it appear denser than the cool shadows on either side. Outside, the sun cut into the trees around the abandoned basketball court, creating an exquisite sunset, brutally so, but I kept waiting for it to vanish so that the room would be equal again, no more separation between light and shadow. Then, at least, there would be the promise of darkness.

CHAPTER 9

Out of Nowhere

Mom was released from the hospital after three months, and that news arrived as gloriously as a war coming to an end. We'd all worried that she was lost to us forever. Then she was at home again, back at the stove. She was doing all the same things she'd done before the hospital, only slower and vacantly.

Two years after her release, we were still missing our slick mother with her razor-sharp comebacks. The woman in her place was reading Graham Greene and Camus. She chain-smoked with jittery fingers. Her voice went from tremble to shriek. She no longer walked; she careened.

For a good while, Mom probably took sedatives. Once lithium became available she steadily improved, and of course there was talk therapy. She hated it. On top of that she feared elevators, making it nearly impossible to go to her psychiatrist's office on the seventh floor, although I don't remember that problem coming up in other places, such as department stores. She had one consistent fear, though, and that was airplanes. Even before her hospitalization, she had been known to drop to her knees and pray the rosary in the aisle of a small plane.

Over those two years, Mom's changes had come gradually. The most obvious one was her confusion about God. During the sixties, she had delivered strident monologues in beauty salons and at the A&P: *Is that what we're paying all this tuition for? Questions? If those Jesuits are so smart, why don't they have answers?*

In 1966 *Time* magazine had asked, "Is God dead?" To which Mom had responded, "Absolutely not!"

Now, in 1970, Mom was deeply conflicted, and God was at the core of that crisis. She seemed to read every situation as an indictment of her worth as a mother, a wife, a woman, and a human being. We would see this even in the way that she chastised us. "And just *who* do you think *you* are?" she would say to one of us, but she sounded so beaten down that it was as if she were getting ready to punish herself.

Meanwhile, Dad juggled a car dealership and eleven kids while toting me to prosthetic appointments and running interference for Mom. I was ten and old enough to see that we had fallen from our place: the proud family on the hill. Our screened-in porch had always been full of perfumed ladies and Jesuits clinking Waterford tumblers of Irish Mist. We still had our aunts and uncles, our grandparents, and the Campbells. They never abandoned us, but Mom had lost some close friends. What she probably missed most of all was bridge. This last was a tender mercy; her concentration was shot.

Finally, the priests stopped coming to our Sunday gatherings. This happened once Mom took her complaints about the clergy to the priests themselves. (Her illness would escalate so that in another year's time, when I was in sixth grade, Mom would show up at the rectory, ranting to the pastor about the devil—which was the catalyst for another three-month stay in a locked ward and more shock treatments.)

In my twenties, I would ask Mom to describe a manic episode. In essence, she said: People don't realize that you remember all of it afterward. You know what you said and what you did, but you could no more stop yourself from doing it than you can undo any of it once it's done.

At ten I had only a vague idea of the complexity of Mom's illness and how, or if, it was affected by my being born without legs. Then, on a sweltering afternoon the summer before I entered the fifth grade, I came inside to find Mom sitting at the kitchen table with Michael's dog-eared copy of *The Fall*. Her fingers shook as she inhaled from a cigarette with an inch-long ash, and yet her leaden eyes were grounded. She was lucid enough to not be psychotic but she was still in a netherworld of her psyche, even if not tortured by it.

This was a couple years after my mother thought she was Jesus Christ and one year before she ranted at our pastor. I hadn't read Camus yet and wouldn't have understood his meaning, but I did know what Mom tended to say of such a book: if the Jesuits were going to hand a boy a book in which people questioned God, they were just "asking for it." So I was surprised when she glanced over the curled pages to say, "He's talking about suicide, about whether to live or die." With her eyes and her voice so matter-of-fact, in contrast to her trembling fingers, she was appealing to me to take her seriously, to forget the worry associated with a word such as "suicide," and instead to explore it with her momentarily. Briefly, I glimpsed inside Joy and found the would-be artist, the woman who recounted conversations from the locked ward with the insight of a sage. "I don't think you're paranoid," she had told the patient with paranoid delusions. "In fact, everyone *is* watching you."

Then there was my perspective as the not-so-average ten-year-old girl: I yearned for a mother who would contemplate darkness, eager as I was to have a substantive talk about my legs and what that meant for my life, even if the discussion was deeply confused. On the word "suicide," I pulled up a chair, starved for details.

There is another angle to this moment, which I'd like to forget yet, in all honesty, must include. That is Mom's distortion of Camus' story. It was right there in her description of the scene at the bridge. She talked as if *the protagonist* contemplated suicide. Until I read the book, later, I didn't realize that it was *an unidentified woman* who jumped from the bridge, and that the protagonist was merely a witness. I didn't know that afterward, in an effort to quell his guilt, the protagonist ranted about people with visual or other impairments (people who even today are called "invalids" by some, or, more universally, "disabled"). Having since read the book myself, I'm conflicted. On the one hand, I cling to that intimate moment with Mom, and yet because of her misreading of the story, I want to demand from that woman sitting in our kitchen several decades ago the real story: "What exactly do you think of this man's rage toward the blind, the crippled, and the homeless? Do you ever think about what it means for me to be without legs?" During this brief window she might have shared her deepest feelings, but after that it would be pointless to ask my mother those questions. She would have fallen back on the usual lines: "What do I think of that man on the bridge? I think he ought to talk to a priest . . . What do I think of your legs? Who said you were *different*?"

As for the idea of someone taking their own life, I think my mother's concept of suicide probably never changed over time. She thought that only someone else could stop a person from committing suicide. In Mom's case, that was Dad.

I hated to imagine relying on another person. What if I reached out and there was no one there to stop me? I looked at Mom. Who would stop her if Dad wasn't there?

There was just one week left before fifth grade started, and I was probably more preoccupied with who would be my teacher than what Mom thought about suicide or disability. I was afraid I might land in Sister Luke's fifth-grade class. Sister Luke was about Mom's age, forty-something, and now after the six o'clock Mass every morning Mom was taking her for coffee at Daily Donuts.

Around school, Sister Luke was notorious for identifying her pets and pariahs. She left no room for those in between, sometimes vilifying the very person she'd been grooming as her pet. In her fourth-grade religion class, I had been her pet, which meant that in fifth grade I would have nowhere to go but down. I couldn't tell Mom my fears, though, because Sister Luke was now Mom's best friend. Anyway, Mom would not have seen this pet/pariah issue as a problem. She'd say it was the job of a nun "to keep you guessing."

Others were afraid of Sister Luke because of her eccentricity. Tall and sinewy, Sister Luke's shoulders curled forward, and she gathered her students with a menacing blow of her whistle before turning her back to the rows of children and darting toward the fifth-grade hall in a side-to-side waddle, oblivious to the thirty miniature penguins in her wake. Eccentricity was not a problem for me. While other Catholic girls my age were monitoring their public image, desperate not to stand out as "freaks"—which in 1970 only meant hippies—I had abandoned any hope of popularity, and with my wooden legs I was lucky to be considered "normal." I even had access to the lunch table of the popular girls, although my place had always been at the farthest edge. Although I was never the one girls raced to sit next to, I wasn't the girl others warded off by throwing their trays into the empty spot and saying, "This one's taken." I would never have tried to sit by an insider. Instead I found companionship with the less athletic girls—girls with good grooming, intelligence, and adequate social skills

For her eccentricity, I might have applauded Sister Luke. It was the pet/pariah issue that disturbed me. In our fourth-grade religion class, she named me president, which made me the collector of UNICEF money. At first I was flattered, but then she forced me to go around the room and shake each person's orange box with its faces of starving children. Based on the robustness of each shaken box, we would bear witness to the student's generosity or stinginess. If the box contained only a paltry handful of pennies, this act would amplify its owner's inadequacies. All too often I had to hold up someone's near-empty box as its owner slumped over the desk while the class heckled them.

Adding to the angst were Sister Luke's slideshows. They each had the same browbeaten male voice narrating parables. A woeful beep would alert her to advance the slide. I was haunted by the story of Saul. In one slide he was a tax collector; in another he was being chased by an angry mob. Finally, he was up in a tree with the crowd jeering, "Saul, come down from that tree!" That slide bothered me the most because, as Sister Luke's UNICEF boss, I was in danger of becoming Sister Luke's Saul.

Like most Catholics, she revered the New Testament. I wondered at times if she had memorized it because she barely consulted the page while reciting whole stories aloud: *Then Jesus looked to the apostle he loved most . . .*

Sister Luke's most vexing trait was her whisper. She spoke so quietly that you had to lean in to hear her. She always greeted me with a slight bow, her bent shoulders dipping as if weighted by a yoke. Her eyes would stay fixed as she bowed, unyielding.

On that Sunday before school started, Mom and I went to the eleven o'clock Mass. Mom then charged for the breezeway to see if the class rosters were posted. "They better have put you in Sister Luke's class," she said.

I was sweating to keep up with Mom, who, in those days, moved in jerky, robotic strides. Her hair was no longer a lacquered crown but a blow-dried Joan-of-Arc cut, not so different from the one I was forever trying to grow out. Before I caught up to her, Mom had already turned back. "Come on," she said, grabbing my arm. "The list isn't up yet."

I had to chomp down on my glee. There was still hope. I might yet find myself in someone else's class.

That same afternoon was the church picnic. The older kids didn't come anymore and Mom eagerly volunteered to stay home with the babies, so Dad had become accustomed to taking us middle children. Inside the park he always bought a long strand of ride tickets, which he divided into four equal strips to dole out to Liz, Frankie, Ted, and me. We grabbed our tickets and took off. Dad would park himself in the beer garden with the other fathers, where he'd recount details of baseball games while the oom-pah band played. He'd point out how a pitcher might flick his wrist on a fastball or how a husky boy—a slow runner—would throw the weight of his body into the second baseman, taking him down before the ball met his mitt.

I went straight for the rides, stopping at the roller coaster, where I assumed that my brothers had also stopped. I'd never gone on the roller coaster alone, and I kept moving forward with the hope that I would find them or someone else I knew.

When my time came, I took the last available spot: a car with a girl I didn't know inside it. I put my left leg, the one with a real knee, over the edge and into the car fairly easily; but because the girl took up too much of the seat I had no space to swivel around and bend my mechanical knee. I'd never met this girl, so I was afraid to ask her to climb out for a minute while I manipulated my wooden leg to fit. Since I was in bell-bottom jeans, she probably didn't realize my legs were wooden. There was also the fact that I wouldn't tell people about my legs. And I was turning ten, the golden age of "I didn't mean to" and "I forgot." Finally, there was my fear of making someone else feel self-conscious.

Instead I strained in my seat, twisted and jerked, but my knee wouldn't bend enough. Finally I gave up and left that foot, clad in its saddle shoe, dangling over the lip of the car. The kids behind me shoved at my back. "Come on! Come on! What's your problem?" The operator, who looked to be about seventeen in his shag hairdo, came up to my car and said, "Whaddaya wanna do here?"

I wriggled around to break out of the car, but it was just as hard to get out as to fit inside. Dozens of kids in the cars ahead of mine turned to stare me down. I summoned every muscle in my stomach to lift myself out, but the wooden leg jamming my path was like a wrestler pinning me down. "Just go," I finally said.

The operator craned his neck forward and squinted as if he hadn't heard me correctly. "What?" He scratched his head. "Just go?"

I nodded.

"Sure?"

"Uh huh," I said.

He broke out in a grin that revealed a chipped tooth. "Okey-doke," he said.

My eyes darted anxiously at the girl beside me, a signal for her to volunteer to get out. She only shrugged. So I grabbed the safety bar, which, because of my jammed leg, was not completely engaged. The girl beside me looked to be about ten also. Maybe she forgot, or didn't mean to, but she did not complain.

"Here goes," said the boy at the control station, and he yanked the lever.

The roller coaster was like any other: the first hill the steepest. You advance by a crank that slowly ratchets each upward kick (chicka-chicka-chick) until you're near the top, where you sit for a moment and look out at the crowd, maybe gasp, and then scream your head off while being jolted downward. Fortunately, this roller coaster was not particularly steep, and that could be why I had let this bad idea go so far. But as we approached the first peak, it wasn't the hill that was threatening me. It was the right-side post, supporting a sign that warned: "Hold Your Hats!" The signpost was only inches from the track, and it looked like my leg would not clear it. All the way up I calculated the distance between that post and my curling foot—a hook waiting to be snared.

During those tantalizing seconds near the crest, I would need to let go of the safety bar with my right hand—my good hand—so that I could hold my wooden ankle as close to the car as possible until we cleared the signpost. This would leave me with only my four-fingered hand, now sweating, to grip the disengaged safety bar as we topped the crest and were thrust downhill. I was near the back of the train. The stillest of moments was already happening for those cars ahead of us. They were crowning the arc, and everything seemed to slow almost to a halt. I smelled the sweat of my palms mixing with the metal of the safety bar and heard only the choppy breath of the girl beside me. I saw her snatching glances at my foot. But then she leaned into the safety bar, pushing all her weight into it, securing it for both of us.

I sighed just as the car picked up speed again. I had a moment as if I were hovering above the fairgrounds, or maybe that's just how I remember it. I see myself laboring not to be distracted by the boys to my left who were rocking a Ferris wheel car so ferociously that they nearly somersaulted in it, nor to my right by a vast stretch of bluegrass where a tuba slogged out an oom-pah tune while polka dancers swirled and weaved through beer stalls around the fathers of boys on baseball teams. My own father might look up from his bratwurst in time to see the signpost rip me from the car and spit me to the ground.

We picked up speed.

My foot cleared the post by about an inch. It happened so fast that I can't say if I had the ankle in my hand or if the post was just far enough away. In any case, I had no time to think before I faced the downward thrust with just my claw hand on the safety bar and a quarter of my body swinging recklessly from the car.

I grabbed hold with both hands and felt my teeth clacking in my ears. My stomach dropped on the descent. Now, having triumphed over this hill, I decided that I was in charge of this game. I was more than a survivor. I could grab or let go as I pleased. The idea that my foot was rattling alongside me, slapping at the car like a dog chasing after a pickup truck, exhilarated me.

When the ride ended the conductor came up to me, took my hand, and yanked me from the car with a congratulatory slap on the back. All the kids who had been staring me down at the start were now cheering me on. Parents stood at the gate with their mouths agape. I bounced down the ramp, my proudest moment ever. I could not wait to tell Dad my story.

From the gate to the beer garden I saw the fathers at their usual picnic table, one of the farthest from the crowd. Dad was not among them. My throat dried up. Would Dad laugh at my bravery? Or would he scold me for not getting out of the car? Maybe he'd put a hand on my shoulder and rub my angel wing, or give me a proud slap on the back.

I was crafting the story in my head: the flopping ankle, the sweaty fist, *Hold Your Hats!* I tapped anxiously against the denim on my good thigh as I waited for a woman with a pram to quit blocking the entrance. Inside, I headed for the beer stalls. And there he was, alone, under the shade of a beer truck, leaning into the counter in a sort of James Dean style with his moon belly over a pair of khakis, graying hair in sideburns that were a tad longer than in previous years though not the pork chops that other men sported in 1970. I had to blink and check again because I'd never seen Dad alone in a crowd. He had millions of friends, old friends from high school and college, and in a place like this he knew dozens of other parents with kids of all ages. Now he looked like an outsider. There was something about the way he stared out at the crowd as if to find someone in particular, while in fact he was probably avoiding eye contact with everyone in sight. People were reaching over and around him at the beer stall. It was time for him to get out of the way, but for some reason he was not going out to join any of the other fathers. I knew that since Mom's hospitalization she had lost friends. I'd heard her cry about it to Aunt Gert. But Dad?

From several yards away I saw Dad strike a match and stop to glance around before touching the flame to his unlit cigarette, as if embarrassed to be smoking. That was odd. Most of the parents smoked. Dad had never seemed ashamed of doing so. Why did he look so awkward?

Dad's oldest friends were not members of our parish. Many of them lived on the Eastside, where Dad had grown up. He met those men downtown for lunch every Friday. They stood by Dad. I hadn't considered that in our neighborhood, parents were taking notice when Mom ranted about the clergy at the A&P checkout counter. The folks here had liked her just fine when she was merely very religious, but now . . .

I limped faster across the line of stalls to get to him, to save him, and to win him over with my story. As I passed the hot dogs and cotton candy, I imagined the deadeye he would give me, the challenge, the glance at his watch: "How long is this story going to take?" Then the transformation, the silent puff of air, the moment of supreme doubt before his laughter would erupt. Dad had a laugh that exploded from the belly. He'd bunch up his face in an effort to tamp it down. When the laughter broke loose, it seemed victorious, although he looked like he was in pain.

He was only a few feet away from me when I reached the popcorn stall. Although he was facing me from the beer counter, he didn't notice me. I opened my mouth to call to him.

Sister Luke stepped into my path.

"Mary. Eileen. Cronin." This was how she always addressed me. "How fortuitous!" she said in a whisper-gasp with a hand to her heart, while I wondered if fortuitous meant "life-threatening."

The crowd shoved around us. She was blocking my view of Dad. Then Sister Luke, still with hand to heart, reached out to my shoulder as if putting a healing hand on me, taking the energy from her heart and transferring it to mine. I heard kids laughing as they skittered past en route to the popcorn stall.

Beyond her wimple I saw two other fathers approaching mine at the beer stall. Dad straightened up to greet them. He shook each hand, talking with a lit cigarette gripped between his teeth, his knees locked to ground himself.

Now Sister Luke was tilting her head, smiling, and again her wimple blocked my view of Dad. Once more I shifted so I could keep my eyes on him, but she was whisper-talking, and I had to lean in to hear her over the accordion and tuba. She said something like, "I'm so pleasedtohave murmur murmur." I didn't understand why she was saying, "Pleased to meet you." I turned from Dad's knees back to her face and struggled to hear her.

Her cheeks glowed red. I could see that she was insulted, so I scrambled for a better response. "Pleased to meet you, too?"

She gave me a puzzled look, her face deepening now to maroon, as she raised her voice over the tuba. "I said, 'I'm so pleased to have—'" The oom-pah song ended, and I heard, "in my class.'" I felt those words like a great gust of wind, and I had to shift so I wouldn't lose my balance.

I remembered Dad, and my eyes darted back to him. He was listening to one of the men with rapt attention, though I couldn't make out what the man was saying. I saw Dad's face go slack as the man raised his right hand, which then swooped down like a bird coming in for a landing, or a roller coaster coming fast down a hill. Dad's eyes followed that hand and grew wider, filling with either horror or awe as he took in the story that I so longed to tell him. I saw the man's pinky bobbing like a broken wing or a leg slapping alongside a car. Dad's wide-eyed horror turned into a constricted face of concern—or was that anger?

"Did you hear me?" asked Sister Luke. She was now screaming over the tuba, "Mary. Eileen!"

That's when Dad jerked his head in my direction. Soon, he and all the other fathers and Sister Luke were looking at me, expectantly. I stood there with no idea of what to say. Each wanted something different. Sister Luke wanted an enthusiastic "I'm so glad to be in your class," which I couldn't give her. The men looked ashamed to be caught talking about me. Then there was Dad. I had come here with a story to top all others, or so I thought. But the astonishment on his face warned of something I hadn't considered. Had my reckless behavior embarrassed him? His life was becoming one endless humiliation.

One of the other fathers waved me over to join them, and Sister Luke stepped aside. "Go on," she said, with a swish of her arms.

Just as I reached my father, another man slapped him on the back. "What a lucky guy," he said. "How many of these girls have you got, Dick? Four?"

Dad lowered his eyes. "Five."

"Five!" The man blew through his teeth. "And all beautiful."

Dad muttered something in an obvious effort to change the subject. Now I was astonished. Did he not see me as beautiful? I was sure he saw Mom that way. My sisters, too. Our eyes caught for an instant, but his face had retreated behind a mask.

Only with age would I see that this man's compliment offered a way out of the awkward roller coaster business. In any case, what happened next was that the mask on my father's face crumpled up in laughter: a titter that built into one of his explosions. I was hoping that this was about my roller coaster story, so I laughed, and the other fathers joined in. I wasn't sure these fathers even knew why they were laughing. When it occurred to me that my father could be laughing at the idea of me being a beautiful girl, my own laughter almost turned to tears.

In no time, Dad was ushering me away from the men. Along the way, he took out his hanky and blew into it, one of those thunderous honks that made him all-powerful in my eyes—a man capable of great noise. But then I began to lament my stolen glory. The roller coaster story was a once-in-a-lifetime event and I hadn't been able to tell it to Dad, the person I wanted to make laugh more than anyone on earth. In my frustration I lashed out. Dad looked so startled that it was as if I had reached over and slapped him when I asked, "And why didn't you agree with that man when he said I was beautiful?"

CHAPTER 10

Passages

For the entire last week of that summer before fifth grade, Mom
and I tussled. No matter how hard I tried to steer it my way,
the argument always went like this: I'd stomp into the kitchen in
a pair of tie-dyed cutoffs, the metal brackets on my left knee bran-
dishing their pincers, while the spindly right leg made me part girl,
part stork. On top, I wore an orange T-shirt that said, "The Devil
Made Me Do It." Because my outfit—purchased for my two weeks
at Ursuline Camp—was not a hand-me-down, I wore it every day at
camp. Finally a nun ordered me to change clothes. Here, at home,
I just kept wearing it.

Standing with my arms folded under the devil on my chest, I'd
say to Mom, "I'm not riding that *retarded* bus this year."

Mom, with a baby clinging to each ankle, would flip another
strip of bacon and say, "Well, you can't walk to school. It's too far
and there's the overpass."

"You'll take me."

She'd raise her brows, smirk, and poke at the bacon with a giant
two-pronged fork. I'd shove my jaw out, indignant. She'd level
those two prongs right at my nose, bacon grease hissing from its
tips, and say, "I told you no. That's final."

My lower lip would pucker. "But Mom! Everyone makes fun of that bus. The people who ride it are *retarded*." I'd say this last word in a whisper.

"So?"

"So!" I'd explode. "So, I'm not re-tard-ed."

"*Who* called you *retarded*?" She would be screaming this, and that's when I'd hear the dribbling basketball outside the window come to a halt, making me cringe at the thought of my brothers' friends hearing the word retarded directed at me.

"Well, that's my point. If I ride the—"

"Never mind!" she'd holler. "We've gone over this a million times!"

In a panic, I'd start in with accusations. "Why not? Why can't you just do one simple thing for me?"

"Look at me," she'd say, pointing the prongs back at her face. She'd look harried, and it would only be eight in the morning. In a thinning nightgown, her skin losing its olive luster, a forgotten cigarette burning on the counter, she'd be impervious to the fact that two toddlers could take her down headfirst into a skillet of sizzling grease at any moment. "Just how do you expect me to get out of this house every morning? I've got three babies on my shins."

"I only count two."

"Where the two go, the other follows. You know that. Now listen to me, I never took a kid to school in my life. God help me, I'm not doin' it. The answer is no. N-O. No!" One of my siblings would come through the kitchen at this point and give me the signal to stop. Rosa was the only child in this family equipped to beat Mom in an argument. I'd use her old trick and throw my chin out as if daring Mom to slap my face, but Mom would barely scoff when I tried it.

"Then I'll ask Dad," I'd say, knowing that I had even less of a shot with him.

Mom would toss her head back with a triumphant laugh, and I would stomp away.

On the day I did follow through with my threat, I found Dad shaving at his bathroom sink. I said, "Will *you* take me to school this year?"

"Nope," he said, with a tap of his razor before he went back to shaving. I whimpered. He gave me the deadeye in the mirror. "Don't pull that on me, Trix. You've got a ride to school. If you don't take it, you can walk."

The school was about a half mile from our home, and my parents had never allowed me to walk that far by myself. I wasn't sure I could do it, not with the overpass and its forty million steps, nor could I continue with the existing plan.

But now, after this three-month-long and still losing battle, I needed to save face. So, as if I'd suddenly come up with a new plan, I shouted at Dad, "That's it! Don't bother to talk me out of it. I'm walking to school from now on!" I stormed off, convinced that he would never allow me to walk that far alone.

A week later I found myself leaving the house way ahead of my brothers, since I would need to gain at least a block on them if I wanted to get to school on time. About seven houses into the walk I was so hot that I had to tie my V-neck around my waist. The matching cable-knit socks had slid down my shiny calves, which I didn't discover until a boy passed me and said, "Pinocchio!"

Swarms of walkers had passed me before Ted came along. He was in second grade and just starting Saint Vivian. He called back to Frankie, "Look at Lear."

"Look at what?" I huffed.

Frankie caught up to us, smiling with pride. "You're walkin' to school."

"So?"

Soon both boys broke into a gallop and rounded the corner ahead. They disappeared only to be replaced by Liz and the girl next door, who zipped past on their bikes.

My books heavy, my brown-bag lunch twisted into a rope, I finally hit the main road. Rush-hour traffic pushed south toward Procter & Gamble and downtown. I headed in the opposite direction toward the gleaming mesh-metal walls of the overpass about a hundred yards ahead, the scariest part of the trip.

By the time I reached the overpass, there were only a few stragglers left on the path to school. I lodged my left foot on the first step and my knee trembled. Instead of my reliable saddle shoes, I'd put on my new penny loafers, which now threatened to slip off. My right leg dragged behind. As I neared the top, I tried not to look down on the cars passing briskly below, and I became mindful of the term "feet firmly planted on the ground." With legs like stilts, I was hardly grounded. I felt top-heavy, as if I might spill over the railing into the traffic about twenty feet below. Terrified by that thought, I next heard the pounding feet of an older boy rushing to make it to school on time. Eighth-grade boys pulled pranks on the overpass. I'd seen them plug up the stairs while a mob of students shoved from behind. If this boy pushed me aside from the left I might go under the railing and down. I shifted my things to my right hand so I could block his push, if necessary, but as I grabbed the railing on the right I dropped everything. My binder plunged to the street, then an apple punched through my brown bag, and a car swerved to miss the pile.

In a panic I turned to the boy, who said, "Geez, that's tough," and stepped up his pace. In the distance, the morning buzzer sounded. School was now in session.

Sister Luke's door was closed by the time I reached it. Inside, lecture underway, about thirty kids sat in desks arranged in rows that squared off to face the chalkboard. Her favorite pupils were assigned the desks closest to hers, and the last empty desk was just to her right: my desk. I started for it when Sister Luke stopped addressing the class. Staring down at her folded hands, she said in a wounded tone, "Mary. Eileen. Cronin. You are late."

I started to explain.

"Does this make you *special*, Mary Eileen?" The perspiration on my back turned to goose pimples. Only minutes into the fifth grade and already I was being dropped from Sister Luke's list of pets.

At least once a month, Sister Luke rearranged the desks in her classroom. By late fall, mine was inching back toward pariah status. And yet when we changed classes she stood outside her door, where she bowed to me as I entered, folding her hands and nodding as if she were greeting the Pope.

We were almost at Christmas break when I was again the last person in the door, and after Sister Luke greeted me with her bow she stopped me at the threshold. The hall empty, she called on her latest pet to lead the class in a song. As my classmates launched into a half-hearted "Waltzing Matilda," Sister Luke wordlessly ushered me down the hall.

Inside the girls' lavatory on this winter day, I had my back to the marble wall. In the warmer months, the lavatory was cool—the place I went to shut myself in a stall, sit down, and close my eyes. It was my sanctuary. About the only place that I prayed—not recited mindlessly, but prayed—was on one of these toilets.

Sister Luke's eyes oozed with disappointment. Why had she dragged me in here? I got up the nerve to ask, "Did I do something wrong?" Then she smiled. Her hand on my shoulder was cold in spite of the radiator's intense heat. Suddenly I was fighting nervous laughter.

"Mary Eileen," she said, "do you know why I bow to you?"

To keep from giggling I bit the inside of my mouth. My voice was high-pitched and quivering when I finally said, "Yes, Sister?"

"You do?"

"Um, no."

She shook her head, gazing upward and reminding me of an apostle from one of her film slides: a man in conversation with God. I decided that she was Matthew, Mark, Luke, and John rolled into one. I clamped my hand over my mouth to contain a worried giggle, which was working up to hysterical laughter.

"You need to take yourself more seriously, Mary Eileen," she whispered.

This advice hit a nerve, and I stopped laughing. A bit of humility might have actually sunk in except that Sister Luke said, "You have a heavy cross to bear, young lady. I look at you and see the suffering of Jesus." She always nodded on the word Jesus, which infuriated me just now, and my shift from panic to laughter to anger happened so quickly that by the time she warned me to stop "goofing off," I was unhinged.

Then she whipped her black skirt around and left me standing there.

On a spring afternoon, following another shuffle of desks, I silently celebrated my placement in the last row. I was especially grateful that this put me right in front of the windows, where a gentle breeze from the pines in the courtyard comforted me. My friend Debbie, a new student in our school, was across the room and also in the back row. Her straight blond hair was parted down the middle. I thought she looked hip, even if she did wear bookworm, blue-framed glasses. This was religion class. On a typical day, Sister Luke moved from "synod" to "sin," consumed with passion, while we fought sleep. To wake us up, she thought nothing of invoking the names of the fathers of her pet pupils. We heard about Dr. Willke's battle against abortion, but mostly she lingered on pornography. She said Charlie Keating battled sinners daily in order to uphold justice and moral decency in our city. If that didn't wake us up, she threw in a bloody martyr story.

I watched Debbie's foot wag over her crossed leg while she examined her hair for split ends and yawned. Her bored response prompted Sister Luke to test her. "Deborah, what did I just say?"

Debbie parroted everything back, and Sister Luke fumed.

Sometime after that, in the midst of my own drowsy stupor, I heard my name called. I straightened up to search the faces of my classmates, frantic for a clue to what was being asked. Debbie's foot had frozen mid-wag. I whipped my head back to Sister Luke, who said, "Well, anyone?" No one responded, so I raised my hand and asked, "I'm sorry, what was the question?"

"Not you, Mary Eileen. I'm asking the class. Does anyone here know what happened to Mary Eileen Cronin? Why doesn't she have legs?"

With that I felt my head tip backward as if it were falling off. I touched my ear, relieved to find it in its place. I looked to Debbie, who had one perfect silk brow raised over her glasses as she twisted herself sideways to get a better look at Sister Luke.

"All right," said Sister Luke, as if resigned to taking on some grave responsibility. "I'll have to explain."

Humiliated, I slumped over in my seat and braced myself for the "suffering Jesus story." Instead, Sister Luke explained to my whole class that my mother had confessed to taking a pill while she was pregnant with me, which caused my legs to shrivel up in the womb. *A pill?* I could barely take in the details. Next I heard a new word: thalidomide. I didn't know what it meant, or how it might be associated with me, but if that were part of my story why was Sister Luke discussing it with my class?

Confused and hurt, I sought compassion in the eyes of children I'd known all my life. But I felt my classmates distance themselves from me as if *I* had said something wrong. Some were even drawn back in their seats. Surely my eleven-year-old classmates must have been as puzzled and helpless as me, but I was hoping for more. Perhaps I expected too much, but then Debbie, the new girl, seemed to recognize Sister Luke's behavior as cruel.

Her reaction grounded me at that moment. I saw her face scrunched into a knot of disbelief, outrage, and everything I was too numb to express myself. In Debbie's face I could see that someone in the room understood my exact feelings: the shame of having my family's secret exposed in class, a secret about me and one that I'd never heard until now. And then there was the matter of trust, my trust in a family and in a religion that had been telling me for years that these legs were no mistake—this was God's choice, and not mine to question.

When the screen door slammed behind me that afternoon, I was almost hoping not to see Mom, but she was at the mirror in the powder room off the kitchen. My confusion, which had escalated to anger, instantly dissolved into guilt. Ever since she had been hospitalized, we stepped gingerly around Mom for fear that we might put her back in the hospital permanently.

Mom was just finishing her makeup and patting her hair when I stomped in to say, "Do you know what Sister Luke told our class today?" Her hand froze at her temple; she locked her eyes on her own face in the mirror. Then she put a hand to her forehead as if checking for fever. Her voice was uncharacteristically calm as she said to herself in the mirror, "What did Sister Luke say?"

"She said you took a pill. She said that's why I don't have legs."

Mom turned to me, her eyes lit up now. "She said that? Sister Luke?"

"Yes!" I said, ready to incite a riot, although I tried to say it as calmly as possible. "That's what she said you told her."

Mom gasped. "I never said that." She stepped out of the bathroom and away from me. She was slipping away. Please don't leave me, I thought. Not this time. In my desperation I pushed harder. "Sister Luke *said* you told her this story at Daily Donuts!" But by the time I finished the sentence, I didn't even believe myself anymore. Was it all just in my head? "You do take her to get coffee after church, don't you?"

"I have taken her for coffee," Mom agreed. She straightened her skirt, smoothing out the creases. I waited for more. Instead, she headed toward the hall. If I followed her, I might regret it for life.

But I needed her care. Despite what I'd heard about my mother that day and what she might have done, willingly or not, she was precisely the woman I needed. Even more than reassurance, I needed her to stand up for me: to say that no one, not even a nun, could humiliate or otherwise tamper with her daughter. No way, not without answering to Joy Cronin. But Mom's last words as she rounded the corner in the hallway were: "Eileen, there's a baby in every corner of this house . . . Donuts and coffee? Since when have I had time for that?"

CHAPTER II

The Last Worst Thing That Ever Happened to Me

A year after I first heard the word "thalidomide," I had all but forgotten Sister Luke's revelation in front of my fifth-grade class. Had it really happened? Then I woke up one morning to hear cries from downstairs, moans mixed with an incoherent language spoken by my mother—signs of another manic episode. The rest of the morning was a flurry of transactions: someone said an ambulance had been called and Mom would be back in the locked ward before school let out; toddlers bawled from cribs in three different bedrooms; someone handed me lunch money; we middle children were whisked out the door. "Just go. Just go to school," we were told. And we left.

My classmate Debbie had moved to another parish, making school lonely again. Having arrived early, I had to wait in a lineup on the playground until the first buzzer sounded. I couldn't contain my anxiety about what was going on at home, and I blurted out to a group of girls in the lineup that my mother had just gone crazy. I said, "They're taking her away right now. They'll put her in a straitjacket and jolt her with electricity." The girls responded as one might expect of sixth-graders: they dropped their jaws, stared in disbelief, and spread the word through the line.

While I waited for our teacher to take us into class, it occurred to me that this was not exactly the reaction I'd wanted. The shock of seeing and hearing my mother in such a state now seemed like a dream, and maybe I had just told a lie. Inside, as I took my seat, I decided that it was probably just as well that I'd gotten it off my chest.

By the time school let out I might have forgotten about my public announcement, except that I was ambushed at home by Liz, who tackled me and climbed onto my stomach. In front of my friend Penny, Liz squished my jaw between her fingers to look right into my eyes. "Did you tell people that Mom was crazy?" Liz had this habit of biting her tongue, as if she were getting ready to bat a grand slam when instead she was drawing her hand back to hit. I looked to Penny, who, as an only child, was utterly defenseless at these times. She started laughing uncontrollably. This would make me furious with Penny until I reminded myself that there was a year when her mother barred her from coming to our house because, in another brawl, Penny had been slapped by an older girl who was visiting our house. I missed Penny so much over that year that I glowered at her mother every time I saw her. Now I was wishing her mother were here to referee. In the meantime, Penny's laughter escalated to a panicked cough, broken only by wheezes.

Liz held my jaw and slapped with the other hand. "Did ya do it?" she asked. "What were you thinking? Take it back. Right now, take it back! 'Mom is not crazy,' say it!"

With my tears flowing against every attempt to hold them in, I screamed, "She's not crazy! I'm sorry! Let me go."

"Not yet," said Liz. She bit her tongue again and thought it over. "Okay, Looney. 'I'm the crazy one.' Say it. 'I'm Looney.' Say it!" Three years before, Liz had nicknamed me Looney. At that time, Liz was eleven and had not yet learned the definition of the term "lunar module," but she heard the phrase and said, "That's you! You're a space animal, a lunar module."

Now, as my fingers tingled to a numb state from her knees jammed into my upper arms, I shouted in a convincingly crazy voice, "I'm LOONEY! OKAY? I'll say anything. Just leave me alone."

A couple of months later, Mom was released from the hospital with a prescription for lithium, and this time she bounced back faster. It was beginning to feel as if these hospitalizations were merely a "time out." Our family rarely spoke of them. If so, they referred to Mom's "nervous breakdowns" as if almost every mother had one. The more frequently the episodes occurred, the less real they seemed to us.

Antiques relieved Mom's illness to a large extent. At the recommendation of her psychiatrist she took up the hobby, jamming our suburban home with Windsor chairs, dry sinks, and corner cupboards. We tripped on braided rugs and tossed our garbage into a modified butter churn.

Maybe she was buying back the life that her father had squandered in his days as an alcoholic gambler. Whatever she was doing, it was a relief from her obsession with the Church. As she bought and sold, bought and sold, she developed self-confidence and a keen eye for oil paintings: portraits of stern-faced adults and granny-faced infants, or ships—the age revealed by the flags' symbols. Eventually dealers called from New England to seek our mother's opinion on the period and value of items.

Dad never complained about the antiques. Fortunately, his Volkswagens had been so successful in the sixties that he opened a Porsche dealership in the early seventies. He'd sent four children off to private colleges and hosted a huge wedding reception at the Cincinnati Club for Bridget. While Mom bought and sold, she complained that *her* mother had not been able to afford colleges, private schools, and receptions in the Oak Room. And *she* had turned out just fine, she said, to which Dad simply nodded. "All right, all right, calm down," he said. "No one is *getting away* with anything here." And this was how all of my older sisters would be married, with Mom griping and Dad agreeing to whatever his daughters requested.

I'd finally reached the eighth grade and was only days away from the high school entrance exam. My sisters had been sent to Ursuline Academy, a girls' college preparatory school on the Eastside. I was eager to make the switch and hoping to meet girls who weren't into sports. Mom had mixed feelings about this school. Her mother had not been able to afford it. "It's a charm school," Mom said, and I wondered why this was a problem now only as I was approaching high school. Besides, the school's reputation had changed with its move from an old mansion in Walnut Hills to a northeastern suburb. These days it was seen as a progressive school for young women with ambitions to build a career. The entrance exam made it more competitive than the parochial high schools, so it drew from all over the city. The girls I knew who were applying were serious students. "Too much freedom now," Mom said. "When do they have time to learn? They're all taking underwater basket-weaving." Since when did Mom care about her daughters' academics? Only the boys' grades mattered to her. Or was this school now *too* academic for a girl?

One evening I helped Mom with the dishes while Dad pored over the newspaper at the kitchen table. Reading was his nightly ritual. He valued it as much as his summer Sundays with the Reds. Suddenly Mom announced that she would be sending me to our parochial high school instead of Ursuline. I'd pinned my hopes on this chance to make new friends, and I wouldn't sit still for Mom's resistance. "Dad, tell her. All the other girls in the family went to Ursuline. Liz is there now."

"That school is getting out of control," Mom said to Dad. "Next they'll be burning bras in that place." She pointed at him. "You watch!"

He nodded and went back to his newspaper. Why wouldn't he speak up? In the meantime, Mom yammered on about "those wild nuns" at Ursuline.

"If she passes the exam, she can go there," he said finally, shooting Mom a look that said, "Hold on, she may well flunk that exam."

It might have been that my parents had argued this point on every single daughter—I couldn't say—but I wished that just once I might make a transition without controversy or second-guessing. My test-taking skills were erratic enough. I'd been tested before kindergarten, according to Mom, and the examiner concluded that I was "half genius and half retarded." My siblings knew to shrug off such comments from Mom, but I always allowed for a grain of truth in what she said. So far I'd had a string of teachers and Girl Scout leaders who had greeted me with the same dubious expressions on their faces. Other than my physical therapist and my second-grade teacher, the two leaders who had inspired the most confidence in me so far were a softball coach and a ballet teacher. According to them, I could do anything. If Mom and I were confused about my abilities, we had plenty of company.

On the other hand, my sisters' futures were without debate. They would go to good colleges, preferably Jesuit schools, and marry Catholic schoolmates upon graduation. Soon I would be old enough to date. My teeth had grown in straight and my hair was styled in layers instead of the bowl cut that I'd had before. I wasn't sure if boys would find me pretty, and I doubted they would want to date a girl without legs.

Then I received an invitation to my first boy-girl party. It was at the home of a boy who gave a chain-link identity bracelet to a different girl every month, a sort of shackle announcing "ROB, forever." I figured that if I played my cards right I might wear my own shackle someday.

On the Friday afternoon of the party, I walked home with my navy blue sweater tied at the waist in my own kickass style, ready to ask Mom about boys. Heading for the stairs to her bathroom, I paused in the foyer to stare at the front door. I'd seen a parade of boys come through that door for my older sisters. Until now I had felt completely cut out of that deal. I was hoping I'd been wrong.

Upstairs, I barged in on Mom. Privacy never seemed to apply to her baths. In fact, we girls tended to approach her at precisely this time of day because we could corner her in the bathtub. She could never lock the door because at any moment a small child might stab a screwdriver into an electrical socket. The bathtub was situated on the right side of the wall opposite the door, with a partial wall encasing it, and to the left of that partial wall was the toilet, above which a ray of late afternoon sun came through the window, making it into a perfect confessional space.

"Can I come in?" I asked, as I closed the lid to the toilet and took a seat.

She sighed, already reading my mind. "What's wrong now?"

I leaned my forehead against the tile wall between us.

"Well?" she said. I heard splashing.

I swallowed and said, "Mom?"

"Who else!" Did she have to scream even at times like this?

"Okay. Mom." There was still time to walk out. I could forget about boys and go back to the idea of becoming a nun. "Mom!" I said.

"What! And don't say 'Mom' again!"

"Okay. Are boys—" The splashing stopped. "You know how Liz gets asked out on dates? Well, are boys going to ask me out in high school?"

There was only silence. Now I rocked slightly, while holding my breath so she couldn't hear my panic. She might have settled this problem by digging deeper. The boy-girl party held a loophole. In our family girls weren't allowed to go to these parties until high school.

I wanted her to say, "What a ridiculous question! Why wouldn't boys like you? And don't get any ideas. You're too young for that stuff." I peered around the partition. She was staring at the faucet as if she were willing it to turn on by itself, her eyebrows scrunched into such bewilderment that she didn't even notice me staring at her. I could read on her face that she had never associated the word "Eileen" with "boys." Mortified, I pulled back. How had I ever considered this boy thing possible?

I stood up to walk out when Mom said, "Oh, I-lean. Maybe you better ask Liz. She knows more about boys these days than I do."

"Liz," I muttered on the way out. "Now why didn't I think of that?"

My friend Doris and I snuck out easily enough to go to the party that night. She was another new girl at Saint Vivian, a rabble-rouser by our peers' standards. Doris loved to provoke their outrage. Lately she was educating me on Dylan and Baez, whose albums we listened to for hours in her bedroom, or, when really daring, in the basement with her older brothers. She had even recruited me to hand out Jerry Springer flyers during one of his campaigns. Now we stood under a red strobe light in Rob's basement, while the boys flirted with the popular girls. For me it was enough excitement just to be invited. The new Paul McCartney album fascinated us more than the boys. All the way home we sang "Band on the Run."

I passed Ursuline's entrance exam with high scores and chatted enthusiastically in school with the other girls who would go there with me. Doris was going to Ursuline's sister school, and we would stay in touch. We contemplated which languages and electives we would choose. My goals in grade school had reached no further than survival, but now I envisioned myself becoming a leader. We were only days from graduating when a group of popular girls going to the parochial high school pulled me aside to say that "Ursu-slime" was for stuck-up girls. The girl who led the pack was a blond, blue-eyed beauty. The best diver at our swim club, she exuded those Germanic good looks that so many Cincinnatians possess, but few quite so well. Every boy was mad about her. We were by no means close, but we went to the same slumber parties. I was flattered that the popular girls had bothered to insult me and wrote the comment off as rivalry between schools, nothing to take personally.

That same day, I followed my routine for the walk home from school. The eighth-grade classrooms were on the third floor, and since I'd been trampled in the after-school rush on the staircase, I always waited for the stairs to clear before I left. The trampling had mostly damaged my dignity. I was safely down half of the first flight of stairs, alone, when I heard feet pounding on the floor behind me. The pounding escalated, followed by shrieks. Three girls rounded the corner.

I glanced back to find the diver and her friends, who surprised me by shouting, "I-wean! I-wean!" Were they imitating a mentally retarded person? That was going too far.

I held onto the banister and waited for them to pass, never imagining that this was a calculated assault, until two girls looped their arms into each of mine to rip me from the banister. My only thought was to get back to that banister, so that I could stay upright and keep my legs and skirt intact. "Let's help you down," they said, in a mock-helpful tone. I felt a shove at my back from the diver, followed by a thrust from the two girls at my sides who held my arms. These sent me airborne over the last half of the staircase. I might have screamed, but I wasn't sure if others would find this behavior atrocious, and I could not find my voice. To me, the only thing worse than what was happening would have been for someone to witness it.

I hit the landing hands first—a hardwired instinct accrued from a lifetime of falls. The sting in my palms was nothing compared to the ache in my wrists that followed. The pain would linger but not so long as these questions: How many times have I fallen? How many falls are ahead of me? Have I ever been pushed before? Was I pushed? What would people think of *me*, if they knew?

On the landing I shook my head, as if that would make them stop. Their laughter escalated to hysteria. "Let me help you up," said the leader. The incongruity of her false voice would haunt me as well. Scorn was one thing, but this falsity only underscored the layers of insult: superiority and hatred. Why now? We were in our last days of school.

They swooped down to lift me up again by the arms, brushing me off as if to be my caretakers; then they dragged me down the second staircase, tossing me again midway and chasing after me. I was in a kind of shock. By the time they dragged me down to the last one, I was only worrying about my skirt flying up.

"What's wrong?" said the leader. "Can't keep up?"

How many summers had I studied her at our swim club? I'd looked up from my towel to find her adjusting the diving board with her foot. Her eyes shone bright blue above the water. I marveled at her poise before the spring and at the verve in her twists and tucks. Courage was what I was known for, but I knew something about verve. For years I'd performed ballet in my head, and I'd fantasize that, given legs for only one hour, I might have lured Nureyev from Fonteyn. In my head, I was that good. When I studied this girl's dives, I felt those twists and tucks and flips in my own muscles. Why would *she* hate *me*?

Finally, I crashed onto the landing at the door. My legs absorbed the hit, and after the slam I felt a vibratory sensation, a sting that radiated from outside into my core. By the time I looked up, the girls had scattered. Through the open doors, I saw the diver turn back to wave. Even then I marveled at how she could run backward. "Stuck up!" she yelled, swiveling into a graceful turn before they took off. The doors closed, and I might have fainted but I was still in shock.

For a second I was relieved. Then, as it became clear what had happened, I pulled myself up and became frantic that someone might find me in this state. My books were missing. I'd dropped them on the stairs. I climbed up to the first flight and found them in their strap, nice and neat. Thank you, Sister Luke. And just after that it seemed important to touch my cheek, which I found hot but dry. This allowed me my one moment of pride. I hadn't cried in front of anyone.

The tears came as I walked home, slow at first then hysterical when I reached the top of the overpass, where the sound was drowned out by the traffic below and no one could see me. I wiped my face against the shoulder of my short-sleeved blouse. Down on the sidewalk again, I turned away from the street, hoping no one I knew would drive past.

I didn't tell anyone about the girls throwing me down the staircase because I was afraid of what my family would say: *Why* would girls do that? Are *you* sure? Did anyone *see* it? I was beginning to meet tragedy with numbness. A few months later I would face an enormous loss: my beloved Grandpa would die, my strongest advocate within the family. Yet I could hardly manage a tear.

CHAPTER 12

How to Build an Empire

I loved everything about high school, beginning with the fact that it was across town. Never again would I have to climb the steps to the overpass. Now I had a carpool. The nuns in my high school valued sisterhood over rivalry. I decided that if I stuck close to them, no one would hurt me.

In Sister Anne Marie's Western civilization class, historical figures became everyday people, so that one day we were dining with La Famiglia de Medici, another we stood on the sidelines at a soiree with Richelieu. A handsome middle-aged woman who might have been Italian or French herself, Sister Anne Marie cut a commanding figure in her shortened black habit. This cardinal was in, she'd whisper, that one out. Who would wear the papal crown of glory? She taught us the dance of power and opened our eyes to the beauty that might come of its by-products, art and architecture—Rococo and Baroque, words that made my mouth water—only to shine the spotlight on the diabolical acts that built those empires.

Sister Anne Marie worked us hard, and the best antidote to her class was the choral room, where Sister Jude actually bounced on every syllable: "fringe on the top . . . (clip clop)." Gone were the power-parable slideshows of my elementary education. Gone were the days of blind reverence for athletics. This was a school where humanities thrived: French and literature, art history, glee club!

On a fall morning, as I scrambled to make it to class, the bell sounded, and there were just two of us girls left in the freshman locker hall. I hustled while the other girl whistled, taking her time. Her name was Phoebe. She had rosy cheeks, impish eyes, and a tumble of dark curls. She barely combed her hair, let alone styled it, and to me she was the prettiest girl in our class. Based on my eighth-grade experience with the popular girls, it made me nervous to find myself alone with her. Maybe she had a posse lurking in the shadows, ready to pounce, but she didn't seem invested enough in popularity to organize a mob. While most girls at this school wore shiny penny loafers, Phoebe wore high-tops with holes in them. While others tucked pens in their blazer pockets, Phoebe tucked a box of Marlboro Reds. She was in my English class, and when the word "insouciance" appeared on our vocabulary list I read the definition and looked right at Phoebe.

Finally ready for class, I slammed my locker shut and found my sister Liz at my back. "Give me that, Looney," she said, grabbing my purse. According to Liz, it was my job to ask Dad for lunch money. She fished out my wallet and found it empty.

"I told you, I didn't have time this morning," I said, and she slapped me. "Get up earlier," she said, and after tossing my wallet, she left for class.

At first the slap did not even register. I had grown accustomed to the notion that Liz was supposed to reset my clock with a periodic flick of the wrist. My lofty ambitions for leadership in this high school dissipated in a cloud of dust. I might as well have been using talcum powder to launch a cannon. Would the new girl, Phoebe, take this as her cue? Was I never to be anything more than an easy target? At Saint Vivian I'd always looked to the new girls, those who lived outside my neighborhood, for friendship.

They seemed to view me differently from the girls I'd known since early childhood. Perhaps it was because they had not known me as a "squiddler," but they viewed me as their equal. Finally I got up the nerve to face my new classmate, and as I turned I saw Phoebe's narrowed eyes tracking Liz down the hall.

"Bitch!" she said to Liz's back. I almost dropped to my knees. She was defending me. "You don't have to take that," she said to me.

"You must not have an older sister."

Phoebe shook her head, dismissing my comment. "What's your real name?" she asked.

I sighed and admitted in a whisper, "Eileen."

"Huh?" said Phoebe.

"I lean!"

"Oh," she said apologetically. Already it felt as if she knew more about me than I knew myself. "'Looney's not so bad," she said. "Where you headed, Looney? We're too late for class. Wanna catch a smoke instead?"

Part of our school's progressive identity was its smoking patio. It was the seventies, and while women were celebrating the right to vote or to go to law school, they also celebrated the right to smoke in public. In an instant, my concern over a tardy slip vanished, replaced by a desire to be embraced by a girl as cool as Phoebe.

After that day I followed Phoebe slavishly, taking up cigarettes and making a career goal of becoming cool. We spent countless weekends at her house because it was more hip than mine. Her older siblings might have protested the Vietnam War, whereas mine might have protested the protesters. Phoebe did spend one night at my house, and Mom had only this to say about her: "That Phoebe is up to no good."

This was fine because I preferred Phoebe's neighborhood to mine. She lived at the border of Hyde Park and Mount Lookout, an area where parks sprang up every few blocks and the tree-lined streets featured signage with flowerboxes. It was a place that valued the arts and social programs. On the other hand, it had a reputation for being so exclusive it bordered on incestuous. Everyone there knew everyone else from the country club. Many of the parents owned summer homes on Lake Michigan, all within minutes of one another, and they frequently took the party north. When the parents went away for weekends, the children threw gigantic parties with hundreds of kids. Word often reached the parents about their children's parties through the country club, and when it made its way to my parents, Mom would simply roll her eyes and say, "Well, that *is* the Hyde Park way."

On a balmy fall evening, Phoebe and I dressed for a party at her cousin's house down the street from her own. I wore a turtleneck under a cardigan with a snowflake design at the yoke, while Phoebe's womanly figure beckoned from a man's sleeveless undershirt, over which she wore a red cashmere cardigan with pearl buttons and holes in the elbows. We walked to what was supposed to be a small gathering. I marveled at the gabled Victorian house. Marijuana smoke wafted overhead. On an expansive front porch, at least two dozen kids leaned into the railing or sat cross-legged on the plank floor. Neil Young's "Cinnamon Girl" spilled from a speaker in the window, while a curtain swayed in the breeze. Some people gripped the necks of beer bottles while others, stippled across an endless lawn, smoked joints. There were about fifty people, and Phoebe wandered into the crowd, shoeless. Her boyfriend was a senior at X, our shorthand for St. Xavier High School. In his frayed Oxford cloth shirt, he reached up from the grass to hold a joint to her lips. She dropped to her knees, took the joint from his hands, drew on it, and leaned into his waist.

I found myself hugging a post on the porch, alone in the crowd. Soon I heard a familiar voice call my name and quickly spotted a glimmer of strawberry-blond hair in the dark. Liz's friend Colette waved to me from the lawn. I carefully negotiated the squatters on the staircase in order to reach her. Colette's pale blue eyes and wide smile always offered me the kind of reassurance that I longed for from an older girl. She was by far the worldliest person I knew. Her father, a famous chef, had come to this city from France. He died when Colette and her sisters were young girls. Naturally inclined to nurture others, Colette advised me on issues such as boys and which classes to take or avoid.

To my surprise, she handed me a beer. I took it, relieved to have found my anchor at the party. She bent forward and whispered, "Someone's been asking about you," and backed away to assess my reaction. Her eyes expanded over a dimpled half-grin.

"Oh," I tried to sound nonchalant. "Who?"

She mentioned a football player. Was she joking? I laughed too loudly.

"Shhh," she warned, just as a towering young man with braces joined us and introduced himself. I gave Colette a nervous look, afraid to face him, but she helped us through an awkward introduction. And I, in the way that a fourteen-year-old might go from feeling like the most ungainly girl on the planet to Queen of the Universe, rose to the occasion. He flirted with me; I giggled a lot. Colette slipped away.

On the walk home I was so intoxicated by the thought of a boy seeking me out at a party that I showered Phoebe with a frenzy of chatter while she stared blandly, unimpressed. She had known this boy since grade school. He was a bore back then, and she was pretty sure he was still a bore. I came to an abrupt halt. Was it true? He was a bore? Phoebe knew so much more about boys than I did. But he was a quarterback!

"Looney, you need to play it cool," she said, grinning at the obvious incongruity of those words in the same sentence. Silently I cursed myself, and yet I was aflutter with nervous energy.

By the following weekend I was scheduled to go on my first date, with Colette acting as chauffeur. The night before my date, Liz knocked on my bedroom door. By now she had her own room, Rosa's old bedroom down the hall. She'd just come from ballet and was still in her leotard and pointe shoes, clutching two empty Coca-Cola bottles in one hand. In the more or less accusatory tone that she generally took with me, she asked, "Looney, do you *know* how to kiss?" She pushed past me and headed for my dresser, where she deposited the bottles and stopped momentarily. When confronted with a mirror, ballerinas are compelled to check the position of every bone, every muscle, so that nothing falls from alignment. As if conversing with herself in the mirror, Liz watched her right arm unfurl—the unraveling of a sacred scroll—to announce her turned-out leg with its arched foot suspended in midair. "Well," she said, "have you ever been kissed?"

She possessed the physical trappings of a ballerina—slim figure, coordination, comportment—but I liked to think that I had the sensibility and motivation. Ballet demanded the subtle energy necessary to convince an audience of the transformation from girl into rose, the same energy that I was certain must be radiating from my core, if not for all the man-made artifice I had to juggle. Walking in these legs had made me an acrobat on stilts, as I saw it. My every move from an upright position was calculated to the most minuscule clamp in one muscle, to the release of another, and so on. These moves were in my hips, my shoulders, my stomach, even my face. Especially in my face, I thought, as I glanced in the mirror. It never failed to surprise me how starkly my stressed body contrasted with my face. Mine was a choirgirl's face. And yet, any girl in wooden legs is in pain about two-thirds of every day of her life, pain that varies from low-grade and chronic to walking on broken glass in bare feet or hauling a large man on her hip. Ballerinas know that level of pain, and they make it all look effortless.

I decided that, given a pair of legs and two complete hands, I might mesmerize a crowd with a twist of a wrist juxtaposed against a lift of my chin.

This argument was going through my head when I saw us next to each other in the mirror, me with inquisitive lines etched into my baby face, and Liz with an elegant posture. "Sure, I can kiss," I blurted out. "Who doesn't know how to do that?"

I'd never been kissed by a boy.

Liz didn't answer right away. Instead, she planted one foot on the ground, turned it in opposition to the other to form fifth position, while she balanced her arms as if to hold a small chick in her hands; at least, that's what she'd been told to do in class. I knew because long ago I had taken those classes, back when I believed a ballet teacher who said that I could do whatever I wanted.

"French kiss," said Liz.

"What?" Was she baiting me? I'd never heard of this.

"I figured," she said, drawing back and stretching her arms and her head to form an arch. Then she snapped forward and grabbed the bottles from the dresser. With an impatient sniff, she said, "Hold this." She handed me one of the bottles. Closing the door behind her, she leaned her silky bun into it and barricaded the entrance.

"This is a French kiss," she said. "Now watch." She held the bottle to her lips and poked her tongue into its rim, wriggling it while tipping her head this way and that. There was a pop when she took it out. "Now you try," she said.

I looked down at the bottle in my hands and tried to do exactly what she had done. It surprised me how smooth the rim felt against my tongue. With a thrust of my tongue, a brief rush of excitement came over me. To think I might do this with a boy! The bottle was sticky and sweet but I could not replicate that pop.

"You better keep at it," she said, going up on her toes and evaluating her posture once again in the mirror. She made one pirouette en pointe, and left.

For all of my worry about dating, this first date was an unremarkable event until the kiss at my front door. That kiss sealed our fate as a couple. He grabbed me by the waist, and I stumbled into him just as he plunged his tongue deep into my mouth. His braces gnashed my upper lip and took a layer of skin with them as he pulled away. But it was behind me. I'd had my first date and my first kiss. For the remainder of my high school years this boy and I might have exchanged ten words, but I wore that torn lip into school on Monday morning like a badge of honor.

The rest of that year was a flurry of parties, football games, and dances. Even Liz invited me into her swanky lair, a bedroom with three white walls contrasting with a Kelly green one. Mine was still painted lavender from when we'd shared it as girls. From her bed, we blew cigarette smoke out the front window and listened to Simon and Garfunkel. When bored, Liz would say, "Call the pharmacy." They would deliver anything. If they had sold alcohol, we would have ordered it. Instead I would ask for *Glamour* and *Vogue*; then, as if it were a last-minute thought, I would add, "Oh, and throw in a pound of peanut M&Ms and a carton of Kents, please." We smoked our parents' brand, not that we needed to cover our tracks. There was no one chasing us down.

Our parents were too tired and distracted to argue over our poor study habits, and we weren't sure if they knew about our cigarettes. Dad had put in hard labor on our older siblings; his only interest these days was in keeping the boys' grades up. Mom would see us going out—often together—and she'd give us a congratulatory nod.

Now, along with my plans to join a convent, my grades took a plunge. I decided that math, inextricably linked with Saint Vivian in my mind, was for future accountants. Phoebe and I held a contest to see who could score the lowest on an algebra test, and I won. I gave up my position in the glee club because Liz played volleyball and, instead of finding a ride home from someone in glee club, I became the scorekeeper for the volleyball team. I even stopped caring about Sister Anne Marie's class. My parents scolded me for my report card that quarter but Liz pointed out, "They don't know what they don't see. Just snatch the report card from the mail before Dad comes home. He'll never notice." I tried that the next quarter, and the next; no one came looking for another report card from me, which led me to believe that I'd been going about life all wrong. I'd been working way too hard. People who coasted never seemed harried, and because of that they were a joy to have around. Daisy Buchanan, my latest idol, was a slacker. Had that hurt her popularity?

In the spring of my freshman year, I was called in to see the guidance counselor, who greeted me with the news that while my entrance exam scores had placed me in the top quarter of my class, my grades now placed me in the bottom quarter. I gave no explanation. Instead I focused on the symmetry in her statement: top quarter/bottom quarter. My thinking had become so magical that I imagined this was merely a matter of flipping quarters.

"This is not going to bode well for your college applications." Until that moment, I had been feeling pretty good about my new life and what I was doing with it.

Shortly after that talk, a sophomore friend told me that Sister Anne Marie had mentioned Liz and me in her class as an example of how sisters *should not* treat each other. "Well, that is ridiculous," I said with a laugh. "She must have seen us wrestling out here on the smoking patio last week. Everyone knows that was just for show. We were horsing around. Sister Anne Marie is too serious."

Dignified, I thought. Sister Anne Marie had conviction, and she cared enough about me to say something. But why would she say this to sophomores? Sister Anne Marie seemed an unlikely gossip. Or was this gossip? Was she instead trying to send me a message about my choices? If anyone knew how hierarchies worked it was Sister Anne Marie, the Richelieu scholar. Perhaps she'd wanted someone who was in neither Liz's nor my class, but someone older, to relay this message to me.

The following year, instead of improving my studies or stepping out of my sister's shadow, I gave up Phoebe. I decided that Phoebe was a pot person and I was an alcohol person. My future would be cut from the fabric of an F. Scott Fitzgerald novel, and hers from a Jack Kerouac one.

That fall I took up with a new friend, Claire. She lived in the neighborhood that Mom's family had moved to after they left her grandfather's house. Although this neighborhood had seen better days, I liked its older homes. Claire put no more effort into her homework than I did, but somehow she had the right answers when called upon in class. I couldn't figure out how she did it, until I realized that she was about the most logical person I'd ever met. She just listened in class, applied reason, and came up with the answers on her own. Initially I'd assumed that Claire, with her broad shoulders and lean legs, was one of those athletic girls with whom I would have nothing in common. But Claire and I shared identical schedules because we'd chosen French and art as electives freshman year. She spoke in a husky voice, the kind that people took seriously, whereas I was still aiming for Daisy Buchanan's persona: vulnerable on the surface, another story underneath. What story was under there I had not quite figured out. I hadn't even understood that Daisy was a tragic character.

Claire and I sat next to each other in art class, and one day she said, "My mother's an artist." This surprised me, because I'd seen her mother when she showed up on campus in a golf skirt. She looked every bit as athletic as Claire. I couldn't imagine an artistic golfer. So I said, "My mother went to art school. She is, or was, an artist. You know those pen-and-ink models for the Giddings Jenny ads?"

"She does those?" said Claire deferentially.

"She has done that *kind* of work." I wanted to be more definitive. "Now she collects antiques."

If there was one thing that we agreed on without qualification, it was that we both adored our art instructor. Sister Catherine was close to ninety years old and had to point to whomever she addressed because she couldn't remember our names or bend her neck to face us. In her lectures on art history she elaborated on the sordid lives of the artists: this one who spent days alone in a studio with a pile of corpses for models, and that one who had sex with royalty. Sister Catherine salivated when she spoke of sex and death, which caused her to spit on words such as "corpse" and "succulence." Once when we took out our sketchpads, she said to Claire with a poking motion, "Don't forget, I taught your mother everything she knows. Your grandmother, too. I taught them both . . . once upon a time." And Claire whispered to me, "Don't forget, I taught Jesus, too . . . once upon a time."

Now in our second year of classes together, there was nothing about Claire that I didn't admire. Her drawings were beautifully executed, especially the geometric designs, while mine were a hodgepodge of anxious erasures and lines too thick or too crooked. The first time I held one up to her, Claire pursed her lips as she struggled to find words. We both had to laugh, and eventually she merely poked a finger at my erasures—her homage to our instructor. From then on, I came to class mostly to entertain Claire with my sketches and for Sister Catherine's lectures.

At home I spent afternoons writing poetry, which I didn't share. Then, one day in class, Claire confided her dream to become an architect, and I said, "That would be a good choice." After some deliberation, I added, "I think I'm more of a writer."

"And that's a good thing," Claire said, staring woefully at my ill-proportioned drawing of a table and chair. Then she looked me in the eyes and said, "I could definitely see you as a writer, Eileen."

We shared a diverse clan of friends. Our group included a math whiz, a ballet dancer, a soloist from the glee club, a pianist, an equestrian, a few girls who smoked pot, three who worked in a concession stand of whom two played volleyball, four who skied, of whom three also played tennis, and a poet.

When I entered Claire's house for the first time, it became clear why we had bonded. I followed her up the back staircase to find her mother passed out on a sofa, legs akimbo and hair matted to her cheek. I looked at Claire, who shrugged and explained, "She's an alcoholic."

"Oh," I said, stunned by her candor. Then I blurted out, "Well, my mom has been locked up on a psych ward, but don't tell Liz I said that."

Claire had two things which I lacked. First of all, she was responsible. Her family had been upper-middle-class, but her father lost his job and finances were stretched thin, so Claire worked in a concession stand at the zoo. She bought her own clothes and art supplies. Secondly, her father was the best mother I'd ever met. He was forever baking cookies and quiches because he knew that his food would draw us down to the kitchen, where he would coax us to open up. He would slip bits of parental advice into the conversation without lecturing. In a satirical voice, he'd cajole us to tell him what we were up to: "Where were you two *ladies of the evening* off to last night? Have another cookie."

Claire's bedroom floor was layered two feet deep in clothes and junk. I spent weekends there for two years before I discovered the royal blue wall-to-wall carpeting underneath. Instead of nagging, her father taped sticky notes to her bedroom door:

Dearest Darling Clairish,
The fire department called about this business of your room: haven't yet located the beds in there. Maybe you could shovel a pile of clothes aside for their hoses?
Cordially,
Adoring Father

Even as I teased "Clairish" about her father's notes, I secretly envied them, especially in contrast to my mother's "I-lean!" (It took no time for Claire to pick up on my mother's intonation; from then on, Claire would always find the precise moment to slip in an "I-lean!") While he was out of work, Claire's father acted in a local theater troupe and starred in comedies. He enjoyed opera and the Boston Pops, which we watched with him on summer evenings. I had cherished those summer afternoons with Dad, tuning in to Joe Nuxhall and the Reds, but now I was hardly at home anymore. I wished I could be as close to my father as Claire was to hers.

I even admired Claire's compassion for her mother, although I couldn't understand it at the time. Claire's mother showed up at mother–daughter luncheons drunk, and while Claire was mortified she also felt sad for her mother. I kept thinking Claire should be angrier about her mother's drinking. Despite her family's woes, their ills would not fester under a deadening silence, nor would they be dismissed as a joke. In Claire's home, even disease might be forgiven.

She had almost no guidance from her mother during high school, but thanks to her father Claire kept her mother's younger, healthier image alive in her memory. Also thanks to her father, Claire had more confidence and self-esteem than most of the fifteen-year-old girls I knew. Now that I was set loose to move about the city, in and out of friends' homes, I was unconsciously building my ideal family from the examples around me. I wanted a family with a sense of humor, not unlike my own family, but one with more compassion and openness.

CHAPTER 13

Birth of Venus

While I spent weekends with friends on the Eastside, the expansion of my family's clan was well underway. Bridget, who was the "sweetheart" of her husband's fraternity, moved with him to a "darling town" outside of Boston. Mom couldn't wait to drive up to see their newborn baby—and pick up a few antiques along the way. Michael, a law student, was marrying the girl he'd been dating since Bridget and Rosa fixed them up in high school. My sister-in-law-to-be was Cincinnati's answer to Christie Brinkley. Instead of appearing in the *Sports Illustrated* swimsuit edition, she sported a white tank suit with a pink monogram on her chest from the lifeguard's chair at her country club.

As it turned out, while our mother complained about "those damn liberals," she made exceptions. Bridget's husband was a "Boston liberal," but Mom adored him. Michael's fiancée's parents were friends and supporters of Governor Gilligan, another liberal. But Gilligan *had* graduated from St. Xavier High School, and the Gilligan Funeral Home was right across the street from Mom's grandfather's old house. Mom was already beaming with Irish pride while some of us recoiled at the prospect of Michael's future in-laws' wedding tradition: they took over the dance floor with an Irish jig culminating in the Notre Dame fight song. We considered this pride a bit aggressive, and as if the image of five Colleens and their parents circling in a jig wasn't enough, this family danced around their only brother, who happened to be a priest *and* the assistant dean of the Notre Dame Law School.

"Gag me with a spoon," I said to Liz.

"Out to lunch," she added, with a roll of her eyes, but Liz was the chosen bridesmaid from our family and she was secretly "psyched as hell" about this wedding.

We were no strangers to competition among in-laws. As Catholics, our mothers ran the Charity Ball. Specifically, our Aunt Eleanor chaired the Charity Ball, for years. Each time Mom would see Eleanor's name in the society page, she'd say, "Welp, I guess that Eleanor is at it again." Of course she envied Eleanor's success, and we hated to admit it but we envied our sister-in-law's flawless Irish Catholic daughter-in-law persona. We even envied her monogrammed swimsuit.

Then we had to contend with Bridget: Bridget and her "Eye-talian" in-laws with grandparents who spoke in Italian accents—Sicilian, we decided, as if we knew the difference. They made wine from their own grapes. Bridget was looking more like Diane Keaton every time we saw her, blue-eyed and satin-skinned. Now we all wanted Italian husbands. Damn these marriages! They would put every girl in our family under pressure to marry a Catholic man right out of college. And worse, we would have to race into pregnancy and give birth exactly nine months later. Now Mom would look at us girls as traitors to the family team if we didn't meet that honeymoon-baby standard.

On this one point Mom was no different than the other mothers from the broader Catholic circle in which we traveled. The dances and parties we attended might have seemed innocuous on the surface, but they were serious business. Marriages were meant to come from these follies, and all by the age of twenty-two. At fifteen I swished away those worries. My priorities included the accumulation of sweaters and friendships, second only to finding out who had parents going out of town and were therefore most likely to throw a party. At one such party, I met James Cabrera.

On an October night, Claire and I sat on a stone embankment, shivering as rusty leaves skimmed the driveway in the chilly breeze. I had to keep patting my nose with Kleenex. There was this guy sitting to my right but we were under a floodlight, which made his face a silhouette. I tried to get a look at him but it was impossible to do that in a subtle way.

Meanwhile, Claire had taken up a conversation with someone on her left. I glanced over the shoulder of the shadowy guy to my right to see who else was around, but there was no getting past his nest of curls. I scooted closer to Claire. David Bowie's "Diamond Dogs" was drowning out her conversation. Finally, I turned to the guy on my right and said, "Hey." A flash of white teeth blinked and disappeared. He said nothing, although he did shift slightly so that I could see his face, which included a bulbous nose and intelligent brown eyes.

His face was what kept me there. I would not have called him handsome but when he grinned, his face twisted into a half-sneer, and something about that face posed a dare. My voice has always been either too soft or too shrill. "I'm Eileen," I finally said, too softly under the music. I couldn't hear what he said back, so I said, "Please?" And he screamed, "I said, 'I know.'"

"Okay!" I said, shrilly.

"You okay?" Claire asked.

"Sure," I said, even as my eyes sharpened into a face that begged, "Don't leave me alone with this guy." She grinned and whispered, "He's kind of cute." Then she went back to her conversation.

I thought about taking my chances and leaping to freedom, but I might lose a leg or break it in half on the landing. The guy's shoulder brushed mine. I smelled fresh-scrubbed boy, all soap and musk. Being from an all-girl school my capacity to smell a boy was extraordinary. My senses were tuned to a pitch so keen it almost hurt, and coupled with that, my curiosity about people often trumped social protocol. In my crowd, a girl would only speak to a boy once he had made the first move. "What's your name?" I asked bluntly.

He straightened up and in a reasonably affable tone he said, "James." He offered his hand, a warm and welcoming palm. His arms were still tan and he wore a golf shirt.

"Aren't you cold, James? James who?"

His eyes shot off in the distance, as if he felt ambivalent about saying more, but he added, "Cabrera."

I'd heard the name from Phoebe, which could either mean that he was very cool or that he was trouble. "You know Phoebe?" I asked.

"Ooooh," he said, stretching his neck as if he'd just set down a sack of potatoes. "I might know a Phoebe."

"You said you knew me."

"Did I say that?"

"You said you knew my name."

"Is that all there is to know?"

I hope not, I thought. Instead I said, "Maybe." This was my attempt at mysteriousness, but I couldn't hide my grin or the fact that I was anxious because of the lingering silence. He seemed comfortable just sitting there, and the more content he looked, the more I talked. "I like to write," I said. What an absurd thing to blurt out, I thought. My claw hand shot up to hide my face. But he asked, "Write what?"

"Poetry!" I shouted, throwing out my arms as if confessing to a crime. Then I started giggling a bit crazily. He turned to face me head on, so that I could see his features. He was trying not to smile. "What kind of poetry?" he asked in a more serious voice.

"I don't know," I said, coming down hard from his seriousness. Besides, I really didn't know. I was distracted by his mouth, which he hardly opened, but I guessed that he'd had braces. Straight teeth mattered, according to Mom, who said that my teeth were straight because God is always fair. If I complained about my legs, she said, "But you have those teeth . . ." Suddenly I remembered one type of poem. "Haiku," I said. "We had to write one in class and I wrote a bunch of poems for my friends to hand in because they hate to write them. Most people do." This launched more frantic chatter until I concluded, "Our teacher gives them As and she gives me Cs."

"Hmm," he said, folding his arms. "Sooo misunderstood, eh?"

"Oh, forget it," I said, looking away. I was such an easy read.

"Maybe your English teacher knows they're your poems. Maybe she's *playing* with you."

I hadn't thought of that. We bantered for a while. I kept thinking that maybe I'd ask him to our sophomore dance, which was coming up in a couple of weeks, but my ride beckoned me to leave.

At home, I asked Frank about James. Frank's friends were all the same boys from our neighborhood, Chief Taylor and Stilts and the whole gang. He'd never left them. To him, James was just another of those Hyde Parkers, our "cross to bear." He said, "He's a snob."

"I bet you don't even know him."

Frank had this way of tilting his head and pushing out his lips, as if to say, "Granted . . . but . . ."

"What?"

Now he shook his head disapprovingly. "Why do you hang out with those people?"

"I choose friends based on how they treat me."

"Well, how did he treat you?"

When I thought of it, there wasn't much to say. I'd done most of the talking. "He's nice. Quiet."

Frank pursed his lips and nodded. "I could see that. I mean, from what I know of him. But he's *on the golf team*."

"Yeah? So?"

"I don't know." Frank rubbed his chin where a few hairs had sprouted. "Isn't that kinda weird?" he asked. "A kid who golfs?"

On Monday, I asked around at school about James. "James Cabrera?" said a girl from his neighborhood. "That boy is always grounded."

"Grounded?" That seemed an odd detail. "Anything else?"

"Only that he's Cuban."

"Cuban!" Lucy and Ricky—already I had us married with baby Ricky on the way. A Cuban boyfriend, what could be sexier than that? And in Cincinnati!

I remembered that there had been one Latino boy in my grade school. We called him the Frito Bandito. Beaten up on a regular basis, the boy was completely ostracized. In the middle of a class in third grade he slipped me a note saying, "I love you," and I slapped him hard across the face. I'd left no doubt in anyone's mind about where I stood, which was as far from Frito as possible. Now, the thought of my cruelty horrified me. I could never apologize enough because of how deeply it hurt me to be treated that way. And of course, my esteem for James Cabrera only benefited from my remorse.

But James Cabrera was an altogether different story. If there had been trauma in his past, there was not a shred of it to be found in his demeanor. More importantly, the fact that this boy, this *golfer*, was somehow different, well, it made me crazy with anticipation. Immediately my mind went to work. Was he inquiring about me?

If so, what would he hear? "Cronin? Which Cronin? One with legs?" Would he fight that all-too-obvious joke that his friends might make about "I-lean"? And what, exactly, made a boy *choose* the golf team in high school? This last one tore me up: a boy who golfed. He did not play football, basketball, or baseball. My father was going to hate him; I was already falling in love.

I decided that if I wanted to ask him to our dance, I'd better act quickly. Word was that he'd dated a cheerleader from my school, who might ask him to the dance. A year earlier that news would have shut me down, but competition now escalated my resolve. I was less afraid of rejection than I was of dialing a telephone and asking for a boy. How would I get the words out? He would hear the tremors in my voice. My throat would dry up, or I'd start blathering again. Aside from that, I was about to do the one thing that Mom always said was *as low as a girl can go:* "Only a desperate girl would call a boy."

On the smoking patio, I explained my dilemma to a friend. I had wanted to ask Claire to call and pretend she was me, but Claire's voice was steady, deep, plodding. Mine raced from high-pitched to a shrill birdcall. Besides, James had met Claire.

On the other side of my friend was a girl named Tracy, who strummed a guitar and sang church tunes. I had to raise my voice over "Blowin' in the Wind" to ask my friend if she would call for me. Tracy silenced her guitar and said, "He'll think you're a coward."

I scowled at her and turned back to my friend. "Look, just pretend you're me."

"Huh?" This friend did have my voice. In one syllable she'd just gone from merely high to an inaudible shriek.

"Come on," I begged.

Tracy butted in again. "Why don't you just do it yourself?"

"Please," I pleaded. This high-pitched, shy girl could possibly pull it off, but she stared at the tip of her cigarette and said, "What makes you think I can do it any better than you?"

"I can't do it. I'll fold. I know it." I tried to think of something to entice her. "I'll call someone for you."

"Naw," she shook her head. "I might not even go. It's just a dance. And what if he says no?"

"I won't blame you if he says no." I held up my right hand. "I swear. But at least I'll have tried."

"No, *she'll* have tried," said Tracy, pointing at my friend.

I shifted my back toward Tracy, who retreated into her strumming. Then I badgered my friend until she capitulated.

I hardly slept that night. Before class the next morning I raced to the smoking patio, bursting through the cafeteria doors. The group of smokers started giggling.

"What's so funny?" I said, jittery from a lack of sleep. The air was nippy, and smoke made me nauseous in the morning.

"Tracy was just out here," said a sophomore provocatively. This girl reminded me of Faye Dunaway, with her high cheekbones and red hair. She was the epitome of cool.

"Okay," I said, resigned. "What did Tracy say?"

They were all silent.

"What?" I tried to sound put out rather than terrified.

"Tracy was the one who called James," said this girl. She even had Faye Dunaway's monotone voice.

"No!" I slapped my forehead. *Kumbaya Tracy?* "Oh, God." Everyone laughed while this miniature Faye Dunaway tilted her head and smirked. She was laughing with me, and if it weren't my problem I'd have been laughing, too. After all, if there was anything to soften the blow at this, my most degrading moment, it was that Faye Dunaway was recounting my nightmare with smoke curling up from her nostrils.

"I guess that's it." I tried to sound accepting. "Did he give a reasonable excuse?"

"Well," said Faye, wincing. "It gets worse."

I had to ask. "What happened?"

She cleared her throat. "He said no to Tracy. He said . . . what'd he say?" she asked another girl, and bit into her fingernail.

"Come on!" I said.

"I think he went along with it. At first. He let Tracy ask him to the dance, but then he said, 'You're not Eileen Cronin.'" She made her voice go deep, like a man's voice. "'You tell Eileen Cronin if she wants to ask me to her dance, she'll have to call me herself.'"

Everyone doubled over in laughter. For the rest of the day I sulked.

That night, I went into Liz's room and collapsed on her bed. I was holding my head, rocking and groaning. She'd heard the story. Everyone had heard the story. "Oh, stop it," said Liz. She lit a cigarette and handed it to me. "Smoke this before you call. It'll calm your nerves." She opened the window and put a Cat Stevens album on the turntable.

We sprawled on her bed, blowing smoke out the window. The nicotine kicked in. I was wired. My throat dried up. "I can't do it."

"Yes, you can."

"No." I shook my head and dragged so hard again on the cigarette that it crackled before I handed it to her. "Will you?"

"Do you want to piss this guy off?"

"That's just it," I said, hugging my stomach. "He's already pissed."

"No he's not," she said, irritated.

"He's not?"

She waved off the cigarette. "Just finish that thing. You always hotbox." She imitated my bent fingers holding a cigarette—not my claw hand but my normal hand. "Would you take a hit from that?" she'd say, holding up my double-jointed fingers. Then she said,

"You're giving up when he never said he doesn't want to go. Why would he tell Tracy to have you call him?"

"So he could yell at me?" I said, throwing up my hands.

She tossed her hair back and sighed. "You're *such* a loser." She handed me the yellow phone that we fought over constantly. It was as if we were the only people living in the house. Now and then someone would pick up from the kitchen and say, "Not you again!" Or one of the "babies"—now in elementary school—would listen in from the line in the basement and start giggling.

Liz pointed to the receiver in my hand. "Look, I'm going to go brush my teeth, and after that I want to go to bed. You call him. Get this over with, you hear?" Then she left me alone to make the call.

I dialed the rotary pad, praying his mother would not answer the phone because surely she would think, like my mother: *desperate girl.* Instead, a boy answered.

He sounded like James but more formal. "Hello, this is the Cabreras. May I ask who is calling, please?" I almost hung up. If this was James on the line, he was already putting me off. At our house we said, "Hello?" and then screamed for the requested party. That was our way of welcoming a caller, and it was an inviting reception. What *was* all this polite talk? Could he *be* any more cruel?

"James?" I blurted out.

"Are you sure?" said the voice. "You don't sound like a James."

"Oh, sorry," I said. The fact that he was playing with me went right over my head, which meant that we were getting somewhere. The bedroom door creaked open, and Liz crept back inside. Where was I? "Hello, may I speak with James?"

The voice grew impatient. "*May* I ask who is calling, *please*?"

Liz stood over me, mouthing the words, "Just say it."

"Um. This is Eileen Cronin."

"Uhleen," he said. "Hello! This is James."

Already I loved the way he said my name. He left out the

incriminating "I" before the "lean." And I forgot what I was going to say next. Why wouldn't he talk? "Well, um. I was going to ask you to go to our dance . . ." Nothing came back from his end. "Hello?"

"You were going to say?" he asked.

Liz sat down on the opposite bed. She was in a terrycloth robe, white with toothpaste-blue flowers on it, completely plain, but every girl in the family had inhabited that robe in high school. Its shared history was the whole point. That robe had put in a lot of phone time with boys. Liz crossed her arms and legs and gave me her implacable face.

"Uh, well, I heard about the mix-up. The other girl called you, right?" I stopped and tried so hard to wait him out, but he only said, "Yes."

"Oooh. Sorry about that. Did she ask you to the dance?"

"Yes."

"And you told her I should call myself, right?"

Another pause. Then he said, "Wait. Which girl?"

"Oh," I said faintly. I'd waited too long. Someone else had asked him to the dance. "Oh," I said again. "So, you're already going."

"Going where?"

Now he was dragging it out. "Look," I said. "I was going to ask you to our sophomore dance. I'm sorry about what happened, but if someone already asked you . . ." Liz's face scrunched up like a fist. She looked ready to belt someone, either James or me.

"I'll go," he said.

"With me?"

"Sure."

I sank into the pillow, relieved. I wanted to hang up immediately, but he cleared his throat, and something about the way he did that made me worry that he was about to set some conditions. His tone sounded tentative when he said, "We should probably get to know each other better. Maybe we should go out this weekend. You want to go out?"

The following Saturday night, James came to my back door, passing Frank and his friends on the basketball court. From my bedroom I heard the boys acknowledge each other tersely. Why had he come through the back? There was always a three-ring circus out there: a pack of children might be chasing each other, one with a bat, someone else might be digging up mud with a soup ladle. Who could say? After all, our idea of a joke, briefly, was to chase one another with an axe, until someone nicked up the walls in our newly renovated basement. And then there were Frankie's friends.

Frank and I had been arguing lately. "You're changing," he said, pointing at me.

"And you are not."

Frank pushed out his lips to think. "No," he said, waving a finger authoritatively. "I am not changing." He tried to make it sound like a commendable goal, and I laughed at him mockingly. After that, his eyes misted over and he went silent.

Now I heard Chief Taylor yell up from the basketball court, "Loooooney! Your *date* is here." I crashed onto my bed and moaned, fighting nausea. Around our house, Rosa had been referring to James as Chi-Chi Rodriguez, and now I heard Mom greeting James in the kitchen. "Come on in," she said. "What's your name? Dick! Come and meet the Rodriguez boy. He's here for Eileen."

"Cabrera!" I wanted to scream from upstairs. Instead I hurried to finish getting ready because I heard Dad clear his throat. "Oh, God," I said to Nina, who had just come in to watch me. "He'll give James the mole face. He's going to peer over his glasses from his newspaper like a chubby rat poking out from his hole."

"I know," said Nina with a thumbs-up to our father. She worshipped Dad, and he tried not to play favorites. But Nina was everyone's favorite. I scrambled to finish my hair, burning my hand on the curling iron. I peeled off my cardigan and snuck into Liz's room where she kept a trunk full of sweaters. I stole her beloved cashmere one and doused myself with her Chanel perfume.

Downstairs I found James's sinewy figure draping the kitchen wall as if he were trying to camouflage himself in the swell of traffic. Mom stood at the stove in a nightgown, petroleum jelly smeared on her black eyebrows. She looked like Bette Davis in *What Ever Happened to Baby Jane?* Dad was eating a bologna sandwich at the kitchen table, completely ignoring James, whose expression was a mixture of horror and amusement.

"Oh, hey," I said to Dad. "You met James." I rushed to James and toward the door, but my barefoot mother leapt into my path. She mouthed the words, "Are you wearing that girdle I gave you?" Then she shook her head with dismay. "I didn't think so," she said under her breath.

"Excuse me?" said James.

"Naaaw," I said. "No. Don't need a heavier coat. Let's go."

I rushed him out and he looked eager to flee, especially when we hit the porch and the dribbling stopped. Eight boys stared us down from the basketball court. "Where you headed?" asked Chief. "Hyde P-p-p-park?"

I saw Frank shoot him a look and Chief nodded, as if to say he would handle this.

"Sump'n like that," said James, adopting the lingo of my neighborhood, although he kept moving. We made it past the dogwoods, a relief until we came to a van in the driveway. "Ohhhh, who left *that* there?" I asked.

"It's mine," said James, opening the passenger door for me.

I could practically feel my leg falling off as I considered how I might hoist myself up there, but James came up behind me and gave me a hearty shove from behind. A jolting motion like that might have broken the suction on my right leg, which would have made a prolonged farting noise, but I was spared. Having navigated the awkward situation, we both sighed as I settled into my seat.

By the time he came around to the driver's seat, a shroud of maturity had engulfed him. He took the wheel with a sobering sense of duty. We were going on a double date, he said.

"Really?" I said, relieved. "Who's coming?" This was good thinking on his part. Otherwise, he'd have to deal with my nervous palaver or panicked silence.

"Will," he said. I liked Will; that was another good choice. But then he added, "And Dodi."

"Dodi?" I said, rubbing my chin. Oddly enough, there were two Dodis in my class. The main Dodi was Phoebe's cousin, her polar opposite. Whereas Phoebe was sensual, Dodi was prissy. Phoebe took herself out of the college track in less than one semester of high school, while Dodi aspired to make National Honor Society. Phoebe preferred to go shoeless, and Dodi probably slept in Papagallo flats. The two girls even looked opposite: Phoebe's dark features and voluptuous figure made Dodi seem a borderline anorexic blonde. Girls were intimidated by Dodi—everyone except for Phoebe, who found Dodi's concerns laughable—so this news made me want to giggle. I pressed my good hand to my lips. James kept his eyes on the road. At the stoplight he said, "What?" But a smile crept over his face.

"It's Dodi, right?" We both cracked up.

I waved it off. "I didn't say anything."

"You didn't have to," he said. He tossed his kinky hair back dramatically to imitate the way Dodi tossed her silky hair, which sent me into gales of laughter. It was not James's nature to join in that laughter. He was more of a repressed performer, all about setup and execution, though there was a nurturing aspect to his delight in my laughter.

After everyone had been picked up the boys took us to a sexy comedy, where James laughed at all the subtle innuendo, most of which I didn't get, but then I was completely focused on his arm bent so perfectly around my shoulder. I wanted to lean my head against his chest, though that might be interpreted as scandalous by Dodi. I did it anyway.

Afterward, James led me by the hand into a party, where we separated for a while. Each time I glanced around, I found him watching out for me from close by. Later he ushered me to my back door, where the porch light was on but there were no longer boys dribbling basketballs.

"Thanks," I said.

He nodded. His smile had changed from what I had first thought of as a partial sneer to one like someone squinting into the sun, head tilted and one eye barely visible. He kissed me as if taking a small bite of some new fruit, first with concentration, then abandon. His teeth brushed against mine, and his hand at the back of my neck clasped a handful of my hair. I wanted to reach up and touch his curls but remembered that Will and Dodi were out there beyond the dogwoods. "I really had fun," I said, hurrying to break away because if I gave in and touched his hair I might not let go.

"Nights in White Satin": that was the make-out song at my dance, and it pretty much summed up the 1975 school year, during which we went to concerts by Santana, Little Feat, Jackson Browne, and the Allman Brothers. Throughout all of it I chatted away nervously, never having gotten over that first sensation of ascending the crest of a rollercoaster every time I encountered him. James was a man of few words, perhaps choosing instead to let his music express what he could not. We needed distractions: movies, dances, parties, games of any kind, because we fell into that youthful pattern of making out as soon as we came up short. We ran out of distractions often. What we never ran out of was a novel make-out session. Like everyone else, we made out under changing leaves, in the snow, and under moonlight. But we also made out once after I threw up in a parking lot.

In the spring we went to a Reds game. He'd come straight from a golf match, and he was wearing yellow pants. I winced and said, "You can't be serious."

James never did buy into an insult. I'd seen kids shrink away after provoking him with names such as "spic." The venomous stare James shot them struck the offender speechless. Within seconds James would be humming a tune to let it be known that he wasn't giving it a second thought. Now he said to me, "They're *golf* pants," as if I were too simple-minded to know golf clothes when I saw them.

"If you say so," I said.

We were sitting in Dad's seats on the third base line, just a few rows from the opposing team's dugout, so you could see exactly what was up inside the Reds' dugout. Here Johnny Bench was always robbing us fans of foul balls, snatching them from over the rail with that huge bearlike mitt. Now, while we watched from behind the Pirates' dugout, the lights coming on mid-game, the smell of popcorn, peanuts, and beer embracing us, James pointed up to the corporate box where his father was partying. My father's seats included four season tickets, but no one had wanted the other seats so they were empty. In the seventh-inning stretch, a man with natty black hair in a red linen blazer came down and took the seat next to mine.

As if the jacket weren't enough to catch my attention, he played a Charlie Chaplin routine, turning his back to me when I turned to him. I cleared my throat, and he popped his head up as if he'd been napping. Who was this guy? Finally, I looked at James as if to ask, "What'll I do?" James bit his bottom lip and shrugged. The man whipped around and pretended to be startled, throwing his hands up theatrically.

Instantly I saw that he had James's face and hair in a darker complexion. His eyes made me think of Albert Einstein, or maybe I just imagined him as a quirky scientist.

"And who is this young lady?" Dr. Cabrera asked in an elegant voice, while offering his hand.

I glanced back at James, who introduced me in his formal voice. Although the prank was over, James maintained what seemed to me an odd sense of formality with his father. But what did I know? When Dad saw a child running past the window wielding a golf club like a weapon, he only called through the screen, "Settle down. That's my nine iron." In our house, irreverence might be tolerated but a failed joke was reprehensible. James's father might have been strict, but it pleased me to see that he had a sense of humor, too.

As soon as James asked me to go to his prom, I got to work on my tan. At school Claire and I concocted a plan to break something fixable on my leg so we could skip biology class and instead "lay out" by the creek. On the smoking patio, we tried to bend a clasp on my below-knee leg by holding a lighter to the metal. Unfortunately, the metal snapped. "Uh, oh," we said, then Claire ran into the classroom and told Sister Theresa that "I-lean" was in "desperate straits" and needed help with her broken leg. I came hobbling in after her. "For Heaven's sake, girl, get her to the nurse. It looks painful," said Sister Theresa. We hobbled away before veering off to a side door and heading down to the creek, where we sunbathed.

That evening on the phone, I bragged to James that I had skipped class. When I described the scheme, he said, "You broke your leg on purpose?"

"Yep."

As soon as I heard a curt sniff, I understood that I'd done something wrong. "You better get that fixed before my prom," he said.

The prom was only days away. Who would I get to drive me to the leg man? "Uh-oh," I said.

"This is not funny."

After I hung up, I went to work on the leg myself with a piece of coat hanger that I fashioned into a clasp similar to the one we'd broken, only this one was roughly constructed so the jagged ends of the wire crossed. They scratched my thigh a bit, but that was nothing a Band-Aid couldn't fix. So I looped it through the strap that wrapped around my thigh, and it held the leg in place.

On the evening of the prom I wore a cotton dress with a tiny floral print and a gold necklace with a pearl at my throat. My waist was small enough that a boy could wrap his hands around it and his fingers might overlap. The prom queen was a blonde with big blue eyes (was there any other kind of prom queen?). When I looked in the mirror, I saw a rosy-cheeked girl with golden brown hair and hazel eyes flashing brown to green. I decided I wasn't so different from the prom queen.

The dance took place downtown. Inside you descended a wide staircase into a posh hallway. In the ballroom, tuxedos and gowns swirled. We stayed on the dance floor most of the night. The boys perspired so heavily that they peeled off jackets, bow ties, and cummerbunds. I was hot myself, but my shoulders were bare and the dress was light. My biggest problem was the strapless bra. It kept falling, and I had to sneak off to hoist it up from my hips. A few of James's friends unbuttoned their shirts, but as usual, James hardly broke a sweat.

The band played "Saturday Night's Alright for Fighting," and the mob rocked in rhythm to it. James gripped my waist and bounced me up and down. The makeshift clasp in my leg broke loose. Worse than falling out, the coat wire slipped inside my leg and lodged itself on the bottom, so that James was bouncing me on the jagged wire, which was as sharp as an upturned nail. I threw my head back in pain, and James stopped. "What's wrong?" he screamed over the music.

I pulled away.

"You didn't," he said. "I thought . . ." He clapped a hand to his forehead. As I watched him register what was happening it occurred to me that my mistake was about to ruin his prom. James didn't know what to do with himself, concern and fury all over his face.

"I'll fix it," I said, hobbling away. With each step the wire stabbed into me. I pushed off of people and tables, toward the powder room.

Inside the sitting area of the ladies' room, girls gossiped about their evenings while passing liquor smuggled in purses. I leaned into the wall as I tried to sneak past them. "Are you okay?" said someone. Inside a stall, I crumpled onto the toilet seat.

"Oh, no," said another girl, her voice lowering to a whisper. "Did you see her face? That girl is about to barf." Everyone fell silent, and a round of giggles followed.

I took advantage of their laughter to rip open the Velcro strap that held my leg in place. I'd been drinking, though I wasn't feeling sick. The stall was dark and my vision blurry from alcohol. I turned the leg upside down and shook it, but nothing came out. Then I found that one side of the wire had pierced the cushioned lining, where it lodged, and the other end was poking up. "What have I done?" I kept saying. In fact, this was nothing a very long pencil and a steady hand might not have corrected, but being a teenager with a few gin and tonics mixed with my reckless drive toward the crest of despair, I couldn't conceive of such an invention. Or maybe the relationship itself was the looming threat: it was hurling too quickly toward love on my part, or worse, uncontainable lust. We were just fifteen and seventeen.

I was literally knocking my forehead against the stall when I heard Claire's voice, distinct and deeper than the others. "I'll just be a minute," she said to someone on her way to the stalls. "Claire!" I called before I stood on one unsteady leg to open the door. "Claire, get in here! Help!"

"Eileen?" she said, jamming into the stall with me. I explained what had happened, and she said only, "That's bad."

"Claire!"

"We'll fix it."

We peeled off the white slipper on my foot, then my pantyhose. "These are full of runs," she said, "Wanna just ditch 'em? Your dress is long. No one will notice." I was probably still beating my head when she tossed them into the Tampax trash bin.

"What's going on in there?" said someone from the sitting room. That was followed by whispers and titters.

Claire tried shaking, then batting, the leg, but we were too crammed in. She shoved the shoe back on the foot and helped me out to the sitting area while carrying my leg in her hand. A swarm of girls descended on us, some to our aid, while those who didn't know me stood at a distance, their chins tucked to their chests, their eyes astonished. A redheaded girl with a boyish haircut and a strapless gown commented, "Well it's a cute shoe on that foot."

Someone offered a chair. Claire helped me into it, before kicking off her own shoes and climbing onto an upholstered chair. She wedged my foot against the ceiling to look inside. She tried to jar the wire loose. Nothing came out. "I see it, but the wire is pinned into that small part. My hand won't fit," she said.

"Oh, god," I said, "He'll never forgive me."

The redhead handed me a lit cigarette. She pulled a small flask from a white clutch with Kelly green piping that matched her dress and shoes, and even the upholstery of her settee. "Just in case it doesn't come out," she said, handing me the flask.

The warm bourbon tasted awful then wonderfully hot on my throat, before I passed along the flask. Now I was sweating out my fate under an air-conditioning vent in a powder room, which was turning out to be more fun than one might imagine. And my heart was breaking. The flask made its way back to me, and I said, "What the hell." I took another mouthful of bourbon.

Finally Claire, who never did fail to ground me, asked me what I planned to do about the leg situation. She could go to such insane depths then jerk back to reality, an enviable trait, but one I probably hadn't even registered because I was still climbing the arc of despair. "Well?"

"I don't know," I finally said. "Just get drunk enough to go back out there, I guess."

"Eileen?"

"You got a better idea?"

She shook her head before handing me the leg. At least now the wire was only stabbing from the side of my leg, so I could walk, sort of. I found James in a knot of people dancing. He gripped me by the shoulders and saw the pain in my face. "You couldn't fix it, right?"

I shook my head. "Come on," he said, his jaw tightening as he led me out of the room. "I'll take you home." Nothing was said until he lifted me into the van. "You don't have to take me home," I said. "Let's go to the party. I don't want to ruin your night."

He rolled his eyes as he climbed in on his side and took the wheel. "It's kind of late for that."

"Oh." I felt my lip quiver. "Oh."

He paused to collect his thoughts. I was pretty sure he was going to tell me this was the end of us. Instead he reached for me. "Come on." He got up and carried me into the back seat. "At least we have an excuse for missing the party," he said. His anger gave way to a hard, open-mouthed kiss. It began almost bitterly and mellowed as if he'd forgotten himself entirely.

So far, in all of our kissing, James had only touched me under my sweater. I tended to gasp at the touch of his palm on my stomach and by the time it worked its way under my bra, I would have to hold my breath because I was afraid he'd hear my excitement. He dedicated hours to exploring under my meager brassieres. I would be gasping for air as if coming up from a thirty-foot pool: *Will I make it? Will I make it?* The rush of excitement and breathlessness made me even giddier. It's a wonder I never passed out.

Most of what I knew about sex came from columns in either *Vogue* or *Glamour*. I had no explanation for why I was literally gushing at times. Did men find it appalling when a woman's body reacted so enthusiastically? Then one of Liz's friends gave her a copy of *The Happy Hooker*. I stole it from her underwear drawer, and when I finished I stuffed it under my mattress. Then I remembered that Candy changed the sheets every Tuesday. Oh, the stories Candy might have told every evening to her sister! This book gave me far more than I needed, but that was the whole point of reading it. James had only put his hand under my sweater. Clothing had not come off. He hadn't ventured anywhere near my legs. And this was due to the fact that invariably, just before things got too hot, we'd squabble. Usually it was me who started it. "Why did you say that at the party?" I'd say.

He'd lift his face from inside my blouse, which seemed most unlikely, but James was all about honor and reputation. "What did I say?"

"You know!"

"That joke about your family?" he'd say, barely concealing his grin.

"Well?"

He would squint. "*You* joke about your family." Then his wet lips were on my breast again, and panic coursed through my veins. Often I would fire into the dark: golf, or the fact that he was Cuban—those were frequent targets, but both I found intolerably sexy, and therefore I could hardly rouse his ire on either. James had almost no visible weak spots, from my perspective. About the only thing that made him vulnerable was the fact that he was grounded for about fifty percent of his adolescent life. These house arrests were a sign of the very short fuse tethering him to his father.

Alone in the back of James's van, with hours ahead of us before either of us was expected home, James kissed me until we had to stop and remember how to breathe separately. We dropped back against the seat. He reached over to my neck and pointed right where that pearl-drop necklace rested. I watched him slide a finger from my clavicle across my chest to lower a strap of my dress. He liked that. And I didn't stop him. So he sat up enthusiastically and lowered the other strap, checking my face for a reaction. I lowered my eyes. He took that as a sign, and peeled my dress down over my strapless brassiere. He stopped to give an approving nod before shimmying it down to my waist. Then he buried his face in my flesh. I cradled his neck and squeezed his curls between my fingers, so lost now that I said nothing when he lifted my skirt.

If I'd wanted to argue, he'd take care of that. He plunged his tongue deep into my mouth. My shoulders rose in alarm as his fingers traveled to my bare thigh. Now his palm, warm and tender, was planted on my skin. We stayed in that place for what seemed hours.

Finally, he took my hand and placed it on his pants, where I felt what I'd been brushing up against for months. I started to pull my hand away. This had always seemed to me the part of the body that men had to bear, and women dealt with—what was I supposed to do with it?

An argument—I needed one, something, anything to break this up. Of course I could have simply said no, but where was the fun in that? Besides, I didn't want to stop. Nothing but anger, raw, in-your-face rage, could distract us at this point.

Even beyond my fear about having sex, I didn't want him to touch the wood of my right leg. If he did, I felt certain the world would close in on us. So I did the only thing I could think of at the time: I shifted the right leg away from where he stroked my left thigh. He stopped kissing me again to look questioningly into my eyes. Once more I could only look down, so he kissed me again before his hand moved to the spot where my eyes had apparently directed him. I jerked as it landed, and jerked again when he slid it under my panties.

Now we were Russia and the United States, both of us only a finger's stroke from detonation.

I pulled back from the kiss and froze. He had discovered my secret. What did he think of me now? Was he going to leap over the front seat and drive me home? Wasn't it true that boys were "turned off by girls with a sex drive"? The Girl Scout den mother said as much in the birds and bees talk that Mom had signed me up for in grade school.

I took my hand from his pants and whispered, "I'm sorry. I'm so sorry. I can't do this." He lifted my straps up and smoothed them over my shoulders, and lowered my skirt. He bit his lip and looked out the window. We sat there a while, just our heads touching, staring off in different directions. It seemed that eventually we would drive home. I wondered if he'd go to the parties by himself after he dropped me off.

In time we both stared ahead. Eventually we found our foreheads touching, as if our thoughts were being transmitted physically through our brains. Then our noses touched. He kissed me. And before long we fell back into the throes of foreplay.

CHAPTER 14

Changer of Hearts

The women in my family were stingy with compliments. When Rosa, who was majoring in art history, elbowed me on the sofa and said, "Eileen, you have a Botticelli face," I braced myself for the punch line. What species was a Botticelli? She pointed to a reproduction of *The Birth of Venus* in her massive textbook.

"Oh," I said. "Thanks."

Flattery or anything that smelled of success intoxicated me; it also caused me to panic. I'd come to believe that if I were naïve enough to see myself as attractive or smart, I would pay in humiliation. The payment might not hurt as much as being thrown down a staircase, or it might hurt worse. Maybe I'd be broken from the inside. In this sense, James seemed a safe boyfriend. Upon threat of death he would not hand over a compliment. On the rare occasions when one escaped from his lips, I could bank on its sincerity. My favorite compliment from James came in the form of a reconfiguration of my nickname. Instead of Looney Tunes, he called me Tunes. Since he cared almost as much about music as he cared about golf, this was as good as being called Her Majesty. And better still, everyone followed him.

In general I was mistrustful of people, and yet for a girl of fifteen

I trusted in myself to an unrealistic degree. Within my family I trusted Frankie, except that we were clashing over our choices of friends; Kevin, but he was away at Notre Dame; and sometimes Ted, but he was only in the eighth grade. Nina, who was about seven years old and shared a bedroom with me, wasn't old enough to confide in; however, she and I lavished affection on each other. On Sunday mornings she climbed into my bed to give me butterfly kisses with her abundant black eyelashes, while I tickled her until she begged me to stop. We'd had only one argument. I don't remember what it was over, but that same day she left a note on my pillow and, because apologies were rarer than compliments in our family, I kept it. The paper is full of angry scribbles and finally the words:

> *Dear Eileen*
> *all my friend think you are party and I do to*
> *sorry*
> *Love*
> *Nina*

During my early childhood, when I wasn't in legs, people viewed me with horror, or worse, sorrow. Many looked away, which made me want to be invisible. Now the message was conflicting. On the one hand I had a hideous defect, and on the other I was frequently told I was beautiful. I didn't know how to reconcile this disparity, so at times I convinced myself that I was better than ordinary: I was extraordinary. And why not? Fairy tales are full of "blind men" who see into others' souls. There had to be something that made me special. The tolerance of pain, I decided. Secretly I scoffed at my peers who worried about things like B.O. or bad hair. I had to keep my head intact, which was hard after a night of boys flirting with me, because I still had to go to sleep that night without legs. The humbling facts always chased me down in the morning. That was when reality hit extra hard, requiring me to talk myself out of bed as if going into battle.

I never thought to tell anyone what was going on in my head. Who would understand?

Simultaneously, I reveled in the sheer joy of being almost sixteen. My girlfriends and I cruised for parties. When we came up short we masterminded capers. One night while we sat in my friend Meg's convertible, looking for something to do, she mentioned that there was an underground house nearby. Meg was the equestrian in our group, and I imagined that she was used to jumping fences. I said, "An underground house is built that way so people can walk on it, right?"

"I'm not so sure they had that in mind," said our cautious friend Gretchen from the back seat.

I glanced over at Meg, who revved up her engine.

Viewed from the road, the underground house was all but invisible: a mound of earth with cylindrical chutes coming up from its core. Supposedly a pond butted up to it, and the people inside watched an underwater scene through a glass wall. Meg and Gretchen pulled me over the fence while a third friend hoisted me up from behind. We had not expected the dog that charged out from a chute, although we did make it back over the fence intact.

Skinny-dipping also involved breaking and entering. We had friends with pools. Meg had her own lake. But that was beside the point. We craved the risk: dancing naked in starlight, water lapping our bodies.

What I loved most about skinny-dipping was that we were alone. I could swim among girlfriends and no one stared at me. I'd learned to ignore the gawking eyes of strangers, but it still undermined the one time I felt utterly free. In a pool I moved without a single compromise because I was liberated from my legs. Without them I became an elusive mermaid, the Venus de Milo spit from the ruins, or a comet firing across an endless sky.

Not far into the summer, I faced my first obstacle with respect to swimming. My latest pair of legs consisted of a hard synthetic surface with metal parts underneath. There was a hollow area behind the knee of my below-knee leg. In a pool it would have filled up and sucked me under like wading boots in whitewater. Whenever a party took place at a house with a pool, every girl was thrown in before the night was over. The boys I knew would not have tossed me in because I might drown in my legs, but I would never admit to a strange boy that I didn't have legs. One time Liz threw herself over the threshold of a sliding door to block a varsity football player from taking a running leap into a pool with me in his arms. Both she and I were too embarrassed to tell him that I had artificial legs. Another time, while James was grounded, his friend Peter snatched me from a boy preparing to hurl me sideways into a diving well.

Maybe because James was grounded the night that Peter stepped in to save me, I hadn't considered the problems that swimming posed for us. I wasn't ready to have sex, so I'd never imagined how James might react to seeing me without my legs. Now swimming— the one sport I loved and could perform with grace—posed a threat.

That summer James and I double dated a lot with Peter and my friend Ginny, the math whiz. They were making out in the back seat of James's van when we passed other friends on the road and pulled onto a side street. James got out, talked to them, and climbed back into the driver's seat. Briefly he hesitated.

"What did they say?" asked Peter.

"A bunch of people are pool-hopping at the country club,"

said James, rather somberly, I thought, for such a festive topic as pool-hopping.

I turned self-consciously toward my window.

"We don't have to," he said to me.

"It's okay," I said, facing him.

He started the engine. "Are you sure?" he said, making a U-turn toward the club.

"Yes."

We both grew quiet. As we neared the parking lot he said, "Maybe you should stay in the—"

"Right." But I kept turning it over. Why? Was Ginny going to do it? If other girls were doing it, why couldn't I? "Maybe."

His mouth dropped open, then snapped shut.

I would at least go onto the deck to see for myself. But there would be boys combing the place to throw the girls in the pool, maybe boys who didn't know about my legs. James pulled into a space. Peter stopped making out with Ginny and glanced around the empty parking lot.

"Maybe we missed it," he said. "Nobody's here."

"We could go by ourselves," said James.

Silence filled the van. I was the one to open the door first, and we all shuffled across the parking lot toward the pool. Ginny and I exchanged nervous glances while James and Peter led the way. Then a night watchman stepped out from between a group of pine trees and held a flashlight to James's face. After a brief exchange, the watchman let us go, but not before it came out that James's father was the president of the country club. "Uh, oh," I whispered, as it occurred to me that, like me, James negotiated two worlds within this homogenous town: one in which, as a Cuban American, he belonged to a minority group, and one in which he was a privileged citizen. That connection probably eluded James, though. He seemed to view himself almost exclusively as a privileged citizen. And for that, I envied him.

On a Sunday night during the same summer, Mom asked me to do the dishes while she stuck around. I'd never known her to be calculating enough to have an agenda, but with Mom, it was best to exercise caution. As far as motherly guidance was concerned, she tended to operate by the seat of her pants or, in her case, girdle, for Mom never went anywhere without one.

"It's not good to date just one boy, you know," she said. She was wiping down the table so I couldn't see her face. Still, I knew that voice: Mom's attempt to get inside my head.

From the window over the sink I watched Frankie and his friends. The thud of their basketball was now a droning noise, child's play as far as I was concerned. Except for Stilts, who was stalked by girls because of his prowess on the basketball court and his blond, square-jawed good looks, the other boys were light years from dating. I heard Mom's sponge scraping the red-and-white-checked vinyl tablecloth, smelled the steak fat clogging the disposal, and felt the oily soapsuds on my hands. "Well," I said, trying to sound casual, "you met Dad when you were fourteen." Even that story, which had once been my favorite fairy tale, was now as trite and false to me as *Cinderella*.

"Your father wasn't the only boy I dated," said Mom rather boldly. She was still wearing her clothes from church, pearls and a mint green suit. Why did she never dress like this when my boyfriends came to the door? The woman who greeted James could have escaped from a locked ward, and everyone knew that Mom had done time on a ward. Because of my own experiences with rejection, I could not allow myself this one teenage girl's rite of passage:

the fantasy of shoving one's mother off of a cliff. Instead, I mostly felt sad for Mom. My inability to express my outrage crippled me, though. On top of that, Mom had been so damn pretty and popular at my age. Tears pushed against my eyes. I never allowed myself to imagine what my life might have been like if I'd been born with legs. Not a ballerina, just a happy-go-lucky girl. What I needed was a woman who could put herself in my situation and just listen, without judgment, to my rage and my sorrow. Did my mother have an inkling of what I was up against? I turned back to the suds and admitted to her in a barely audible voice, "No one else asks me out."

"And that's exactly my point," said Mom, throwing down her sponge. "They won't ask you out."

"Mom?"

"It's true!" She tossed her arms up in frustration. "They won't ask you out if you're just dating one boy." She lowered her voice. "They'll think you're going steady."

"No one 'goes steady' anymore."

"Well, isn't that what you're doing?"

"No. We're just, well, going out." Even as I said it, I doubted my own words. A boy at a party had recently asked, "Are you and James getting serious?" His tone hinted of warning, and I understood that this was based on the Cabrera men's popularity with women. But I decided that if I was about to go down I would do it my way: flames ablaze, fireworks, and ashes. Wasn't that, after all, a sort of grace under fire?

And yet, because of my dramatic and flighty nature, this conversation with my mother was taking root. Even as I told myself I was emotionally more advanced than my peers, I couldn't quite trust that I knew anything about myself, or boys, or sex. My mother held the advantage of experience.

When James called that night, I told him I was going out with my friends. I tried to sound nonchalant, even reluctant about seeing him. Mom was within earshot so I took the phone into the den, where I glanced back to see her straining to listen.

James offered to bring Peter along for Ginny, so we could all meet up.

"Hmm," I said. "We'll see."

"What's up with you?" He sounded miffed.

"I don't know," I said. My neck was suddenly hot. "Maybe we see too much of each other." I said this loud enough for Mom to hear.

"You think so?" His voice was almost inaudible.

"Maybe." I said this with a mixture of guilt and glee as I imagined myself the one who would now dictate orders.

He had only to clear his throat. Something about that gesture made me doubt myself each time he did it, and this time the message rang as clear as a door slamming in my face. I was no match for James.

That night my girlfriends and I drove in circles. Bored by ten, we caved in to meet up with James and Peter. The minute we pulled up to them, I saw the difference in James's face. The half-sneer was now a crumpled squint, as if he were weighing his prospects. He seemed torn between hurt and a desire to punch something. Still, the two boys climbed into our back seat with a twelve-pack between them. James immediately wrestled for the advantage, obviously uncomfortable in the back seat of a car, much less one driven by a girl. My friend was driving her ancient Buick sedan with a front seat that stretched like an old sofa to fit the three of us. She called her car Bessie. Since she never drank herself, she ordered James to "drink up." Now James was calling my friend Bessie, which made Ginny and me laugh. We patted her shoulder. "Bessie! You're Bessie now."

James took a languorous swig from his bottle right in her line of vision in the rearview mirror. "Do you always drive thirty miles below the speed limit?" he asked. "Step on it, Bess." He clapped her on the opposite shoulder. Bessie was our glee club's best soloist, but she had a tendency to snap at us like a grandmother in her efforts to stay on the right side of every choice. Our mothers loved her. If they wavered on whether to allow us to go somewhere, we only had to mention that Bessie was driving. From beside her in the front seat, I smelled the beer from James's breath clash with her White Shoulders perfume.

"Where are we going?" she asked. "I've been driving all night. Gas ain't cheap, in case you hadn't noticed."

"Pool-hopping," said James. He took another swig and sat back to stare out his window.

"I don't think so."

"You don't have to go," said James, dismissively.

Peter shot him a corrective glance, and James bit his lower lip.

"You're right. I don't." She jerked the wheel to whip into a parking lot, where she slammed on the brakes, even cranking the emergency brake. James leaned forward again, whispering, "We need you, Bess."

"Tunes?" She shot me a pleading look.

"I don't know," I said. I glanced bitterly over my shoulder at James, who fell back against his seat as if shot down from his throne. He wouldn't look at me.

Ginny popped a huge bubble out her open window. "Well," she said, "where's a pool?"

"Riordan's in Michigan," said Peter, whose eyes twinkled at the thought of skinny-dipping with Ginny on a lavish estate.

"Riordan's house," I said, remembering that Peter had wrestled me from the arms of a boy who wanted to throw me into the Riordans' pool. "Hmm. A place like that would have a caretaker, wouldn't it?"

"And when were *you* there, Tunes?" James asked in an imperious tone.

"When *you* were *grounded*," I said, turning back to glare at him. He could be so haughty.

He slumped down, folded his arms, pulled into himself.

"I don't know," said Bessie, her eyes flickering back at James as if she expected him to argue with her, but James was lost in his sullen mood. Suddenly, she threw the car in reverse and said to Peter, "Which way to Riordan's?"

We drove about twenty minutes. Halfway there, James eased out of his sulk and talked us into going to an apartment complex instead. "It's closer and less risky."

Minutes later, we stood on the deck of a pool that would have been pitch black except for the moonlight shimmering on the water. I looked up with regret. That moon might as well have been a floodlight pointing accusingly at my legs. We girls were hanging back near a low brick wall while the boys peeled their shirts over their backs.

"You're going to keep your skivvies on," Bessie ordered them.

James and Peter looked at each other. *Skivvies?* Then James threw off his pants and dove in before we could get a good look at him. Peter followed, a stockier silhouette. The boys came up from the water, hair swinging. James's spongy mop hardly released a drop. Ginny and I stood speechless on the deck. Now it was our turn. Behind us, Bessie must have burrowed into the shrubbery while Ginny and I stared at each other before glancing longingly at our boyfriends. They had inched toward us to wait in the shallow end. I was relieved to see that they'd kept on their underwear, and I told myself that underwear was no different from a bathing suit. Or was that even my concern?

"Come on," said Peter, reaching out to Ginny. "I'll close my eyes."

Ginny giggled nervously, but then her smile turned fearless.

"You're doin' it, Gin!" I said, pushing harder than I intended on her thin shoulders, almost knocking her over. In my excitement I tasted something salty, and it was a while before I realized that I was on the verge of tears. Ginny whipped off her T-shirt and stepped out of her shorts. I fingered the tie at the bust of my sailor top as I realized there was no graceful ending to this game for me.

Ginny was in the water now, and Peter latched onto her hips to pull her closer.

I stood staring at James, knowing that the water would be up to my chin while it only met his belly button. "I'll close my eyes," he said, putting his hands to his face. My breath heavy, I edged closer to the pool.

"I lean!" said Bessie from the bushes. She lapsed naturally into my mother's role.

"Oh, shut up," I said. I pulled the shirt over my head, and with my arms above me, I checked James's eyes. Pointless, I thought; everyone knows how to peek through their fingers. I had curvy hips, tight breasts, and arms like a tennis player: all in all, not a bad torso. I may never forgive myself for this, I thought. Then I sat down and worked on removing my pants and legs as noiselessly as possible. The time this took dragged out my horror. For the first time that night, James was being patient. I lowered myself into the shallow end and dropped underwater, knowing that above me were my legs in a pair of painter's pants and Topsiders. Could I just stay down here? When I came up for air, James still had his eyes closed. He wasn't reaching for me. Was it up to me to show him that it was okay? I gave up and swam to him.

His embrace was more welcoming than I perceived it at the time. The brevity of our kiss might have been due to the fact that all eyes were on us. A blanket of silence dropped over the pool. Finally James's big teeth broke into a smile, and we kissed again. I felt something hard against my thigh, which offered reassurance along with the standard threat of sex, and we separated.

The drive back to the boys' car was subdued. Ginny sat beside me, arms folded as if to restrain her contentment. I couldn't look back at James because I was certain that this must have been a disappointment for him. Why was he being so quiet now? This was the worst torture: guessing at what he might be feeling. I never wanted to see him again, and at the same time I felt trapped by the inescapable fact that I needed something from him. Was it reassurance? Love? I wasn't sure. Whatever it was, I could bet that he was not about to hand it over.

The following week, word spread that Dodi and her best friend, the other Dodi, were organizing the event of the summer. Ginny phoned me with the news. "The Dodis are planning a canoe trip on the Little Miami." As I weighed the risk, I groaned. Irrational as it might seem, I felt as if the Dodis were holding me over a banister ready to drop me several flights. In reality, they were only planning an outing.

When James called, I picked up in the kitchen. "You coming on Saturday?" he asked.

At the oven, Mom poked a fork into one of her roasts. If only she and I could talk about these problems in a meaningful way. My choices boiled down to two intolerable options: wear my legs and potentially drown in an overturned canoe, or take my legs off in front of all of James's friends in broad daylight. Even I lacked the daring for this one. When I told him I couldn't go, James sounded miffed. "You're sure about this?"

"Yep," I said, trying to sound pert even as I was telling myself, I will never get over this.

He left me with another clearing of the throat. "Well, goodnight."

I knew he wasn't angry *at* me, but that was what frightened me. He might have been angry because he could see the dead end up ahead.

Every friend I had would be out on the river all day, except for Claire, who would be sweltering in a hot dog stand at the zoo. The night before the trip she said, "Don't worry. There are so many parties. You can miss one." She was right, I decided. Claire had missed dozens and it hadn't hurt her.

Still, I awakened the next morning with dread. The whole day it felt as if someone was holding a pillow over my face, allowing me to breathe just enough. That night I washed my hair and put on the bathrobe that Liz had passed on to me. I can still feel my wet hair on the terrycloth collar, soaking into the fabric and drenching my neck as I sat on the basement couch, surfing the television for distraction. Our basement had paneled walls, a bumper pool table, and a wet bar that was Cincinnati red. The place was always freezing.

I couldn't find a good movie. Even the couch I was lying on made me think of James. Once when we made out on this sofa, we discovered the "babies" spying on us. We'd chased them off, all three giggling and racing in separate directions. As they ran up the stairs shrieking, we went back to kissing. Minutes later we heard faint laughter and looked up to where they had climbed into separate window wells, crouching and gaping. Now, in an odd way, the image of three children squished into three wells reminded me of a row of fetuses in jars. I'd seen anti-abortion propaganda hanging in the breezeway at Saint Vivian. James had once told me that his sister's class talked about euthanasia and someone brought up my name. I hadn't the nerve to ask what the class had decided about my life. At a time such as this I hated to imagine how I would vote on my life, given the choice.

My mind had gone straight to every fear that haunted me: fears that I'd been putting off, stumbling onto again, and shoving away once more. Aside from the issue of sex, there was the issue of motherhood. In biology class, Sister Theresa had discussed various causes of birth defects. She told the guidance counselor to ask me if I wanted to be dismissed from those sessions. I'd looked at this guidance counselor, who had been trying to resuscitate my academic potential for two years, and said, "Why would I do that?" If only I had trusted the guidance counselor enough to tell her I was terrified, not only of biology class, but of life.

Months ago I had been sitting on this same couch watching *Butterflies Are Free* on television, riveted, when James's call interrupted the movie. I desperately wanted to get back to it except that James was on the line, so I watched and told him what was going on in the film. That was the closest we had come to discussing my "disability." I didn't tell him that I saw myself as the blind man and James as the Goldie Hawn character. I felt certain that Goldie was going to leave the blind man, but I didn't tell James that. I said, "Goldie just told the man's mother to back off," though I didn't mention that Goldie also told the mother that her son needed to have sex, and lots of it. I definitely withheld Goldie's opinion that this same son needed to have his heart broken so that he might grow up, and that probably she would do just that, break his heart. So I told James that it had gone to a commercial and turned the television off. I couldn't face Goldie's departure. Except for conversations I'd had with Claire—at times heavily intoxicated—this was the most intimate conversation I'd ever had about my legs.

All of this was going through my mind when a call came in. Mom answered it in the kitchen. "Eileen?" I heard her say. "Dick, where is that girl? Did she go out?"

"Down here."

I was breathless as I lifted the receiver. "Hello?" I said, trying not to sound too eager.

"Uhleen?"

I was afraid to speak. James's voice quivered uncharacteristically. Then he went silent. Finally he said, "I can't talk long, but I won't be able to do anything tomorrow."

"Okay," I said, holding my breath so he wouldn't hear me wheezing.

It seemed he would never speak, until finally he blurted out, "You should know that I, well, I made out with a girl today."

"Oh." In the months we'd been dating, James had never given me cause to feel jealous. That a boy from what was rumored to be a long line of ladies' men had never stirred this emotion in me was probably more shocking than the news that he had just broken his clean streak. More troubling was the idea that he might have had sex with this girl, and it was not so much jealousy that I felt as a profound sense of loss. I didn't want to ask him the next question, except that everyone else already knew: "Who was it?"

He cleared his throat, I bristled, and he told me the name of a girl in my circle of friends, not a close friend but a pretty good friend. "Oh," I whispered.

"She feels really bad about it. We don't. It wasn't. You know? I was drunk. They put her in my canoe!" He stopped.

"What are you saying?" If he was trying to put this off on the Dodis, I could see right through that. "I thought you—" I wanted to say that I thought he cared more for me than this, but his behavior suggested otherwise. "I'm so confused," I said.

"You weren't there! It wasn't like we planned it . . ."

Someone picked up. "Mom?" I asked. How childlike I sounded. Instead of my mother, a man cleared his throat, and James immediately said, "Yes, sir! I'll be right off."

There was a click. Had James hung up?

"James!" I said, panicked.

"I have to go, Uhleen." Another silence. "I can't see you for a while."

"You're kidding me? I should be saying that to you!"

"No. It's not that . . . I have no choice. I'm grounded. That was my father. I'm not even allowed to talk on the phone."

"What now?"

"I wrecked a car on the way home. Two, actually. I sideswiped someone."

"Are you all right?"

There was a pause. "Sure. I'm fine. Look, I have to go."

"James," I said, and although it was the last thing in the world I wanted to do, I imagined my mother saying, "Hang up right now and never speak to that boy again." I said, "Listen, maybe we should break up?"

I wanted him to beg me to change my mind. There was only more silence.

"So, you agree?"

"This thing that happened wasn't because I wanted to be with someone else. We were drunk. It wouldn't have happened if—"

A tear dropped at the base of my neck, startling me. I pulled my robe closer to my throat. My hair was almost dry but still cold against my back, and I fought a shiver. Since I couldn't make myself hang up, I held the phone away from my mouth, preparing for the inevitable clearing of his throat, but that didn't come this time. Finally, he said, "If you want to break up, I guess that's best. I can't go out anyway. I'm not even supposed to be on the phone."

I couldn't answer because I didn't want him to hear me crying.

"I have to go," he said. "Goodnight."

CHAPTER 15

When a Pop Diva Comes in Handy

At seventeen I was the oldest girl at home, driving myself to a summer job, and so preoccupied with my own life that I completely missed the signs of chaos roiling in my home. Claire and I had been working in a concession stand in 100-degree weather that weekend. As I pulled in late on a Sunday night, I didn't notice that Dad's car was gone.

I entered the kitchen and found my mother in her sleeveless pink-and-white-checked dress, leaning against the countertop at midnight. Every light was on. What was she doing up so late? Mom usually fell asleep by ten. Was I in trouble? I'd mentioned I was going to Claire's after work.

Calmly, she said, "Your father's left."

"What time's he coming back?" I asked warily.

"Eileen, I'm telling you he left. He packed up and moved out."

I stopped just inside the door, my head tilted. "What?" Was this a joke? I went to the kitchen table and sat. "Just start from the beginning. What happened?"

On a Sunday evening not so long ago I had seen Mom, in this same dress, storm out of the house after dinner. Snatching up her keys, she told Dad that she was "leaving for good." As I followed her out the back door, I couldn't help but notice how her olive skin radiated against the pink. If I looked that good in a dress I might just leave for good, too, I thought, as she zoomed away in her Scirocco. Was she just blowing off steam? Why wasn't Dad chasing after her?

An hour later she came back and tossed her keys hard into the cabinet where she kept her cigarettes. Dad glanced over his glasses from his station at the kitchen table. "So you're back" was all he said. I'd thought that was the end of it.

Now Mom explained what she knew. For years, Dad had been trying to run a business and hold the family together. He shielded us from the effects of skyrocketing interest rates on his business. The Midwest was suffering, the auto industry among the hardest hit. The Beetle generation had been replaced with "Buy American." Dad now owned two foreign-car dealerships. Because he rarely spoke, no one knew the pressure he was under. He announced to Mom that, while he would never abandon us financially, he could no longer call this his home. In fact, he said, he'd prefer to never set foot in our house again. He took an apartment, something temporary until he could figure things out.

"Never again?" I asked. "An *apartment*?" Was she talking about the same man who had stayed up all night to take my broken leg apart and put it back together so I could go on a field trip with my fourth-grade class? That was my Dad, not a man with an apartment.

Mom shook her head. "I don't know. I don't know."

"He's not going to see us anymore?"

"He'll be by on Sundays for the babies. I'm supposed to bring them outside."

"Huh?" I slapped the tabletop. "What about the rest of us? He's just gonna wave as he passes by the house? What did we do wrong?"

In her church clothes with her hair coiffed, Mom looked both fragile and elegant. On the night she left, she had stood in the same dress right where she was currently standing, but she'd been angrier then. Now, with her hands on her hips, she looked for a moment as if she might have the grit necessary to weather this crisis, but in an instant she started waving her arms, revealing the strain it took to match her words to her racing thoughts: "What'll I cook for dinner tomorrow? Who's gonna pick Tim up from baseball? Has Matthew been to the dentist lately? I don't know anything anymore, Bridget. I mean, what's your name, Liz? Oh, Eileen! My I-lean. What'll I do, Lear dear?" She reached into the cabinet and took a pack of cigarettes from a carton. Without warning she pitched them to me. "I know you steal 'em, anyway," she said. "You might as well smoke in front of me."

I caught them midflight. My fingers trembling with self-consciousness, I opened the pack and lit up. "What's going on with Dad?" I said, trying to sound older. "Why is he doing this?"

"I don't know." She glanced out the window above the sink and for a few seconds she was silent, almost contemplative. Mom pursed her lips and squinted before she confessed, "He told me he had to pull over before coming home some nights." She paused. "Oh, Dick," she said sadly, pressing her fingers to her lips. Then she admitted what was too horrible to keep to herself. "He said he cried every night before he could walk in the house."

There was only one other time in my father's adult life when anyone had knowledge of his tears. Rosa had told me about the day Dad introduced me to my siblings. She said he brought me home by himself because the doctor kept Mom in the hospital after I was born. Rosa didn't explain why Mom wasn't released, but I wondered if Mom had had a nervous breakdown. Rosa said that when Dad handed me over to my siblings, they tore off the receiving blanket and cried, "Take it back." She said that Dad had broken down in tears.

Shocking as the news about Dad's recent sorrows seemed, it rang true. Dad might have pulled over to cry for a few months, or years. "Why now?" I asked Mom.

"I guess I've hurt him," she said, as if thinking back to something that happened years ago.

I tapped my cigarette even though there were no ashes and started to ask her to explain, but decided against it. Her tone sounded too intimate and her guard was down. She might tell me something I would regret hearing.

Every night for almost a week, I sat there with Mom, smoking and listening. At first she rambled. Anyone in her shoes would need to vent. The rambling turned to a drone, then a whir. I'd start to say something only to be run over by her rapid-fire talk, which mixed with laughter, then rage, then tears. She couldn't sleep and took on a bedraggled appearance over the next week, while she plotted to win Dad back.

As she slipped into mania, I grew furious with my father. Yet I had to admit that if I were him I might just keep my foot on the pedal, too. I could see both sides, but being a teenager I needed to level my frustration against one party. Dad became my target.

I'd seen Mom survive two manic episodes. The third was only a question of time and stamina. How long before she would crash? Daily, older siblings called in for updates on the sly. Aunt Gert also checked in several times a day. She might have tried to talk Mom into signing in to the hospital, but Mom would have viewed that as betrayal.

Since Frank was commuting to Xavier University, I tried to help out by running errands for Mom. My car had an extra accelerator on its floorboard so I could accelerate with my left foot—not so different from any other car—but I was a nervous driver. Thus far I'd had almost no practice with an adult in the car because Mom had a habit of slamming an invisible brake on the passenger side while gripping her door and rearing back in her seat. I couldn't pass the parallel-parking test until after Claire and Gretchen took me out to practice.

Days after Dad left, I drove to the shopping center to pick up school supplies for the babies. As I made a left turn into the shopping center, I misjudged the speed of an oncoming car and in a panic crashed into a car that was pulling out, just before being slammed by the car I misjudged. No one was injured, but three cars plus my self-confidence became casualties in what was turning out to be the summer of sorrows. And yet, like other tragedies I'd known, within an hour my car had been towed, a friend of the family had driven me home from the shopping center, and we were on to other things. Mom was unraveling fast.

At the end of a grueling week, my brother Michael said he'd sit with Mom so I could go out with a boy I'd recently met. In the year since my breakup with James, I'd gone out with a couple of boys, but no one as compelling as James. The first one had been one of James's oldest friends. When he asked me out I said yes but only to hurt James, who then asked out one of my friends and suggested we double-date. Watching James make out with my friend made me think twice about doing this again. And yet there were more failed attempts at a similar mix with other friends. At times James and I went out alone, but those evenings culminated in arguments. This new boy was from a public school across town. Better still, he didn't know anyone I knew and I didn't know anyone he knew, which was a combination that could not have made me happier. People knew him by a nickname, but I think of him as Lance. He was blond and blue-eyed and might have been the most handsome boy I'd ever met. On top of that, he was the most humble boy I knew. In another girl's life he would have made a perfect Lancelot—for a story, I imagine, with a happier ending.

I was nervous about leaving Mom, whose speech was so rapid it was incomprehensible. She was not sleeping or eating. As the oldest daughter at home, I felt territorial about Mom and knew that Michael, as our oldest brother, tended to take everything over. Now he was in law school, married, and a father. We still referred to him as "Special Boy." Most of us viewed him as our second father; in fact, he commanded more authority than Dad. A few of us believed him to be nearly perfect, while others saw him as bossy. I leaned toward the latter, but had to admit that he had his own life in order. In a crisis, Michael seemed the best person to have around.

When I came downstairs to meet Lance in the den that evening, I found all three babies climbing my date's six-and-a-half-foot frame to grip his head. "Egghead," they called him. He laughed at this nickname and tossed the "babies" from his shoulders onto the couch.

At the party Lance glided seamlessly into my group of friends, who were happy to entertain him while I mingled. Under the bright lights of a tennis court, his hair shimmered above the crowd. I kept glancing back to where he and my friends chatted, nervous that he might not be having fun, but Lance was a bubbly, entertaining boy. "Does he never stop smiling?" I thought. "And it's so genuine."

Before I knew it, I came face to face with James. It had been several weeks since I'd last run into him. His stern face made my hands shake until I almost dropped my beer. Every time I saw him now, my throat dried up and my hands shook. The meaner he looked, the more I wanted him back.

"What's up?" he asked.

With James, I had never outgrown my nervous chatter. I saw him and my darkest secrets flooded the space between us. "I totaled a car and my parents are getting a divorce," I said in a quivering voice. "And Mom's cracking up again."

"What?" he said, waving off what he assumed was a joke. "*Your* parents splitting up?"

"I'm serious."

"Come on," he said, leading me through the crowd with that golfer's stride, always a man surveying his prospects. This was my chance to say no to him, and yet my only concern was that no one saw us as we left the tennis court. He took my hand and we climbed a hill in the distance. From there I saw Lance glancing around for me. I should get back to him, I thought. Instead I laid out the details of my family's crisis for James, who reached over and put his hand on my back right below my neck, the same place where my father used to rest his hand. The smell of cut grass reminded me of those Sunday afternoons with Dad on our screened-in porch, Joe Nuxhall on the radio. In my confused state, James was so like my father that I wanted to bury my head in his arms and sob, but his familiar reserve kept me planted at some distance.

"You want to go out tomorrow night?" he asked. I missed him so much. And yet in the middle of a crowd down there was a clear-eyed boy who laughed openly at my jokes, whose kindness and affection came without reservation. I said to James, "Pick me up after work. I have to get back now." I scrambled to stand up while defeat sank in, and with a self-conscious wave goodbye I stepped into the mob.

After the party, Lance and I pulled up to my house. He kissed me goodnight in the driveway, my neck straining to meet his lips as he stooped over me. Suddenly my brother Kevin stepped out from between the dogwoods. He'd come to ask Lance to sit out here with me since there was "kind of an emergency" going on inside. Lance assured him that he would do that. Within minutes I sent Lance home so I could rush into the house.

In the kitchen I found Mom under the dim glow of the stove light, lost in a netherworld. There was no communicating with her. Her language was a garble of nonsense syllables. Seeing her like this, knowing that she had fought her way back from this place twice before, my heart ached for her.

"Eileen, you shouldn't see this," said Michael, so I looked to Kevin, who said, "There's nothing you can do."

"We have to help her," I said, dropping to the floor to hug my mother. She didn't seem to recognize me, and gathering her in my arms was harder than holding a frightened cat. Her eyes moved in a chaotic pattern as if synchronized to her scrambled words. "Why isn't Dad here?" I said, bitterly.

"Go to bed," snapped Michael.

"Come on," said Kevin, leading me out to the stairs in the front hall. "Michael knows what he's doing."

I had to admit that Kevin was right.

In the darkened hallway I said, "You have to call Dad." But Kevin said, "Dad needs a break this time. He might look better off than Mom, but he's not. Aunt Gert will be here any second. She'll call the hospital. Too many people around will only make it worse."

I gave in.

Later, from my bed, I heard Mom being taken against her will by the paramedics. She had made it out of the locked ward twice before, but she'd never had to do that without Dad waiting for her at home. I doubted that she would make it out this time.

Over the next twenty-four hours I hardly left my room. Instead I wrote a poem about a battered crystal at the mercy of a raging ocean. James never called. It's possible that he'd been grounded again. Or maybe he saw that his reappearance would only result in more heartbreak. I decided I would never trust another man.

Later, during a fitful sleep, it occurred to me that I would probably break my promise.

By Christmas, I had made an enemy of my father. He'd clenched his teeth through three months of parenting us while Mom was in the hospital. Over that time I botched dinners and complained about a sore under the back of my knee. Periodically Bridget called from Massachusetts and told me to make a list of chores and get everyone to pitch in. She didn't pry into whatever was making Dad upset, but whatever it was, she wanted me to stop. The problem with this last piece of advice was that I didn't know what I'd done to Dad, other than my acting the bratty teenager. In the past I'd been Dad's "Trixie"; now I was a no-good lout. As far as I was concerned, Dad had turned into a mean and scary guy, but a man I desperately needed.

Then there was the problem of Frankie and me being in charge. No one had ever seen us as having any authority. We certainly didn't see ourselves that way. The babies balked when we told them to go to bed. Ted laughed in our faces.

Adding to my growing sense of ineptitude was the fact that the sore behind my knee throbbed every time I stood up. Aunt Gert took a look at it and told me there was a boil where my weight rested on the leg and it should be treated by a doctor. Dad said I was only trying to get out of school. Based on my grades and the time I'd broken the clasp, his conclusion was logical, but in fact I had never stayed home from school due to pain. I took offense at first. Then, in my irrational mind, I got him back by *not* seeing a doctor. Besides, if I walked long enough, the boil went numb.

Within a few weeks, Mom was released from the hospital and Dad was back in his apartment. Because my sympathy was with Mom, I calmed down. To everyone's astonishment, life at home ran smoothly with Mom back at the helm.

For me, school became a welcome retreat. Even my grades rose. I had joined the glee club and our Christmas concert was coming up. From the telephone next to Liz's bed, I called Dad to invite him to come. I was as nervous calling my father as I had been when I called James that first time to ask him to my dance. This is my father, I thought, it's crazy to be so nervous. Then Dad surprised me again. "No," he said. "I can't come to that." There was a lengthy silence while I took this in. Too shocked to speak, I waited for an explanation. None came.

"But I have a special part this year. Only a few girls made it into the vocal ensemble." Already I was sobbing while my father waited on the other end in unyielding silence. "Pleeease, Dad!"

"Honey, I just can't do that." He didn't say so, but he couldn't show up to an event where so many of his friends would want to know why he'd left us. People would shun him. Still I wanted him to do this for me, and I interpreted this slight on top of our ongoing struggle as an indication that he wanted to punish me. My tears erupted into an adolescent scourge. "You've never come to anything of mine. No one ever comes to anything of mine. You hate me!"

"Honey, I don't hate you."

"You hate me. Oh, yes, you do. Everyone in the family hates me." My nose running, chest and shoulders heaving, I screamed into the telephone, "And I hate myself!" Then I hung up. I stayed there for the longest time, trying to calm down, waiting for the phone to ring. He never called back.

Without warning, and a few months into his first year of college, James called and invited me to go with him to a Christmas party at the home of a mutual friend. The familiarity of that ritual would tie me to a happier past, I told myself. On the other hand, given my fragile state, a date with James was not advisable. I quickly agreed to go.

This time I prepared myself for the aftermath by doing the one thing I knew best: I would sit down and write him a letter, in which I would admit defeat. I'd say that I knew our relationship, whatever it had become, was hopeless. I'd confess that I loved him, *as if* there had ever been any doubt. I told myself I had no delusions about his reaction to this news: if I could go through with this, he would definitely flee.

Convinced of my own maturity and resolve, I failed to see the uncanny resemblance between my sophisticated plan and the lyrics of two songs by the pop diva Olivia Newton-John.

We drove to the party with another couple, maybe because James's father had taken away his license again. The girl sitting up front was not Dodi as in Will and Dodi, but her friend, the other Dodi. The party itself blurred by years of preceding parties at this house, I now recall only what happened before and after it.

Before the party: Mom put on a cream-colored silk dress and pearls, becoming the mother I'd lost years ago, while Dad broke his policy and came into the house to deliver his gifts to us. I remember well the pink blouse that tied at the neck and the white sweater with a snowflake design. Since he'd chosen these gifts on his own I wore them often, feeling both closer and farther from my father—in colors appropriate for a girl younger than I saw myself at seventeen, but with a bow at the neck to herald the career woman I might someday become.

And after the party: James kissed me in the back seat of his friend's car for the whole drive home. For those twenty minutes I burrowed my fingers into his curls and touched his face, saying to myself, "Last time." I didn't care that one of the Dodis was in the front seat. More startling to me was that when she glanced back, I could have sworn that her expression was sympathetic. As we pulled into my driveway, I slipped the note from my purse and set it on the seat between us. James stared at it, bewildered.

"For later," I said, pushing the note his way. I told him not to walk me to the door, but he insisted. On my back porch, he searched my face with questioning eyes. Then he kissed me goodnight as if he understood this was the end.

I assumed that I wouldn't hear from James again, and the next day I sulked in Liz's old room while listening to "Bridge Over Troubled Water." I must have played it forty times, when the phone rang. I picked up, heard James's voice, and rolled off the bed, taking several books down as I attempted to grab hold of the bookshelf on my way.

"What was that?" he said.

"What was what?" I said from a pile of books on the floor, my breath choppy with nervous energy.

"Never mind," he said, and then he threw me off by going right to the thing I had not imagined he would ever discuss. "Listen, do you want to talk about this letter?"

I hesitated for an instant. How likely was he to do any of the talking? Or what if he said he didn't have the same feelings for me?

"No," I said.

"No?" I heard disbelief in his voice.

I wanted him to say he felt the same way, or that we were too young, or to at least acknowledge that my feelings were understandable. But, just as in my relationship with my father, there was an awkward silence coming from the other end of the line. Please tell me yes, we have to talk about it! But nothing came.

This time I tried to sound harsh. "No."

"Okay," he said.

Unable to grasp what had just transpired, I found myself drifting on to gossip with him. We laughed about mutual friends in the same way we had when we first met. It seemed as if nothing had changed. The tone as we hung up was not unlike other conversations we'd had, except that once I set the receiver in its cradle I knew that we were really saying goodbye.

My mother's walk grew sturdier as she gained confidence in herself, dressing up daily as if she were going on a date with Dad. She pulled herself together with silks and linens, an up-do, lipstick. When Dad drove up on Sundays, she came out to the car. Sometimes she chatted and left. Other times, she invited him into the house. He consistently rejected her offers, but she kept trying.

Over the next year, Dad began to shop for a house of his own, one large enough so that he could take custody of the youngest children. Then, in a preemptive strike probably prompted by my mother, all eleven of us children met with her psychiatrist. The smallest children yanked at their clothing. Tim, the toughest of them, shielded his face with his T-shirt, his shoulders shaking as tears soaked the cloth, while the eldest of these three, Matthew, looked on with the face of a forty-year-old man. Nina, our brown-eyed love bug, so tranquil and pale-skinned, was frazzled. Seeing our "babies" in pain made us older kids feel inept. We'd all played a role in raising them and, as I glanced around the room, I found other faces reflecting my own consternation.

Dad must have picked up on our anger. Maybe it forced him to weigh his options. He started to accept Mom's invitations to come into the house when he dropped off the kids. I was afraid to hope for it, but I wondered if, given a little space and time, even his wound might heal.

CHAPTER 16

Venus Rises (Having Gotten a Lift from Dr. T. J. Eckleburg)

Through the leaves at the head of the trail, I glimpsed the last rays of sun as they lit up the dance floor inside the fraternity house. "At least it's a Hawaiian theme," I said to Gretchen. "We can pretend we're somewhere else." It was the last month of my freshman year, and I still had not accepted the fact that I'd had to stay in town for college. Gretchen shook her head in disapproval. She was happy here at the University of Cincinnati, or maybe she was remembering our spring break. "Don't get any big ideas on the dance floor tonight," she said. "It's getting hard to keep track of all of you."

My disco story was still traveling across campus, an incendiary bomb which I'd launched myself in what was turning out to be a successful attempt at damage control. People I'd never met were now greeting me with gusto: "I heard about *your* spring break!" To which I would say, "Took my legs and threw them over here . . . took my chest and threw it over there." Some people would laugh at my reference to the scarecrow, but others would look at me as if I were describing an incident too brutal to mention in public. Either way I felt somehow superior for having survived the experience. Indignity, I was finding out, could be worn as a cloak of fame, at least in college.

After the last hearty push from Gretchen, I reached the top of the path and stepped into the Betas' backyard. It was a year since the boil had formed. I was still jamming the leg on, sinking my weight into it despite the shock of pain, and waiting for numbness to take over. Numbness had become my closest ally, if not my greatest threat.

To this party for my pledge class I wore a sundress—red with white hibiscus flowers. My hair was pinned up on one side with a white flower; the rest was a tumble of curls. Optimistic young Betas handed us each a glass of punch, which—I should have known by now, my second semester—was always a mistake. Invariably they spiked the punch with grain alcohol. Often, to Liz's horror, I would suck the drink down. This night was no exception.

The tradition in our family until Liz, Frank, and I graduated from high school was to go away to college. Liz and Frank didn't mind staying in town because their friends had stayed, but most of my friends were away at school. I wrote tear-stained letters, usually after a party, to Claire in Louisiana. "Get me out of here," was the repeated refrain on those pages, some dappled with cheap wine.

After sunset, the party crowd thinned or moved into the house. On about my third glass of punch, a blurry vision crossed the dance floor. "Not James," I said, blinking. James belonged to a rival fraternity and was dating a sophomore. I still couldn't take in the fact that he had been set up with Liz's "little sister" from the sorority. Whose idea was that? I didn't want to ferret out that information. Maybe James had just seen this girl from across the room and had to have her. But did it have to happen just before I arrived on campus? And just before I was funneled into Liz's sorority? Because everyone in the fraternity system knew Liz, there was no other sorority that was going to take a chance on me. The others assumed that of course I would join Liz's sorority. That assumption was partially correct. No one revered Liz more than I did, which made the combination of her "little sister" and James particularly painful. As a result of this setup, Liz's sorority became the last sorority I needed to join. Now I saw the couple everywhere, usually sweeping out of the sorority parking lot in James's brother's Camaro. Worse still, my apartment—actually my bedroom—overlooked that parking lot.

A wiser girl might have left this party upon spotting James. But two things kept me there: one was the downhill path in the woods leading back to my apartment. I couldn't possibly make it down alone. Then there was the apartment itself. My life there was a calamity, and I was doing my best to avoid going home to it. My choice to move in with Liz and two of her friends was a mistake that had seemed harmless at the time. Now, on weekends when Liz's boyfriend came to town, I would have to sleep on the couch, which was awkward with roommates coming in at all hours, my legs on the floor, and boyfriends stepping over them. My brilliant solution was to inebriate myself and pass out on the couch, making it less awkward for boyfriends and whatnot to step around me. I aimed for memory loss. Given the potency of the Betas' punch, I was now half a drink away from my target point.

Why was I in this apartment in the first place? Liz had thought it would be good for me. She pointed out that a dorm might be awkward since I didn't have legs. I'd actually been looking forward to making friends in a dorm, but I had to agree that that was something I hadn't considered. Our parents agreed, so much so that Dad gave us a car. Unfortunately, it was a stick shift, which was impossible for me to drive as I could only use one leg to drive. Maybe it was the only car on the lot. Or maybe he gave us one that I couldn't drive because he was afraid I would crash it. That would have been a reasonable assumption at the time. In any case, the campus and especially the apartment became in my mind a prison.

I would complain to Liz, "You never said I would have to sleep on the couch." To which she would say, "What's the difference?

You stagger home every night. Half the time you don't even know where you are."

I could hardly argue that point. So I made running lists in my head. People make lists when they are disoriented, preparing for change, and/or about to die. I had at least two of those factors pressing on me, and my lists included these four keys to my survival: one, writing short stories; two, taking in the German- and Italian-inspired architecture around campus so that I might conjure the feeling of being far from home; three, watching *General Hospital* with a roommate, who was, thankfully, Colette; and four, plotting my escape.

As for writing, I preferred the oak table in the library at the sorority house, where I used the electric typewriter that Dad had given me for my high school graduation present—his olive branch. "You should have this. You should write," he'd said economically—I heard that word a lot in my writing classes, all taught by men.

Having grown up in a busy household, my creativity flourished in a room where people milled around like shadows moving with the sun. Sometimes I would look up to summon an image or a smell, only to find James holding Liz's little sister's hand in the window seat. If he happened to catch my eye or vice versa, I'd smile at the page where I took my revenge: James in various guises, posing as a devil and smelling of fetid fruit . . . no, of death.

My second-favorite escape came in the form of architecture. As a small child I'd learned to focus on the buildings in Walnut Hills while Mom pulled up to the leg man's shop. A good stained-glass window takes the edge off when you know an ancient man is about to knead wet plaster over your thigh. The university is between Walnut Hills and Clifton, both areas full of Germanic houses with thatched or tiled roofs. Down Clifton Avenue is the Gaslight district, where Italianate Victorians were offset by an old-fashioned ice cream parlor, a German bakery, and a florist. The architecture transported me, but then there were the familiar faces within those walls.

No matter where I turned on this campus of roughly 20,000 students, I managed to find James in all his glory. His father, who taught at the medical school, had bought a house for his sons, which happened to be right next to the sorority notorious on our campus for girls who graduated with the largest diamond engagement rings—a perfect setup for the Cabrera boys, who would be shoe-ins at the medical school. Welcomed everywhere, apparently, James moved through the Betas' party as if it were for him. Upon seeing his face, my throat dried into a knot. I'd never lost this reaction to him. It was bad enough that we kept running into each other, but did he have to keep pointing out my newly acquired foibles? The "freshman ten" I'd gained, the endless drunken stupors, and the yoke of self-hatred I refused to take off.

Earlier that year, over Christmas break, James had called me at my parents' house to see if I wanted to go on a double date with his friend. "I think we've already tried that combination," I thought, but I agreed to go, only to get drunk across the table from James and Liz's little sister, after which he and my date watched me do a Dick Van Dyke somersault over the sofa before my date gathered me up and drove me home.

Here on the fraternity patio, a naïve Beta handed me a drink. Then James was in my face. I backed up and fell into a rosebush. He reached in and plucked me out. Fresh scratches on my arms began to weep.

"You're drunk," he said.

"Don't you have a girlfriend to pick on?"

The look on his face suggested that maybe he didn't.

"You need to go. I'll take you home."

"Economical. Concise," I whispered to myself as he led me around the side of the house.

I saw his car and started limping away, losing a limb in the shrubbery of the side yard where thankfully only James was my witness. "Who said you could boss me around?" I whispered as I fastened on my leg and climbed up to a standing position.

"Just get in the car."

Then, with arms outstretched in a martyr pose that rivaled my mother's, I screamed, "I'm not going with you!"

"You're gonna walk down that hill by yourself?" He pointed to the dark trail at the mouth of the woods.

I got in his car. At a stoplight I escaped. I'd like to think I leapt out; instead, I opened the door and toppled out.

James, determined to do the right thing, followed me home. Driving on the wrong side of Clifton Avenue, he tried to talk me down. I was gleeful as he faced two-lane traffic head-on and only disappointed that at this late hour there was no traffic. I passed his house and half of fraternity row until he whipped into a driveway, cutting me off. I turned to limp in the opposite direction, but this time he got out and ushered me back to the car. "You can't even walk," he said. "I'm not leaving you out here."

Having decided that I'd made him work hard enough, I got in the car. As we pulled up to the apartment, he lingered. I couldn't make myself leave. Just go, I told myself.

Back in the late summer before school started, Liz had introduced me to her little sister while James stood there holding the girl's hand. I got drunk, went home to our parents' house, and swallowed a handful of pills. I didn't know what I'd taken. I hoped it was a painkiller from a pulled tooth or a sports injury. More likely it was an outdated antibiotic. Ill-conceived and impulsive as this gesture might seem, the relief washing over me as I drifted off was an indication of my sincere intent. The pills were my recognition, not of a failing, but of an innocent mistake of circumstances. Life in my body was too difficult—not the physical part but the almost certain disappointment involving other people, their disappointment in me, mine in them—and I was ready to concede that.

My head floated on my pillow. This was the right thing to do, I thought, just go. Then I fell asleep.

It never occurred to me that Nina, at ten years old, would have been the one to discover my body in the next bed, nor could I foresee a future where wonder and joy might replace loss. Whatever pills I swallowed caused no more than a cramped stomach in the morning. I didn't tell anyone what I'd done. I'd left little evidence of wrongdoing. There was only my knowledge of having come really close to leaving. If I were to tell someone about it, I would have to relinquish that option.

Now, drunk and alone with James, I could see that if this argument gave way to sex I'd come undone entirely. Sex was the one thing I hadn't let him take from me, and sex was the only thing I wanted from him by now. Sex and insecurity were propelling this repetitive loop. So I fell back on my oldest defense: I started an argument. Of course James had the better poker face. (The Pillsbury doughboy had a better poker face than I did.) But we were both middle children from large Catholic families, which meant that we had the predatory instincts of serial heartbreakers.

James advanced his position. "I'm thinking of asking out Colette."

"Colette?"

He nodded.

Colette. Every day I'd rushed home from classes to watch *General Hospital* with Colette. Smoking cigarettes and watching soap operas with an older woman was my idea of being nurtured. That year Luke raped Laura in a disco scene, which was replayed weekly in flashback. Each flashback unfolded a new insight into the couple's conundrum. Colette and I would ask, "But wasn't that rape? Why is Laura dating Luke now? How can they be in love?"

Beginning with my first date, Colette had been the older woman I sought for advice on boys and men.

Now I said to James, "Colette. Why not?"

"Yep," he said, eyes lit with pride.

Spawn of Satan, I thought. Then I said, "Great idea. Come on. She might be home from the restaurant." An eerie calm masked my rage as I led him up the winding staircase and into the apartment alcove where Colette slept (apparently nude). When she opened her eyes to see me standing over her, James peering over my shoulder, Colette sprang up and cursed us out in both English and French, wrapping herself in her sheets and chasing us off.

James—having had two women gesticulating madly at him in one night—took to the stairs. He loped down in strides of two or three steps at a time. I leaned over the railing at the top of the staircase, howling with laughter. My voice echoed after him in a frenzied cackle until I heard the door slam, at which point I sank to the floor sobbing.

By the following summer, Mom had won Dad over. Not only could she manage the household herself, but she had a whole new wardrobe. Earlier that year, my parents had gone away for a romantic weekend on their anniversary and then taken a trip to Ireland, their first time abroad since the trip to Germany when Mom was pregnant with me. Upon their return, Dad moved back home.

This same summer I visited Claire in Louisiana and surreptitiously scheduled an interview at Newcomb College, the women's school at Tulane University. After an encouraging interview, I came home and announced my wish to transfer schools. My parents quashed that plan instantly. They offered one alternative: a Catholic college with about 100 female students surrounded by cornfields.

In the fall I returned to Joselin Street, moving into the sorority house this time, while Mom and Dad started their lives over by buying a house in a neighborhood where they didn't know anyone.

In January of my sophomore year, Joselin, a slope of a street, was covered in ice. Gretchen and I were on our way to a party. In a pair of clogs, I skidded. Gretchen caught me. The precariousness of my situation was magnified by the surgery I'd been healing from since Christmas break.

The surgery came after Gretchen, now my roommate, had seen the boil. By then it was a golf ball-sized cyst that swelled to the size of a baseball when I wasn't jamming it into my leg. "You have to go to a doctor," she said. "Now!"

I capitulated. An elderly doctor took me as his last patient before retiring from surgery. He studied the wound through his Coke-bottle lenses, incredulous. "Two years?" he asked. Even as he chastised, Dr. Perlman seduced my mother and me. Turning to Mom, he said, "She's had this cyst for two years, Joy?"

"I know it, Dr. Perlman. I wanna wring her neck."

He squeezed my mother's hand tenderly, as she fought a grin and tried to look soberly into his lenses. "Don't wring it just yet," he said.

Mom gulped audibly; he turned back to me. "Eileen, Eileen," he said, lifting my chin so that I faced him. "Promise me you won't ever do anything like this again."

Mom and I exchanged glances. "Don't you just love this man," our expressions said.

It was his next statement that made the deepest impression: "You might have lost the rest of your leg."

Now, with my wound barely healed, Gretchen and I raced to keep up with our girlfriends. We were on our way to a party over in the med students' apartments. We'd already been to a series of parties that day and during one of them, I would soon find out, I was apparently drugged. Back in high school, my mother had warned Liz and me: "Don't ever let anyone slip you a mickey." We'd laughed in Mom's face.

When we pulled into the apartment complex, I cowered in the car as a silver German shepherd, on its hind legs, scraped the glass and growled at me with a vengeance. Gretchen got out and called to me from her side, "What are you waiting for? We're here."

"But that dog," I said, pointing and shrinking. She had to be nuts to go out there with that beast charging us. "Get back in the car!"

"What dog?"

"You can't see it?"

"Eileen, there's no dog."

"No dog?"

"My god," she said, "did someone slip you a mickey?"

"But he's right—" The animal salivated as I gazed into his shimmering blue-gray eyes.

"Let's go," she ordered. She came around to my side, standing right where the dog had stood. "No dog. See." She extended an arm. "Come on. I've got you. And why you have to wear those damn clogs is beyond me."

Inside, Gretchen found a clearing along the wall and propped me up. "Don't move. I'll be back in a minute," she said. I was wearing a trench coat with jeans and a cashmere sweater. Leaning against the wall, I rocked in my clogs. Someone handed me a drink. My hair was a tangle of curls, with combs jammed in at odd angles to pull it off my face.

I wasn't on the wall a minute before I sloshed David from Buffalo three times. "A tie?" I said, and spilled. "Oh, clogs," I said, then splashed. "And what's that?" I squinted into his round glasses to find . . . what? Brown eyes. Oh, boy. I pressed my index finger to the bridge of those glasses and said in all earnestness, "Are you Woody Allen?"

"A jokester," he said with a laugh. "Naw, I'm his good-lookin' brother."

"You're from the twenties," I said. "The eyes of Dr. What's-his-name?"

"Eckleburg. Dr. T. J. Eckleburg."

"A medicine man who knows Gatsby?" My jaw dropped. I leaned forward. "Snazzy, remember?" I asked him this as if he and I had once driven through West Egg together and stopped by Myrtle's husband's gas station for a cool drink.

"Right, old sport. And how 'bout Gatsby?" he said. His voice softened, and he leaned into the wall so that our faces were inches apart. "Am I Jay Gatsby?"

"Mmm." I jerked my head back to check him out and banged it on the wall, then steadied myself to reach into my pocket for my cigarettes. After fumbling with the lighter, I doused him and my trench coat again. He took the drink from my hand. "I think you finished it off that time." He put the cigarette to his own lips to light it, stifled a cough, and handed it back to me. I inhaled and focused on his face again: too dark for Gatsby. But those eyes? "Maybe Nick," I said. "Yeah, I like Nick. You're Nick." I leaned back, proud of pegging him so neatly.

"Which would make you Jordan."

Oooh. Jordan, I decided, was now my favorite of the Gatsby characters: the sultry Jordan. I leaned forward to stare into his eyes and whispered, "You know her, too?"

Then I blacked out.

Later, David and his friend drove me home while Gretchen followed in her car. They carried me up the frozen staircase into my sorority house. Gretchen told me this the next day, adding that David insisted on waiting downstairs until I was safely in bed.

"Watch her," he'd said, to which Gretchen said to herself, "Now, there's an idea."

He called the next day to see if I was all right and to ask me out.

David tended to greet me with a gift, usually a book—Sartre, Joyce, and Faulkner being among his favorite writers. He read up on all of Cincinnati's best-kept secrets and courted me on Valentine's Day in an Italian restaurant as small and intimate as a grandmother's parlor. He collected wine, learned how to cook Vietnamese dishes, made his own yogurt, and wore bow ties. On weekends he wooed me with jazz. He taught me that Cincinnati had a vibrant jazz scene, and introduced me to a network of back alley clubs. The scenes of my stories began to include a philosophical Sartre-like character with Woody Allen's voice, hanging out in jazz clubs.

It was on one of those evenings of discovery, of seeing my city and myself through David's eyes, that I decided I was ready to face sex. We'd gone to see Mr. Spoons in a club downtown, and I made this call on my second gin and tonic while Mr. Spoons thrummed on the table next to us before working his way up to a waiter's elbow. Actually, I'd been toying with the idea earlier that night. I'd worn a black skirt, a white silk blouse, and perfume behind my ears. With my hair now cut in a Cleopatra bob, I tried to convince myself, as I brushed on mascara, that this is how a woman faces up to sex: in bangs and mascara.

On my fourth drink, Mr. Spoons played his utensils to a bass rhythm on my head, moving down my neck and arms. I never took my eyes off of David. Perceptive young man that David was, he rushed me back to his apartment. On the sofa, he cradled me on his lap. I felt dizzy.

He kissed me as he worked the minuscule buttons on my blouse. He'd taken his glasses off, but he had the eye–hand coordination of a surgeon already. I looked up at those gentle brown eyes and saw two Davids looking back at me. I closed my eyes as he went under my skirt to peel off my tights. At this I let go of his neck and pretended to fall asleep.

"Ah, jeez," he said. "Are you out?"

No answer.

He whistled in my ear.

Nothing.

He froze there, with a warm palm pressed to my belly. Would he pursue this thing even though I was drunk? I turned limp as a rag doll on him—my test. I'd learned the "limp act" from trying to dress Nina as a toddler. (It's impossible to dress an infant in the midst of the limp act, and Nina was a pro.) He waited. I waited longer.

"Okay," he said, finally pulling his hand out of my skirt.

Then, just to throw him off, I pretended to be coming to and said, "Hmmm?"

"You awake?" he asked optimistically.

I opened my eyes, saw two baffled Davids staring back at me, and closed them again. "I don't feel so good." This was the truth.

"Okay," he said, flustered. "Okay." He lifted me up and carried me into the bedroom. "I'm going to put you in the bed, you understand? I won't do anything. It's just to sleep."

I nodded.

He set me on the edge of the bed. I opened my eyes as he knelt in front of me. "I'm just taking the blouse off so you can sleep."

"Mmm."

Then, in a sort of package deal, he yanked the skirt, legs, and tights off at once. He held them momentarily as if someone had handed him their baby before jumping off a bridge. What to do? Finally he just tossed them aside. When he tucked me in, I was down to pearls and panties. I closed my eyes again as he whispered in his gravelly Buffalo accent, "Ya dodged a bullet this time." He kissed my forehead. "You're a beauty." I couldn't believe my good fortune.

In the morning, he showed me things about a woman's body that I hadn't known existed. I would never again rely on popular literature for advice on sex. And what was all this nonsense about sex in wooden legs? In this man's bed I would become a treasure spit from the ruins.

After that, I spent most of my nights with David, coming back to the sorority house only for clothes and mail between classes. We studied for hours in the library. While he rose to first in his class, I began to see that it wasn't so hard to make the dean's list. All you had to do was open your books and read them—not just the ones you enjoyed. It didn't hurt to show up for class. From there it was merely a matter of organizing assignments.

Soon David was walking me through my upcoming appointment at the student health center. I would get started on a contraceptive. He read up on the different forms to help me decide which one to choose. Did other girls have boyfriends who studied the side effects and the efficacy of birth control? I doubted it. This time, I told myself, this time I'm not going to mess it up. David was about the best boyfriend a girl could have, and I was finally mature enough to appreciate my good fortune.

In the spring, David took me to New York City. We stayed with his college roommate in Soho. Because it was my first time in the city, David planned for me to hit all the tourist spots. We visited the Metropolitan Museum, saw *A Chorus Line*, ate dinner in Chinatown followed by cannoli in Little Italy, and shopped on Fifth Avenue. I never wanted to leave. "We'll come back," David promised. Then he bought me a sexy dress with a plunging neckline and thin straps, "Because you have to take something of New York home with you."

A week later, as I shimmied into the dress David bought me, I realized that I'd fallen in love. David could tell me he loved me so easily, but those words conjured fear in me. That night on the dance floor he pressed his cheek to mine, posing for a photo with the satirically somber face of a man leading his partner in a tango. My expression could have been the same one I wore at age ten when I'd faced the sign at the crest of the rollercoaster: *Hold your hats!*

From their table behind us, Colette and James, who had started dating, cheered us on. James and I were both in better hands now. I would not only survive college; I'd come away with fond memories of it.

CHAPTER 17

Ancestral Knowledge

On a Sunday afternoon that same spring, David drove his Toyota at a hectic pace, taking a pothole rather hard on the highway north to my parents' house. "Are you nervous?" I asked.

"Not a bit," he said, squeezing my left hand.

My parents' new house, a replica of one in Colonial Williamsburg, fit into a hill, so that it was three stories on the back, a Cape Cod on the front. This neighborhood was known for its Protestant roots and lately its Jewish families. It was the perfect place for my parents to rebuild their lives.

The entry was a sight more welcoming than our last house, where toddlers had been known to jet down the driveway on scooters into traffic. At this house you were greeted by a border of peonies and a white picket gate set into stone pillars with urns spilling impatiens. I poked my head in the back door to find Mom at the kitchen counter slashing a head of lettuce with a steak knife. She'd never bothered with proper kitchen tools.

"Mom," I said, stepping inside, "this is David."

She set the knife down by her martini, wiped her hands on the gingham apron I'd made as a Girl Scout, and as she shook his hand she offered David a drink.

"Scotch on the rocks." He sounded relieved. "Please."

I tried not to look worried while I searched for my father, who had been displaced from his reading spot at the old kitchen table, which was now downstairs in what was a party room for the grandchildren. From the dining room, Mom eyed David suspiciously as she poured a drink from the bar she'd set up in a dry sink. Her antiques gave this house the feel of a roadside tavern from a couple of centuries back. Dressed in slacks and a sweater, her town-and-country look, she seemed an average suburban homemaker. Her hair was neither the lacquered crown from the sixties nor the Joan-of-Arc from her Catholic-vigilante phase. Now it was a smart cut, no fuss, and without any gray—no coloring, she was always quick to point out. After she handed David his drink, she got right to the point. "David, you're in medical school, right?"

"Yes, ma'am."

"Tell me this. Is my grandpa Bruehl still hanging in the lobby?"

"What are you talking about?" I said to Mom. Was she going to bring up some embarrassing family history?

She acted as if she hadn't said anything. Again I wished Dad would show his face, but he was hiding on the sofa downstairs among the middle school kids and a handful of grandchildren. From down there a television blared, a pinball machine rang bells and flapped oars, a ball slammed a wall, a baby cried, another child laughed, someone scolded him, and all that was capped off by Dad's snoring.

I leaned into the kitchen counter. Mom had never mentioned this grandpa Bruehl. Would this story involve a hobo?

"Your mother's talking about those portraits in the med school lobby," said David. "I guess her grandfather is one of those guys."

"Have you seen him?" asked Mom. She poked David hard on the shoulder and said, "Gustav Bruehl?"

"Huh?" I asked.

"Sure, I've seen him," said David. "He was one of the founders of the medical school."

"What?" I directed this question to Mom, who now fingered the shreds of lettuce like confetti. She'd never mentioned this grandfather. "Mom, is this true? Gustav Bruehl, who is *he*?"

She shrugged. "He's my mother's daddy . . . Or he might have been her grandpa."

I wondered how she could not know whether he was Ida's father or grandfather when our father's family history was constantly brought up by our grandmother Katie. At her house, Katie frequently whipped out a black-and-white photo of a woman with a beehive hairdo, heavy black-framed glasses, and a tragic smile. She'd say, "This is my cousin Joan," before fixing her eyes on me and adding, "Spitting image of you, Eileen."

Now Mom was feeding David and me the same line she always gave me: "My mother died when Kevin was a baby. Ida Bruehl Fanger."

"I know all about Ida," I said, before she could launch into the saint story. "But why didn't you tell us about your grandfather?"

"You eat steak, don't you?" Mom asked David, changing the subject.

The meal itself was uneventful. Afterward, Dad slipped away as quickly as possible. He still hated making small talk with boyfriends. I came into the kitchen from clearing the table to find Mom and David like roommates, hip to hip at the sink, giggling while they washed the dishes. Suddenly and awkwardly, Mom turned to him, staring right into his eyes, and said, "You're Jewish, aren't you?"

"Yes, I am."

"You are?" This had never occurred to me. I would not have even thought to ask. What prompted Mom to ask David? It occurred to me that she might even ask if we were sleeping together, so I said we had to get back to school and left.

In the car, I wondered what my mother would think about David's religion. To me, having a Jewish boyfriend was almost as exciting as going away to college. Anyway, the world had moved on from Ricky and Lucy. In 1980, even *Bridget Loves Bernie* was passé. But not to my family, nor to me. I still swooned every time I saw the Bernie character in later roles.

"Why didn't you tell me you were Jewish?" I asked.

"I'm not that observant." We were both silent a while before he added, "You have this HUGE Catholic family. I guess I didn't want to make an issue of it. It's not an issue for me."

"Okay," I said. "I get it." I certainly didn't enjoy when people identified me by my legs, nor did I enjoy being called out on the size of my family. Those were in fact two points that I'd worried about with regard to his family.

"Is this going to bother your family?" he asked.

"I don't think so," I said, sincerely believing it. How could my family not love anyone who loved me so much? "Well," I added, "it's never come up before. We don't even know any Jewish people." My parents had moved to a neighborhood with many Jewish families, but they made their new friends through the Catholic school and the church.

I was hung up on the question of how my mother had guessed David's religion. This would hound me over the years, as more questions would follow. For instance, why had Mom never mentioned her grandfather's achievements? She had every reason to throw them in our grandmother's face. Katie boasted that she was related to Oliver Ellsworth, a drafter of the Constitution, and Ephraim Ellsworth, an advisor to Lincoln. "Oh really, Katie?" Mom would say. Then she'd mutter under her breath, "Were those the same Ellsworths who ended up in that igloo in Minnesota?" Katie never even blinked at Mom's jabs. Instead she'd calmly insist that Mom had her own ancestry all wrong. "A common mistake," she'd say.

But what did Mom know about Jewish people? Why did Mom always say that "all doctors are Jewish"? Was her grandfather Jewish? Was this why we didn't know any of Ida Bruehl's family?

Then there was the bantering on our screened-in porch almost every Sunday for years, as Katie claimed her Ellsworth ancestry. After practically declaring that she had been born on the *Mayflower,* she'd say to Mom, "Joy, you're not German. Your mother was Alsatian." And she'd turn to Grandpa. "Don't you agree, Charles? Didn't Ida *look* Alsatian? Those dark features?"

Mom refused to go along with it. "No, Katie. That's not it at all. I'm German on both sides."

"French, Joy. A common mistake. Alsatians are French, not German. Your mother was Alsatian."

"I know what my own mother was, and my mother was German! Ida Bruehl was German through and through and, by the way, I never even heard of this I'll-saint-ya place."

At this point, we kids would burst out in laughter from behind the Dutch door. Then we skittered away. Until now that argument had seemed as ludicrous as I'll-saint-ya. I'd assumed Katie's insistence on this French heritage came from an anti-German sentiment left over from the war. Now I wondered if Katie was spinning Mom's possible Jewish roots into Alsatian ancestry.

Many years later, I researched Gustav Bruehl's biography and found in him an ancestor anyone would be proud to claim. His name is spelled as Bruehl or Bruhl, even Brhl, in the records I found, but all have the same history. He was born in Hersdorf, Prussia, in 1826 and came to the United States in his twenties after earning degrees in medicine, philosophy, and history. As a physician, he performed the first laryngoscopy in Cincinnati, but he was known around the world for his contributions to anthropology, ethnology, and archeology. He studied the remains of indigenous cultures from Alaska to Peru and wrote a book, *Die Kulturvölker Alt-Amerikas*, still in print, in which he claimed that the indigenous Americans first greeted the Spanish interlopers as gods. In his dissertation on "The Pre-Columbian Origin of Syphilis," he concluded that Columbus's team brought syphilis to Europe from the New World. This theory, which was met with both condemnation and acclaim, is still debated. He also excavated the remains of an American Indian tribe buried in southern Ohio. After examining the skulls, he determined that this tribe had not perished from fever but had been attacked by blows to the head with instruments of blunt force, probably in their sleep.

Gustav was also a poet. Under the pseudonym Kara Giorg, a tribute to the Serbian warrior "Black George," he published five volumes of poetry in German. He took an interest in public education and was the first president of the Peter Claver Society for the Education of Negro Children.

I was not able to determine Gustav Bruehl's religious background, but he came to Cincinnati in the 1840s when an influx of Jewish immigrants fled persecution in Germany, including Isaac M. Wise. Wise and his contemporaries opened the Reform Temple in Cincinnati, which then had one of the highest populations of Jewish citizens in the United States. The city became home to Hebrew Union College.

Was Gustav a Jewish immigrant who converted to Catholicism instead of launching the Reform Temple with the others? Some Jewish immigrants in Cincinnati made that switch. I've asked Mom if Gustav was a convert, and she has neither denied nor confirmed it. Instead she said, "Did I say he was my grandfather? Maybe he was a great-grandfather, or an uncle." After some research I found that Gustav was Mom's great-grandfather. Mom inherited his walking stick, a black cane with a carved gilt head, which she has passed on to Ted.

I was never able to confirm whether Gustav was Jewish, but I did find a reference to a marriage certificate for another Gustav Bruehl in the Jewish Records Index in Poland.

Maybe family history is made only of the parts we remember or choose to believe. But what happens to the part we ignore? Does it vanish? Or is it announcing itself everywhere we go? Could it become the story that everyone else knows about us and we are the last to find out?

CHAPTER 18

Swan Song

After pushing through the heavy brass doors of the Dixie Terminal, a building with marble walls and barrel-vaulted ceilings, I was plunged into humidity so thick that my cotton dress instantly stuck to my back. This was the last day of my job in the summer of 1980, and I would leave the next day for Buffalo, where David was working in a hospital.

I'd worked as an account rep in a recruiting business downtown, which meant that I spent the whole day on the telephone drumming up jobs for people, and it was not easy given the recession. Because of my habit of people-watching, I enjoyed commuting from my parents' house to downtown on the bus, but the ride was about an hour long and involved a tiresome walk home. I wasn't halfway to the bus stop when I stepped into a phone booth and called the house.

At the time, Mom and Dad were on a ranch outside Las Vegas with Dad's brother and other car dealers. This was part of my parents' victory tour, having survived their separation and coming close to the end of their parental responsibilities. The difficult years were almost behind them. Together they were on the verge of finally becoming Dick and Joy, jetsetters.

In their absence, my brothers and I enjoyed being the oldest kids at home, throwing impromptu pool parties, grilling steaks, and holding our own cocktail hour. I couldn't wait to dive into the pool. "Come on, come on," I said, praying that one of my brothers would pick up. Finally Frank answered.

"Please come and get me," I said. "I can't take the heat on the bus tonight."

"Where are you?" he asked, only slightly put out. I heard him grab the keys, unlike what Ted might have done. Ted, who was now calling himself a Marxist, would have said, "You're not above the working class, Looney. Ride the bus."

Within twenty minutes, Frankie arrived on the corner of Fourth and Walnut in the Beetle with its top down. He'd never looked so good. Clear skies reflected off the silver car, tinting his hair blue. I tossed my purse in the back, and if I could have I would have leapt over the door. On the highway, we cranked up the stereo.

We were both celebrating. Recently turned twenty-one, Frank was completely in love with his first girlfriend. Having gone on exactly two dates in high school, both awkward, he had recoiled from girls. Our family read that as a sign that he was surely our priest. Then, on a spring break in Florida with Stilts and the Taylor brothers, he met Sarah Jane from St. Louis. For two years now he and Sarah Jane had traveled between cities. She was expected to arrive in a few days and Frank was happy.

At first I slumped low in my seat while Frankie sang the words to Bob Seger's "Night Moves." As he crooned off-key, I couldn't help but compare him to Ted in my mind. For some reason I did this a lot growing up. If they fought, I rooted for Frankie, although Ted usually won. As we grew older, I favored Ted and felt guilty about it later, because Ted was handsomer, wittier, smarter, and more athletic. As for singing, Ted could do a perfect tongue-in-cheek imitation of the Moody Blues. Frankie, with his crooked teeth, his lips curled in song, had no voice. Then there was the matter of guile.

Everyone still teased Frankie about his handling of Mom's stew, the "witch hazel" that she simmered in her "cauldron." While Liz and I had connived to hide the meat in dozens of ways—inside an extension of the table, or (Liz's favorite) rolled and stuffed into a bottle of A.1.—Frankie would not waste food because of the starving kids on the UNICEF box that Mom strategically placed at the center of our kitchen table. An hour after dinner, we would be lying on our stomachs side by side with our eyes locked onto *The Patty Duke Show*. I'd glance over at him to find that he still had meat stored in his jaw. "Spit it out," I'd say, and he'd look away, embarrassed.

Now, in the Beetle, I shot up from my slouch, excited. I was leaving town. My hair whipped against my face as I joined Frankie in song.

That night I sat in front of the television, folding laundry for my trip. There were windows on two sides of the party room downstairs, one facing the path up to the pool, and the other, my side, facing an isolated patio rimmed by a stone wall. This patio wasn't connected to anything else in the yard, which made it my favorite thing about the house. Frank came down and handed me a long-necked Hudepohl. I sipped the beer, thin and sour. "Why do you drink this stuff?" I asked.

He didn't exactly abide my slights; he simply never registered them. Instead, he brought up his plans for the coming week with Sarah Jane. When would I be back? Did I still want to have a pool party before Mom and Dad came home? As usual, he stared at the television screen while we talked, only this time a smile crept over his lips.

"You like Sarah Jane a lot, don't you?" I said.

He pushed his lips out to hide his giddiness.

Sarah Jane was a lucky girl. "You gonna marry her, Frankie?"

"Maybe." He took a sip of his beer and looked me in the eye, his almond eyes crinkling, then moved them back to the screen. He puckered his lips to stifle a proud grin. Frank's life plans were clear and simple: he would graduate from Xavier University in a year and stay in Dad's service department, where even the most irate customers were soothed by Frankie's sincere desire to be helpful. I'd spent one summer answering the phone there and fell asleep between calls, but Frankie whistled his way to a perch on the service desk.

He might have already proposed to Sarah Jane. Or maybe he would do it on this next meeting. That grin implied that he was at least close, although trying to "breast" his cards, as Grandpa used to say, so I didn't press him.

"Good," I said, folding the last T-shirt. The clothes were warm and smelled of clean cotton. I smoothed a hand over the stack, the way Mom would when she finished folding laundry.

As for David, Frank was kind to him but he thought I'd do better to choose a guy from the old neighborhood, someone Catholic. Other than Michael and Bridget, few of us siblings practiced Catholicism in our young adult years to the degree our parents expected. Many of us lied to our mother about going to church, except Frankie. He attended Mass every week. "You gonna marry David?" Frankie blurted out, his voice cracking on David's name.

For me, it wasn't the way he said "David" but the word "marry" that touched a nerve. David had one married friend in medical school, and that couple looked miserable. Marriage was a possibility for us, but not for a few years.

"Well?" said Frank.

"I guess so. Someday." I sipped my beer.

Then Frank asked me in a coy voice if I wanted to get fixed up with one of his friends. The young man in question was a beefy guy called Bubba Punch. "He likes you," said Frank.

I sighed.

"What?"

"Nothing." I tried to sound gracious. "Really?"

"Well," said Frank, "I'm just saying . . ." When he chose to, Frankie could read my body language. "I mean, if you ever break up with David . . ."

That hardly seemed likely. I couldn't wait to see David. Ten weeks earlier, while David packed up to leave for the summer, I cried so hard I was slobbering. He handed me a key to his apartment and said, "Come here whenever you want. That'll make us both feel better about being apart." At first, I didn't think I would last a week without him. I came by his place often, sometimes with a studious friend who was taking a summer class. Back at my parents' home, because of Frank and Ted, my evenings were turning out to be fun.

The trip to Buffalo made it even better. Over the following days, David took me to an outdoor performance of Shakespeare, a nightclub with magicians in training, a beach house on the Canadian side of the lake, and more jazz clubs. His mother welcomed me warmly into their home. Still, members of both families were showing reservations about this relationship.

Since my parents weren't due home for a few more days, I figured I could get away with a day or two alone with David before anyone would expect me home. His apartment smelled of decay when we entered. Over the last month I hadn't made it there at all. His ferns had rained brown leaves everywhere. We were so tired that we collapsed onto the bed sideways. My legs were hanging over the edge, and I kept meaning to do something about that. Instead, I rattled off the highlights of my summer: fireworks on the river, Frank's friends hanging out at our house, and a canoe trip with my girlfriends.

We held hands, and I told the story of Frankie's scheme to fix me up with Bubba Punch. David laughed in the midst of a yawn. He wasn't offended by Frank's attempt to thwart our relationship. In fact, he'd negotiated any resistance from my family with finesse.

"Punch what?" he said. "With that name, the guy could pitch for the Reds."

"Or go on *Big Time Wrestling*."

"That Frankie," said David.

I sighed. Falling asleep felt as safe as it had with Frankie back in our old room while he endlessly calculated RBIs, like revisiting a time before I even knew what worry meant: before Trent on the playground, or Mom's downward spiral. How freeing it felt to break clean of those dismal memories.

We awakened to a pristine September morning, which was cool but warming up. After we went out to breakfast, we bought groceries and stopped by the sorority house to pick up mail. Gretchen wasn't awake yet, but a girl there said she'd tell her I'd stopped by to see her. I jumped in David's car out front. "Let's scram," I said, afraid that somehow word would get back to my family that I was in town.

We were unloading the groceries in David's kitchen when the phone rang. "Should I answer?" he asked.

"Your parents probably want to know that you got home."

He grabbed the receiver from the wall and took it into the dining room. "Hello . . . Oh, hey, Gretch."

"It's Gretchen?" I asked, ready to take the call.

David didn't answer me. His face hardened. I'd never seen that look on him. I stopped unpacking. "What is it?"

"Okay. I got it. Thanks." He hung up and briefly the stunned face lingered.

"What?" My heart raced. "Am I in trouble?"

"I don't know. Gretchen just told me to get you home right now. Come on." He grabbed his keys.

"Gretchen said what? I have to put these away first."

"Forget it."

The head of lettuce, fresh and crisp in my hands, dropped to the counter. David took my hand and rushed me to the car. Along the way I worried. My family must have called the sorority house, where someone must have told them I was in town. This meant that my family would know I was sleeping with David, and while I was pretty sure that I wasn't the first sibling to have premarital sex, it seemed that I would be the first one to be caught. Already I was crafting my defense.

The radio came on briefly in the car and David stuffed a tape into the deck before starting the engine. "Watch it. You're gonna break your new tape deck," I said, just before the underbelly of his car brushed the lip of the curb. "Ouch!" I was eager to get this over with, too, but David seemed to be taking this so hard. "What can they do?" I said.

David was silent. Some ominous piece by Mozart played. I kept thinking, this is ridiculous, being so nervous about spending a weekend together. I remembered the first time he'd driven to my parents' house.

"We could just tell them it was too late to drive home so I slept on your sofa."

"Sure," he said, distracted.

What would David say to my family? Should I even bring him into the house?

Finally we turned onto my street. As we neared the house, I saw cars lining the curb out front, which was odd because people usually parked in the lane, but as we made the turn into the lane we found more cars. "What is it?" I said, releasing my seatbelt. "It has to be Katie." My heart sped up even faster. Grandpa had died about six years before. Maybe it was Katie's turn, but ninety is a good many years, I thought. And then I remembered my parents. When were they due back? I opened the car door before David could stop.

"Wait!" He slammed on the brakes.

I jumped out and he called after me. Maybe he said he would

park the car, or he asked me to wait for him. My attention was fixed on the screen door into the kitchen. Mom had to be on the other side of it. She could punish me or slap my face, I would still hug her. It was an old door, and I couldn't see into the house through the warped screen. Voices were there on the other side, and the door inside was open. Still, I found myself knocking as if this were someone else's house.

Michael's wife came to the door. Her hair was wet and she wore tennis shorts, as if she'd been playing with her kids in the pool. Maybe this was a party? Except that she had this harsh expression on her face. Her blue eyes drilled into mine, the lines on her jaw tight. "Come inside," she said.

"Is it Katie?" I asked, almost crying.

"Come in the house," she said, softer.

"Oh, God. It's Mom and Dad?" I started shaking uncontrollably.

"Please," she said sternly. "Eileen. Eileen!"

"No!" I snapped, pointing at her. "You tell me right here."

"It's Frankie," she said. Her eyes, swelling with tears, told me that he was dead.

I heard a long scream, and it wasn't until my head started pounding that I realized it was coming from me. My knee wobbling to the brink of collapse, I took off in the direction I'd last seen David driving. At a tree down the lane, I stopped to beat my forehead against the trunk. Something tugged me back. It was David. He was telling me he had me.

We were there in the neighbor's yard, David soothing me, when I heard whimpering from someone other than myself. Out in the lane, I saw Ted, his arms folded over his face, sobbing. It was like hearing the news all over again.

On the day of the funeral, Dad called us all into the living room: Mom, the priest, children, and grandchildren—in total more than twenty people. As we held hands, he delivered a heartening talk before we faced the service. Despite his normally terse style, there were times when my father spoke and it seemed as if he'd been born for that moment alone, his words so stirring that we were prepared to face a battle. We didn't know that Dad had been sedated in Las Vegas and required a wheelchair to get on the plane, that inside he felt he'd just faced his last defeat. We had expected Mom to fall apart, but she was holding her own. Already she said she'd had a visit from Frankie in the form of a dove. This seemed to relax her enough to get through the days ahead.

A wake was held. I don't remember a single image or conversation from it, except that there was a closed casket. Frank had been killed in a car accident while his friend drove home after they had been drinking. Gretchen had heard the story on the news that morning, and called us. Everyone insisted that Frankie was sound asleep on impact, never felt a thing, but for months afterward I imagined him waking up at the last second to face that telephone pole. At the very moment he died, I might have been talking about Frankie to David, just before I fell asleep.

I have only a fleeting memory of the funeral service. The mass took place at Saint Vivian because it was bigger than the church in our new neighborhood and because Frankie belonged to that world. I couldn't have made it down the aisle to the front pew without David holding my hand. I see the jammed church and the candles in their brass chandeliers lit on a cloudy morning. I recall bursting into tears during the gathering back at our house when I came upon a group of Frank's friends, among them Chief Taylor, Stilts, and Bubba Punch.

Otherwise, I remember only two images from the limousine immediately after the service. First, I glanced out the window and saw the friend who was driving when Frank died. He was standing away from the church, scratches on his cheek, petrified, waiting as if he expected the crowd to come out and sentence him.

The second is an image I must have dreamed, in which David sits beside me on my left and on my right sits Frank's fiancée, Sarah Jane. I picture her in a window seat wearing an off-white dress, the driver of the crashed vehicle outside in the distance. I see her freckled cheeks and the cut of the dress, which couldn't have been white, I think, but that's what I see when I picture all of us there in the limousine.

Some days I awakened to the realization that I would never again see Frankie. I could only roll over and go back to sleep. David kept as close as anyone could be to someone encased in a protective shell. I rarely left my room in the sorority house. Frank's death was changing me in fundamental ways. I understood none of them. When I think of that year, I see the bottom side of the upper bunk, where a girl named Kitty slept. She slipped out gently every morning and spent most of her time in the library. Across the hall from us were Gretchen and Pam. On a good day, I joined them for *General Hospital* or a game of hearts. More often I stayed in the lower bunk with the blinds drawn and the lights off, just staring.

I'd had big plans for junior year. At the end of the previous term, I was elected social chairwoman of my sorority. It was hard to conceive of a time when I'd had it together enough to win anything, let alone an election. I considered asking my opponent to take over the position, but she was Liz's little sister and I couldn't bring myself to concede. I groaned every time the phone rang. Out in the hallway I'd hear, "Has anyone seen Eileen?" Our house mom, Biddy, would reply, "Don't disturb her." Jamming my mailbox were requests from fraternities to schedule parties. I put off calling them back as long as possible.

On campus, I arrived late for a meeting that I'd scheduled with a professor. From outside her office, I overheard her asking a classmate, "What's happened to Eileen Cronin? She was strong in my debate class. She hardly shows up for this one."

I wasn't doing any better in my part-time job. I'd worked since I was sixteen and, thanks to the examples my friend Claire and my sister Liz set, I typically balanced work and school fairly well. Now my hours in the bridal registry at Pogue's downtown were being whittled away, which might have had something to do with the fact that I leaned into the counter and drew designs in my breath on the glass case.

Everything had gone askew. I was afraid to get out of bed for fear that I wouldn't land squarely on the floor but instead slide on slanted ground, slippery and endless.

Finally I came up with a plan that would take me, emotionally, to a better place. I became a hostess in a historic German beer garden in Walnut Hills, which had been transformed into a four-star restaurant serving nouvelle cuisine. As the manager, Liz was initially against the idea of hiring me, but Colette, who was a captain, talked her into giving me a chance. Because of its location near campus, a lot of professors and physicians came in for lunch. Dr. Cabrera stepped into the bar one day with James and another son during the lunch-hour rush.

"We'll sit in the bar," said the father, striding past me toward a booth.

"It'll just be a minute before we have a table cleared," I said, flustered and making an effort not to look at James or his usually flirtatious brother and father. They seemed particularly business-like that day.

"This is fine right here, thank you," said Dr. Cabrera. "We're in a hurry."

I rushed upstairs to find Liz setting some extra tables. "Please," I begged, "the Cabreras are down in the bar. They want to eat there. I can't wait on them. You know I'll mess it up." Liz stared blandly as she smoothed a white tablecloth. She'd seen me topple a tray of peach coladas under the grape arbor. She followed me down.

From my hostess podium only inches from the Cabrera men, I tried not to notice them in a huddle, plotting their next moves. I envied James for the guidance his father gave him. Who would be my mentor? A car dealer? A homemaker? I wanted to be a writer. If I didn't take myself more seriously, who would?

That may have been the last time I saw James. My grief over Frank clouds my memory, but I know the precise point on campus where I was walking with a friend when she mentioned that James had gone away to medical school. I couldn't say which season we were in, whether the leaves were red, if there was snow under our feet, or the air was dense with pollen, yet I see the two of us walking toward Clifton Avenue. We'd come down the hill in front of McMicken College of Arts and Sciences, a Georgian building with a spire and stone lions at the entrance. I had seen so many friends leave town, but I'd never expected James to go.

We faced fraternity row, where James lived, or had lived. I pictured him driving the wrong way down Clifton Avenue as he tried to talk me back into the car the night we fought. Had that been our last conversation alone?

The wounds from Frank's unexpected death reopened. Back in high school, when I was ambushed by my father's leaving, I confused that loss with my first breakup. I'd almost given up over those losses. But Frank had viewed me as his equal. At times, he'd even looked up to me. I wanted to see myself through Frankie's untarnished eyes, to become someone I admired. Instead, I was shrinking back into a timid and fearful girl.

All around me people were moving on. With every friend or sibling who left town, I craved new adventures. What was stopping me from finding my own?

CHAPTER 19

Taking the Plunge

Late in my junior year, a flyer showed up in my mail slot at the sorority house, announcing a meeting of the Disabled Students' Union. I shredded it immediately and tossed it into the trashcan, bothered by the notion of anyone associating me with the word "disabled." The paranoia this flyer stirred up signaled a problem that dogged me for days, then weeks, until I did something about it.

First, I became a candy-striper at Children's Hospital, transporting patients to and from physical therapy. Soon I met Susan, a twelve-year-old girl whose legs had been amputated below the knees. When I wheeled Susan back to her room, her nurse tapped the girl's dozing father and said, "This is Eileen. She has two artificial legs." The man's strained face softened into hopefulness. "Susan could walk that well?" he asked.

"Probably better," I said. "She has both knees."

"But not tomorrow," cautioned the nurse. "She has to get through rehab first."

I stayed in touch with Susan after her release, taking her to movies and other activities so she would get used to going out in public. This helped me to heal from my own grief, and I hope it helped her. Meanwhile, I researched graduate programs and discovered a field known as rehabilitation counseling. Boston University had an excellent program. Bridget lived nearby. Ted would be about two hours away, at Williams College. This would allow me to go far from home and still have family close to me.

Dad supported my decision from the start. I came home one Sunday, and he folded his newspaper in the breakfast room to set it aside. "You really like helping this gal, don't you?" he asked. I could see from his smile that he was pleased I spent time with Susan. This touched me because he smiled so rarely after Frank died. The grief that had engulfed my father came in the form of a ferocious silence. In the past he might have laughed out loud at an article, or groaned, but now it was as if he'd been cut off from his voice. I treasured the moment he set his paper aside to chat, even if it was brief.

Often, while I sat upstairs near the top of the staircase writing, Dad read alone in the breakfast room, and I could hear in his breath a broken heart. It was so subtle that one might easily miss it. Once he blurted out at the dinner table, "There is not a one of you who is half as good-hearted as Frankie." I was hurt by the comment, but later I saw how sorrow had affected Dad. He did not feel worthy of outliving his child. The thought sickened him. Aside from that, he was right. Frank had invested more in his friends and family than in himself, while the rest of us were a competitive lot. Maybe Dad regretted his role in fostering that competitiveness, although I doubt that he knew any other way to lead this gigantic gaggle of children.

Mom reacted differently to my news. Her face went pale. She stammered, "Well, well, why would you do that?" She looked completely terrified at the prospect of my going to graduate school, and to study what? Rehab. Why would anyone do *that*?

David shared her skepticism. I told him while we were rushing to his car to catch a movie. "What about writing? Didn't you just get honorable mention in that contest?"

I rolled my eyes. "The guys on the magazine said my main character was a 'fairy.' They wouldn't publish the story."

He stopped and held up a hand. "Hold on," he said. Cold air whipped through me, and I just wanted to get into the car. "Those same guys who assigned you the mascot story? You're going to listen to them?"

I had been writing for the campus magazine and had recently pitched my idea to do a story on sixties architecture that I thought was inspired by *The Jetsons*. I chose buildings with entrances like Jetsonian launch pads, and I planned to talk about how in the sixties we had all envisioned ourselves one day flying around in our own private saucers, but here in the eighties we had a fuel crisis and a floundering market for a surplus of ugly architecture. "That's very interesting," the magazine's editor-in-chief had said. "Now go interview the Bearcat."

I sped up my pace. "It doesn't matter if I write." We were climbing in the car when I added, "The point is I can't make a living at it."

Inside, David nudged me and eyed my unbuckled seatbelt. I fastened it while he said, "Doesn't matter? You don't just stop *being* a writer. It's not a *choice*. And you don't have to worry about money. I'll support you."

Anyone in their right mind would have embraced this man, but I decided that he must not "really know" me. If he did, he would see why I needed to confront the world of disability. Aside from that, he seemed to be moving toward marriage.

I knew so many women who were coming home to marry and start families. Liz and Rosa had recently married. Claire and two other friends had asked me to be in their weddings. Almost no one left Cincinnati for good. Their children and grandchildren would go to the same schools and the same parties. This was their dream.

Given the disappointments I'd known, marriage seemed one

more setup for disillusionment. I wasn't ready to trust anyone that much. As for my dreams, they were satisfied by writing, at night and alone, often with alcohol and cigarettes. Based on what I knew about marriage—wives promptly gave birth and raised children—what kind of a bride would I make? My mind had shifted. It was now focused on accomplishments—my accomplishments, not my children's or my husband's accomplishments.

One night over dinner, David told me that he had helped deliver the baby of a mother who smoked. "It's an awful mess," he said. "I don't want to see you that way." And I thought, "I don't want to see myself that way." But my next thought was this: why aspire to motherhood when one might aspire to live like Dorothy Parker instead?

About this time, a sibling with an alcohol problem told an anti-Semitic joke with David at the table. We didn't talk like that in our family. Three times Mom said, "Stop!" Embarrassed, my father apologized to David, but I regretted that I didn't take David's hand and leave the house instantly. David was so easygoing about the fiasco that I'd let it go, or so I believed.

For days going into weeks afterward, I turned this incident over. It was my responsibility to take a stand for David and for us as a couple, but I was not deft at handling aggression. If I could have managed this situation with maturity, I would have asked my sibling to call David to apologize and then make an apology to the rest of the family at another dinner. Eventually the day came when I received an apology, and I accepted it. There was no apology or discussion with the family, though. As for an apology to David, it would become clear that I was the one who owed him that. Before that I would return to my earlier ways, where I would destroy my own dreams before I'd allow anyone else to destroy them, so I poisoned my confidence in a relationship that was the healthiest part of my life to that point.

The poisoning began with me turning things over obsessively: *But why is David so good to me? Is he my Pygmalion?*

Yes! Now, get over it.

Just think of the hours he'll be gone.

Hours to be spent at the typewriter.

As soon as I'm attached, he'll destroy me.

Are you sure it won't be the other way around?

It was exhausting. In no time I would forget about David, about Frankie, about everything but a fictional world in which "an underachieving lover picks up a birdcage at a flea market but it's the woman (a rich college girl who slums in a jazz club) he wants for his collection. In the end he's the one caged by his obsession." Even my stories were turning into obsessions.

My worries snowballed. Aside from my belief that I was helpless to prevent our religious and cultural differences from being trampled on, I had not even begun to face my fears about birth defects. Were mine genetic? I could not simply hope for the best. If I wanted technical answers explained in scientific terms, I would have to seek them myself. I understood that if thalidomide had caused my birth defects, my pregnancies would be at no more risk than anyone else's. David talked as if children were in our future. But my mother was telling me she'd never taken the drug. If she knew that I had these fears about passing along the defect, she wouldn't persist in allowing me to believe in some other cause, would she?

For better or worse, I was reevaluating my priorities. The promise I had made to myself to hold onto this gift of a relationship with David was now as remote from my consciousness as a promise made to a fellow Girl Scout around the campfire. Life had jerked me at the last second too many times. But if any good had come of

Frank's death, it was that I was beginning to take myself seriously. I needed to believe in myself. I wanted to prove to myself that I was a strong person, not the feeble-minded, weak-spirited girl I saw when I thought back on my life so far.

And God help me, as Mom would say, I broke up with David.

In the fall of 1982, I moved to Boston for graduate school. While I might have been forging a lonely path, I thought I could control my fate.

As an intern in the Developmental Evaluation Clinic at the Boston Children's Hospital, I attended Friday afternoon lectures on every birth defect known to man. From those lectures I struggled to construct my own philosophy of birth and illness, childhood and death. On Friday nights, if my roommates had dates and I was alone, I called my mother, almost in tears. Disease was a scary business, especially on Friday nights.

I couldn't admit to Mom that I was lonely. Instead, I would throw tough moral questions at her. "Mom," I said in one such phone call, "have you ever heard of Tay–Sachs disease?"

"Tay who?"

"Babies, Mom. Mostly Jewish babies. They're born with a genetic disease that will kill them."

"Really?" she said. I heard her gulp. Was that a martini or fright? "Well, what's the cure?"

"None. No cure. They die. It's a painful death, and they die in their infancy."

Silence.

"You there?"

"I can't hear this," she said in a whisper. "It's awful."

"It is awful. They die, Mom. But doctors can detect this disease before the baby is born. Let's say you were the mother, would you abort?"

"No!"

"Mom, the baby is going to die." I hear in my voice that I've gone beyond the hypothetical issue, but I can't stop myself. "*Your* baby is going to know nothing but pain. And you're telling me you won't abort?"

"Listen to me," she said in a raspy voice. "You have got to get out of there. Why are you doing this? What is happening to you?"

I started sobbing.

"Oh, no," she said. "Another kid in tears. Why do we let you kids go away? You all get homesick. I can't help you when you're so far away. Look, just come home. Forget that stuff."

I took a deep breath. "I'm okay," I said. "It's been a long week. I'm just tired."

By my twenty-second birthday I was one month into school and reading articles on social stigma and disability in my bedroom, where I felt as if I was living in a futuristic horror film. Every article validated a truth about my situation that I'd only vaguely acknowledged. Now I took each paper as evidence of an entire world with false notions about people like me. I saw myself as helpless in the face of those beliefs. Between my classes, my internship, and my part-time job as a sales clerk in a clothing store, I had no time to write fiction or poetry anymore.

The doorbell rang, and seconds later my roommate knocked on my bedroom door. She handed me an arrangement of fall flowers with a subscription to *The Atlantic*. The card read: "For my writer. Love, David."

"Oh, no," I said.

"What's wrong? I just handed you flowers," said my roommate. "Looks like he has good taste, too."

"No one knows that better than I do," I said, but inside I called myself a liar. I had to admit that David was perfect for me in every way but one. He suffered from loving me. That I could not appreciate love from a man was not a good sign—and a greater threat than my paranoia over the flyer from the Disabled Students' Union—but there was so much to sort out about motherhood and disability. Boyfriends now seemed a simple hurdle in comparison.

I was equally vexed by David's reference to writing. Writing was my one unconditional love, and I'd let it go as well. For weeks after that night, I debated whether I should switch to an MFA program instead. Every evening I'd step from the trolley on the corner of Harvard and Commonwealth and think, "How would I support myself as a writer?" Halfway home I would decide, "Journalism school." Before I reached the stoop of my apartment building I would be facing dozens of reasons why I would never be hired.

Until now I'd had almost no connection to disability, mentally or emotionally, but it dictated much of my life. If I did not learn as much as I could about something so crucial to my existence, I would remain at its mercy. I had to prove to myself that I could earn a living. The vast majority of journalists in 1982 were men, and to earn a living at writing I'd need to be working for a newspaper or magazine. Women complained about how difficult things were for them, but a woman with a disability writing for a newspaper? Or a fashion magazine? I hadn't actually sought interviews, but my instincts told me to forget those jobs. Given that I generally did not back down from trying things, I had to listen to my gut.

Then I read a study by Robert Kleck, of Dartmouth. He found that in the presence of amputees, able-bodied people stood at a greater than customary distance and even manifested symptoms of panic. For me, this information validated years of fighting an invisible wall during some of the simplest transactions with strangers.

I'd seen fear on their faces when I was swimming, because I wasn't wearing legs.

Maybe this is why people with missing limbs often end up on the streets. How does someone who evokes such fear get hired? Artificial legs in 1982 cost about $10,000 per limb without insurance, and legs need to be replaced every few years. By 2002, they would cost $75,000 without insurance, and $85,000 by 2012. People with amputations may not be able to afford prosthetics, but worse, they are less likely to get a job if they don't have them. That becomes a vicious cycle. Now that I knew this, it seemed selfish of me to contemplate fiction. As I saw it, I owed it to people who were not as lucky as I was to advocate for them.

Fortunately I had roommates, Tish and Donna, who periodically shook me from my monologue of sobering disability facts. Tish, who was studying social work, giggled in a teenager's voice and had a teensy flower tattooed inside her wrist right at the place where you dab perfume. Cursing and laughing the whole way, she would plow her ancient car through mounds of snow. I'd never met anyone so energetic, and yet she often chose inertia as the topic of her papers. Donna was an ICU nurse who grew up in Newton and graduated from Boston College. Another Catholic girl with about ten siblings, Donna understood what it meant to be part of a huge clan. Neither woman dismissed my heated diatribes on disability research. In most cases they validated my conclusions. But they also let me know that I needed to ease up a bit.

Together we escaped to the islands. We spent a spring break in Tish's father's seventeenth-century farmhouse without electricity on Block Island, where we slept by the woodstove at night and scaled the jade hills on Tish's dirt bike by day. In the summer we visited her mother and stepfather on Nantucket. Although I thought it unusual that Tish and her sisters had several homes to stay in—a historic house in town and several by their mother on the coastal cliffs—I never inquired about their family's good fortune. Mostly I relished the remote beach that Tish drove us to, with its sand soft as flour, where we swam topless in a secluded cove. By the end of the summer I felt almost like my old self.

After Tish's sisters backed out on a trip to Jamaica the next Christmas, her stepfather, Walter, flew me down in their place. Years later, I would hear a man on NPR talk about being one of the few black men living on Nantucket and how Walter Beinecke was the only person to give him a job. "Walter," I said, turning up the radio. "Tish's Walter Beinecke?" I hadn't known in my twenties that Tish's stepfather was famous for his philanthropy, not only in the restoration of buildings and industry on Nantucket but for his family's endowment of the Beinecke Library at Yale University.

My life might have been hurling toward tragedy, but it was offering me a seat in first class.

CHAPTER 20

The Gravedigger's Granddaughter

In my second year at Boston University, I interned on a spinal cord unit. Patients there had flown from motorcycles into stone walls, skied into trees, or dived into unexpectedly shallow waters. These folks faced similar or even tougher questions than the ones I'd been pondering for the past two decades. On top of that, they had to confront theirs all at once. My supervisor explained how I fit in on the ward: "Upstairs the beds are filled with bikers, skiers, athletes *your* age, almost every one of them male, and they are now in wheelchairs. You're twenty-three, a woman, *and* you have a disability. Up there, you're a walking Rorschach."

The first question patients asked their physicians was usually "Will I walk?" The answer was generally no. The second question was "What about sex?" The good news was that sex was a viable option for most. Psychologists and interns did whatever it took to get talks about the future going, so as to reduce the possibility of patients grieving in the isolation of their homes after discharge.

Physical and occupational therapists would complain, "Why do you want to bum this guy out? Last week he was feeding and dressing himself; this week he's cocooning." (The term "cocooning" meant that a patient pulled the sheets over his head and refused treatment.) Inpatient rehab was limited to three months, so a cocoon made a safe house to survive the psychological trauma of the injury during that time. Based on my own experience with grief and disability, I could see why a person needed to insulate himself before facing a life that required so much effort just to survive.

Because rehab works best with creative talent at the wheel, the psychologists on my unit offered a workshop called Sexual Attitude Reassessment. These workshops included porn fests, encounter groups, and frank discussions about sex. It was heartening to see that beyond the unit there was a thriving community of folks in wheelchairs. At the end of the year I joined the Boston Self-Help Center so that I might contribute and learn from others about advocating for the rights of people with disabilities.

The intensity of this work took its toll, but it forced me to follow Tish's advice. She'd warned me that mental health workers should undergo psychotherapy themselves. I had asked for a referral from my supervisor when I was at Children's Hospital. For the past year, I'd been rising at dawn to take a bus to the corner of Harvard and Longwood, where I saw a psychologist named Joel, who worked and lived just blocks from the hospitals. Joel, my Freud, smoked a pipe while I told him about my losses: Frankie's death, Mom's hospitalizations, other details of my childhood, and leaving David without understanding why my feelings for him had evaporated. Eventually I would have to face the pain I'd inflicted on others.

It was late in the summer when Joel greeted me as usual at the door to his apartment. I hurried past him into his office. Before he could light his pipe, I launched in. I'd met a guy who asked for my number at a party and never called, though I later ran into the same guy on a beach thirty minutes away. "And I didn't have my legs on," I said, checking for Joel's astonished reaction.

He only nodded.

"My friend and I were trespassing. It was a private beach on the

North Shore." I glanced up at Joel's degrees. My Freud had gone to school in Texas? "We were basically in this guy's backyard," I added.

"Mmm." He lit the pipe.

"He took us sailing."

"Yes?"

"Yes! And I didn't have my legs on because we were swimming. Did I mention that?"

"He must have thought you were a mermaid."

"Mermaid?" My heart quickened.

"Like in that movie—"

"With Tom Hanks. Yes," I said. "I'm a mermaid. I'm a mermaid who washed up on the beach. Maybe he saw me that way." I left that session in a daze. The city was alive with summer, which is Boston at its best. The schools are out, the beaches are nearby. Down at the harbor, the sea salts the air. On Harvard Avenue in Brookline, the scent is of onion bagels baking.

Late in the fall, as I came from the bus stop, I saw why I had been referred to Joel by my supervisor at Children's Hospital. A girl not more than eight years old came out of Joel's building on crutches, her body twisted with a muscular or neurological disorder that looked painful. But she was smiling as her mother pulled up to the curb. Lucky her, I thought. What I could have accomplished with Joel when I was eight!

So much was coming together for me at the time that I couldn't shut my brain off. There was wonder in everything. And, oh, did I talk. If I wasn't reading, I was talking. Sometimes I was talking as I read. Other than papers and notes in charts, I had stopped writing. But that was okay, because words moved straight from my head to my tongue, completely unedited. Free association, this was what I was learning, and it was the result of beginning psychotherapy on top of having two separate hours of analytic supervision weekly. The freedom was such a relief that I didn't care if I talked too much. In our group supervision, a different intern was reduced to wailing in each session. Sometimes our leaders sobbed. This was Boston in the eighties; self-analysis ruled, but equal opportunity mattered as well.

One morning, I looked up from a chart to find a group of medical students on rounds. A face in the crowd smiled at me. The next day, this same young man stepped onto the campus shuttle and walked right to my seat. Because of my chatty nature, it wasn't hard for him to strike up a conversation. His name was Daniel. We quickly discovered two obstacles to dating. For him, there was a family obligation to date only within the Conservative Jewish faith; for me, it was an impossible match because Daniel had been offered an internship in Cincinnati. Even during my loneliest moments in Boston, I could see that my time in Cincinnati was behind me.

In our short time together, Daniel listened while I gave him the rundown on my life, not to mention the ever expanding list of papers I would one day write. I had never met anyone so patient. One spring afternoon, after a walk through Back Bay, we rested on my futon in the sunlight.

Daniel asked, "Why don't you move back to Cincinnati? I'll be there. Your family is there."

"I can't go back."

"Why not?"

I tried to conjure an analogy for my feelings. "Imagine growing up in a town where everyone was exceptionally good at keeping secrets—that is, keeping secrets from the one person who really needed to know them, and that person was you." I rolled onto my stomach and rested my chin on my fists so I could look into his pale blue eyes, just one of his calming influences. "You know the classic tale about the bastard son, the only one in town who doesn't know which man is his father?"

"Sure," he said with a hearty nod. Then cautiously he asked, "Is this . . . does this have anything to do with thalidomide?"

I dropped my forehead. Why couldn't I talk this freely with everyone about the t-word? "Yes!"

"I think I understand the problem."

It turned out that Daniel's father, a physician in Los Angeles, knew someone who was an expert on thalidomide. He referred Daniel to a book written by a task force connected to the London *Times*. Daniel found it in the library and brought the book straight to my apartment. I recoiled when I saw the title: *Suffer the Children: the Story of Thalidomide*.

"Oh, please," I said.

"Just read it. Those are nothing but words on a page. Do you have to talk about everything? You talk about sex all day in that job. Just have sex. You talk about papers. Just write them. But thalidomide . . . well, just read it." He tossed the book on my bed. "I want you to finish that book by the end of the week." And from the hallway he said, "Start now. I'll let myself out."

I sat on my bed and opened the book. There weren't any pictures of the victims. If it had contained those exploitative photos, I wouldn't have read it. At that time, my only knowledge of thalidomide came from tabloid stories, some with tragic and some with happy endings, in which the "thalidomide baby" or "victim" was so stereotyped that I never believed them. This book was not invested in sensationalism; it was about the cover-up. Until then I hadn't known there was one.

By early afternoon the air had grown stagnant around me, but I was too engrossed to open a window. The book explained that the wife of a German lawyer named Karl Schulte-Hillen gave birth to a child with missing limbs shortly after Karl's sister's child was born with missing limbs. The lawyer looked into genetic causes and found no clues. After he checked around, it became clear that there was a rise of birth defects occurring in Germany. His wife recalled that she had taken a sedative in the first trimester of her pregnancy after her father died. Karl reported what he knew to Dr. Widukind Lenz, who began to investigate. Simultaneously, a physician named McBride in Australia was looking into an increase in birth defects there.

The eventual discovery of thalidomide's toxic effects on the fetus occurred three to four years after the drug was put on the market in Germany and two years after I was born. I knew that Mom was pregnant when she went to Germany in 1960. What I had never known was that Richardson–Merrell, a *Cincinnati-based* company, supposedly handed out over two million tablets of thalidomide to US physicians beginning in 1959, after signing a contract with the German manufacturers, Grünenthal. The book claimed that Richardson–Merrell had failed to report side effects from animal studies, and that they had distributed thalidomide to more than 1,200 physicians throughout the US while they were applying for FDA approval. An estimated 20,000 women in the US were given thalidomide on routine office visits, in many cases without consent forms being given to them. This last information came from a legal deposition. Years later, these findings would be republished in a book called *Dark Remedy: The Impact of Thalidomide and its Revival as a Vital Medicine*, by Rock Brynner and Trent Stephens.

The excerpt from the deposition was the first place I saw the name of Dr. Ray Nulsen. The authors of *Suffer the Children* suggested that Dr. Nulsen had been chosen for a special role in the study because he had been in a fraternity at the University of Cincinnati with Don Merrell. Dr. Nulsen's role was to enlist physicians to hand out thalidomide, convincing them that the drug was well-researched and so safe that there was no need to document any side effects. That information was included in the second book, as well as in a third book titled *Hooked: Ethics, the Medical Profession, and the Pharmaceutical Industry* by Howard Brody, MD. In the deposition, Dr. Nulsen admitted to keeping poor records of the drug's dispensation; his secretary's records were later proven to be inaccurate as well. Dr. Nulsen's secretary testified that she would put tablets in unmarked envelopes in the mailbox, to be picked up by women after office hours. The tablets were not yet named.

What I learned next was mentioned in all three books. Using Dr. Nulsen's name, a Richardson–Merrell executive attempted to publish an article in the *American Journal of Obstetrics and Gynecology*, intended to prove the efficacy of thalidomide in the treatment of insomnia during pregnancy. This was part of a move to push for the approval of thalidomide for expectant mothers. The journal's editor questioned the findings.

Dr. Nulsen himself would deliver at least three living babies with severe side effects from thalidomide and two stillbirths, one without arms and legs, according to both the *Times* writers and the *Dark Remedy* team. Yet he testified in 1964, according to the *Times* task force, that he did not deliver any child with thalidomide-related deformities. Throughout this time, Frances Kelsey, the director of the FDA, was unimpressed by Richardson–Merrell's application, and was requesting more clinical data. She also raised doubts about the safety of thalidomide during pregnancy.

Eventually the Australian physician, Dr. McBride, wrote a letter to the British medical journal *The Lancet*, inquiring about an increase in birth defects. The link to thalidomide was soon revealed. Shortly after that, the US clinical trials were shut down.

In the US, the number of thalidomide-related birth defects is estimated at as few as seventeen and as many as forty. Who can say how many people may have been affected but are not included in the reports? Was I one of those people? The effects of thalidomide are so diverse that they were difficult to identify in the early days of diagnosis. The drug has been said to cause heart irregularities, blindness, deafness, mental retardation, facial disfigurement, genital deformities, and a host of limb malformations. Its precise effect depends on the timing of its interference in the development of the fetus. The hallmark characteristic was the flipper-like limb, which I did not have—raising my own doubt about whether my mother had taken thalidomide. If she had taken it, in the grand scheme of things I was lucky. My injuries were minimal in contrast to others.

Now I had another problem, the issue of a lawsuit. The lawsuits, as described in *Suffer the Children* and *Dark Remedy*, were horrendous affairs. Individuals went up against major drug companies. US suits had favored the plaintiffs, but only after lengthy and demoralizing battles in court. The account of a California case raised the issue of the statute of limitations, which in that case ran out in 1971, just nine years after the child was born and five years after the parent had figured out that thalidomide was involved. At twenty-three, I assumed that the statute of limitations had long since passed for me.

Nothing could prepare me for the chapter on some of the families' reactions. I read that one mother tried to suffocate a severely disfigured baby in the hospital. A British couple murdered their infant; they were acquitted before a jammed courtroom. The crowd applauded that decision. Husbands left their wives, blaming them for the misfortune. Some parents committed suicide. I'd heard from the sadder versions of tabloid stories about "thalidomide children" who had no hope of being adopted. Here again, I had to admit that in contrast I was lucky. I did not feel lucky, though. I'd just been pummeled by facts that would never be substantiated by my only firsthand witness, my mother.

CHAPTER 21

One Door Slams, Another Opens

S leep failed me for several nights after I read about thalidomide. My father might have offered up the truth about my birth—if he knew the truth—if I were to ask him straight out. But he was seriously ill. Doctors were running tests to determine the cause of his endless fatigue.

With Frank gone and Dad ill, my relationship with Ted had become crucial. Unfortunately, he was studying in England that year. Now more than ever, I needed someone in my family to understand my fears as well as my disillusionment. Bridget lived nearby, and part of my reason for choosing to move to Boston was that I longed for a relationship with an older sister like her. She had been born ten years before me so I didn't know her well, but I knew her to be gentle. Bridget had grown up with younger parents and more structure. As I saw it, she'd never had to defend herself in a brawl, nor had she been embroiled in one of our sessions of taunting and ridiculing one another. That kind of behavior seemed foreign to Bridget's upbringing. To me, it wasn't that Bridget was better than the rest of us, but she had been better off.

People in the family always said that Bridget took after Dad and Katie, which meant that she tended to keep her thoughts to herself. That was an asset. I felt that I was utterly incapable of editing myself before I opened my mouth. During the tumultuous years between our mother's hospitalizations, Bridget had been away at college or married and living up north. I suspect that she'd felt ambivalent about having moved away, because her eyes misted at every family gathering when one of the "babies" mentioned an event that she'd missed. Bridget loved family—ours, hers—and like Katie, she focused almost entirely on its good parts.

When I had first moved to Boston, Bridget would talk with me about my studies and even about the issue of disability. This was a topic I'd never been able to share with a sibling, except lately in letters to Ted. By now it was clear to me that Ted and I shared a similar narrative about our family. We loved our family but we saw its problems.

Living in Boston, I was able to spend weekends with Bridget's family. I adored her children. I loved seeing Bridget as a young mother. It brought the best memories of my own childhood back to me. When her eldest daughter, at six, danced to "Let's Get Physical," I couldn't help but see Liz and Rosa doing one of their Barbra Streisand acts, only now the girl sang in a Boston accent, "Lemme heah ya body talk . . ."

Earlier that year we were swimming in Bridget's backyard when her three-year-old son came out the back door waving his light saber. I had just come from the pool without my legs on when he pointed his light saber at me and asked in his Darth Vader voice, "Who destroyed you?" Bridget blushed, and I laughed. Here was a three-year-old who looked up to Darth Vader. Like Captain Ahab, Darth was a "gimp with a grudge." This was an ideal opening, so I told my sister about Kleck's research on amputees, which explained why Darth Vader was such a fearful character. I would have preferred to be direct and tell her about my own experiences, as well as what I had learned about thalidomide, but I was intimidated by her restraint. This time, however, her blue eyes grew glassy with tears. She described the awful experience of strangers staring at me wherever we went. That was in the days before I could walk with prosthetic legs.

I squeezed my eyes shut; someone in my family understood.

Then she gasped and tightened her knees against her chest. For a second, her typically stoic expression splintered, and I realized that *she* had felt under scrutiny. After that, I was afraid to bring the topic up again.

Adding to this awkwardness with Bridget was a rift with Liz, which had been expanding since my first weeks in Boston. The problem started when a friend from Cincinnati mentioned that she thought Liz had been gloating to our mutual friends about charging things on Dad's credit cards and signing my name on the bills. I should have dismissed this immediately. It was coming second-hand. My friend might have mixed it up, or Liz might have been talking about something that had happened years ago. Aside from that, Dad never complained about the charges on his credit cards. He must have figured there were too many charges coming from so many children that it wasn't worth chasing them down, and for the most part we acted responsibly when we charged things. But this story nagged at me. After all, I was struggling to make my own way. The other girls in our family had married soon after college with no plans for long-term careers and I didn't want Dad to think I expected him to take care of me forever.

The mature thing to do, I decided, was to wait and take it up with Liz in person, over my Christmas break. Admittedly, I worried that maybe I was just putting off the confrontation. Deep down I didn't believe I could stand up to her. I'd let myself be manipulated by some of my siblings so often that if I didn't say anything it would never stop happening.

Maybe there are some things we should not take on, and for me, that thing was Liz. I was incapable of summoning my courage while at the same time modulating my anger. I had too many memories of Liz taunting me or slapping me in front of my friends, of feeling defenseless and demoralized. In fact, my efforts to stand up to Liz thus far had been so laughable that they only proved her point: I became Pinocchio Gone Wild.

On Christmas Eve, when Liz and I were upstairs in my parents' house, I realized that I might never have a moment alone with her again, so I opened my mouth and my anger spilled out in the worst possible way: "Liz, you cold-hearted bitch." Before I could say any more, she burst into tears and ran out of the house, her husband at her heels. I chased after her to explain, but she was too quick. And that was when Rosa raced up the stairs, blocking me and saying, "Why did you just attack Liz?"

This was the third Christmas I'd ruined. At four, I cried during the vacation movie. At twenty-one, the sibling with an alcohol problem whispered to me on Christmas Eve, "Help me. I'm dying. Pleeeeease help me," which led to my screaming, "HELP! Somebody get help!" Although our sibling began recovery the next day and has since lived a healthier life, my reputation suffered from the outburst. At twenty-one, I'd become the quixotic "I-lean." By now I heard the negative version of my name in the voices of my older sisters as well as my mother. Not only was I the wettest blanket any party could possibly include, but I was on my way to earning the identity "Snarleen."

Now, just as in the other fiascos, no one asked me why I had exploded at Liz. She was well-liked within the family and was Mom's favorite antiquing buddy. She was the very opposite of Snarleen. While Liz donned the Barbara Bush pearls, I took on Rosie the Riveter's fisted pose. I might have asked Ted to defend me, but his endorsement would probably do me in altogether because, after all, Ted was "the devil himself," a tag that he laughed at from the depths of his belly. Given my snarly nature, I could have used some of Ted's cast-iron stomach.

Dad was the only adult who supported me after Liz left the house. When I holed up in Nina's bedroom, sobbing, he came upstairs and said, "I don't know what you said to Liz, but I'll bet she had it coming to her."

I've asked myself hundreds of times since then why I did not just tell him what had happened, but I didn't want to betray Liz. I thought it was between the two of us.

"Why don't you just call her tomorrow and apologize?" Dad innocently suggested. "Put an end to this thing."

I called the next day, but Liz's husband told me that Liz couldn't talk. I flew back to Boston, confused and feeling as if my tongue had been removed clandestinely while I was under anesthesia.

Weeks later, Liz called me, likely at Dad's urging, to say she wanted to come for a visit.

"Great!" I said, nervous but looking forward to talking this out. She said she was coming into town on a Friday. I had class, so I suggested she take a cab to the Prudential Center and I'd meet her at the bar.

When the day arrived, I was both eager and terrified to see Liz. She called from an airport bar, upset because she was delayed in Newark. That evening, I found her at the Prudential Center, glamorous in a miniskirt with a cropped sweater. The restaurant manager had been pouring her drinks while they chatted. I think he'd even offered her a job as his assistant manager.

As we hugged, her muscles tightened beneath her sweater. Of all the daughters, Liz looked the most like Mom, with high cheekbones and dark, dramatic features, except that Liz's green eyes lent her a savvier façade than Mom's hush-puppy eyes gave Mom. Finding so much of our mother in Liz's face now made me aware of her vulnerability. Our talk was probably weighing on her. Liz hated social awkwardness. This trait, and possibly only this trait, was where I had excelled as a child in contrast to Liz. I had no fear in the face of awkward situations. Already I'd lost a foot, midstep, as I came off the trolley in Boston, and I'd had to ask a strange man to help me cross Commonwealth Avenue to get to my job. He ended up hoisting me over his shoulder like a sack of potatoes. And that was the least scary of my "lost foot" adventures. Liz had never had to cope with such indignity and vulnerability on a routine basis. I stored those situations close to my heart, saving them for cocktail parties, where they made me the belle of the ball. I had reached a place where I knew many women who respected me for it. That had made all the difference in bolstering my self-esteem. As long as I'd known Liz, she had worked hard to polish herself. She was a middle child looking for her own way to shine. I could hardly blame her for that.

Once again, she was throwing me a curve ball. Now she was boasting to this manager, "We serve four, five hundred a night. And it's a four-star restaurant." Was this a bolder Liz?

"Should we get a table?" I asked, pushing myself between her and the manager.

She shook her head. "Listen, I gotta go to bed," she said. Then she looked me in the eye for the first time that evening and said, "I'm loaded."

I sighed and led the way down to the street. In the cab, we sat close to each other. With the exception of Frank's funeral, I had not seen her looking this forlorn since I was five and she was seven years old. We had been playing in my friend Penny's backyard when Penny's mother called her in and said she could invite only one friend into the house. "I'm sorry, but you'll have to choose." Penny chose me. I squiddled past Liz so torn up that I leapt onto Penny's sofa and stared out the window at my sister for what seemed like hours. She had dropped to her knees, staring ahead, her face so impassive that I couldn't tell if she was crying.

Now I wanted to scoop her into my arms and hug her, but I had too many years of losing to her. When we were children, she had often led the charge to race up the stairs. It would be dark in the basement and after the others reached the top, someone would close the door and lean against it. I was not a stoic loser. I'd scream from the dark basement until someone opened the door. At twenty-three, I still had not outgrown my fear of being left behind.

As I opened the door to my apartment, with its cheap furniture, bamboo shades, and faux-wood paneling, she said, "Oh," and stepped back.

"You mean I gotta sleep on that thing?" She pointed at the musty sofa.

"Yep," I said on my way back to my room, shocked at myself for not volunteering my own bed.

In the morning, over coffee, Liz said, "We're going to Bridget's, right? How do we get there?"

I was unprepared for this shift in plans. "Don't you want to see the city first?"

"I've seen it before. Let's call Bridget."

I had to stifle a moan. "But I thought you came here to see me."

"Bridget lives here too, you know."

I might have pressed for our conversation then, but I still believed that my every need boiled down to a selfish request.

Liz looked terrified and hung over, her hands trembling as she hinted that I was holding her hostage in my ramshackle apartment. I wanted to hug her—well, slap her then hug her—but I needed her to have the upper hand. I don't think I could have handled it if she had broken down and said she resented growing up with a crippled little sister. On the other hand, if she believed, like Mom, that "baby Jesus chose me to carry the cross," why had she never thanked me for carrying it for her?

On the train out to the suburbs, she wore dark sunglasses. Angry as I'd become, I also felt sorry for her. She might have mastered her fear of strangers, but she had not mastered her fear of me.

As she rested her forehead against the windowpane, I imagined that she hoped to numb her hangover against the cool vibrating glass. I'd done it myself on dozens of subways.

We never did have our talk. Throughout the rest of the weekend Liz and Bridget went antique shopping, while I lagged behind. It might have been my imagination, but by the time we dropped Liz at the airport on Sunday, I could have sworn that Bridget had begun to show signs of frostiness toward me.

A year later, I called Rosa, who was pregnant for the first time. She had been inviting me to visit her in California for months. Until then, I had viewed Rosa as nothing if not direct. Perhaps she would share with me what Liz was saying about her trip to Boston. I hoped she would employ that authoritative voice of hers to influence Liz to at least listen to my point of view.

When I called to schedule my visit, Rosa told me she'd changed her mind. I shouldn't come because I did things to people. "Like what?" I asked. She pointed to the Christmas Eve when I went off on Liz, which struck me as odd coming from Rosa, who had more than once coached Liz on how to taunt me.

What was even more confusing was that Rosa had been encouraging me to stand up for myself. I might have told myself at this exact moment what Mom had been telling me as a child when I cried to her about Liz and Rosa: "That's just girls, I-lean. Get used to it."

Instead I shrieked, "You've gotta be kidding me! You kept telling me that I should stand up to Liz!"

Rosa told me she had no idea what I was talking about and hung up the phone.

The next day I heard from Mom, who asked what the heck I had done to Rosa. "She's so upset. Honestly, I-lean! I don't know what's gotten into you."

I'd read about families who had broken up over thalidomide, and I wondered if these explosions in my family weren't a delayed reaction to my talking about my disability, trying to find out what caused it, and standing up for myself. As I saw it, I could never go back to being the girl I'd been in Ohio. That girl had tried to kill herself. Maybe she had been more successful in doing so than I'd ever imagined. A new woman had replaced her.

I decided to go home over spring break, since I would not be going to California. For some reason, I had an idea that everyone in my family had changed along with me, that suddenly we were a family who talked through our problems. Also, I wanted to see Dad. The news of his illness was only getting worse.

At home, I kept putting off my plans to talk with Mom. There were problems with Dad's kidneys and more tests to be run. I was nervous for Dad, for myself, and, on top of everything else, it had not been long since I'd learned things about thalidomide that I'd never wanted to know but needed to find out. If I didn't ask Mom my questions, I would spend more sleepless nights back in Boston.

On my penultimate day in Cincinnati, I found myself alone with Mom in the kitchen. "Mom," I said, "I want you to understand that I would never blame you if you took thalidomide. You couldn't have known what it would do. No one did. But I have to ask you this before I leave. Did you take thalidomide?" Her eye twitched and she stepped away from me. "I never took that drug!" she boomed. She backed away again, banged her head into the phone on the wall, and glared at me as if I were wielding an axe.

"Mom," I pleaded. "I need to know this if I'm going to have kids."

"We get the kids we get!" She threw up her arms.

"Please stop yelling," I whispered, self-conscious.

"I told you I loved you the minute the doctor handed you to me! Stop badgering me. You're just upset because you're alone. If you had kids of your own, you'd know that!" She left the room, raising a fist to the sky and muttering through clenched teeth, "Why you want to do this instead I'll never understand! You sow what you reap, I-lean!"

Alternately ashamed and angry, I didn't even catch the fact that she'd turned the proverb around. How can you sow what you reap? If this had been Ted's argument with Mom, he would have laughed in her face and by dinner the conversation would have become a story with Mom laughing until she cried.

I could have gone upstairs to share some of this with Nina, but she was only seventeen. She and Liz were the last daughters left in town, and I worried that she would buy into the notion that I'd become intolerably negative. Nina's lovely disposition had deepened. With her black hair and white skin, she could have worn a tiara and called herself Snow White. Nominated for homecoming queen, May fete queen, and prom queen, she lost all three elections. She laughed heartily when Mom called her "the triple crown loser." Who could be upset with Nina? But I couldn't rely on a teenager for the kind of support I needed.

The next morning, Mom and I stood at my gate in the airport, both at a loss for words, until she said, "Are you sure you want to go back to that school? You used to laugh."

"I'm happy," I snapped.

"You know," she said calmly, "men don't like intelligent women. Your father might not tell you that, but I know how he thinks. It's not good for you being in school so long. At some point you have to grow up."

I got on the plane and worried that she was right.

In the spring of 1984, my parents came to town for my graduation despite the fact that Dad was on dialysis. His face swollen from steroids, his fingers trembling, he drove a Volkswagen bus, stopping at antique shops along a five-hundred-mile trek. He'd refused to accept a donor kidney from one of us, and was on the waiting list for an anonymous donation.

At the end of a weekend spent at Bridget's house, Dad dropped me off in town. After he pulled up to the curb, there was an awkward silence. Dad bit his bottom lip and stared straight ahead, which I took to mean that he was in a hurry. I said goodbye and hopped out. As I reached in for my overnight bag, he asked, "Eileen?"

"Yeah?"

His eyes darted from the road over to me, but only for a second. "Honey, I'm proud of you."

"Really?" My voice cracked.

"Okay," he said, pulling away before I could thank him.

As I watched him drive off I worried about him.

Since I would be consulting in three states for my first job in rehab, I bought a car, a white VW Rabbit. Then I went to the Boston Registry of Motor Vehicles to get a Massachusetts driver's license. I was waiting in line after handing in my current license when a police officer motioned to me and said, "Come hee-ah." I followed him into a lunch room, where about four officers were sitting around a table. "What's the problem?" I asked, panicked.

"We was gonna ask you the same," said one of the officers.

"Whaddaya mean?" I tried to sound indignant. By now I knew that only the loudest and most infuriated drivers were taken seriously in this town.

"What's this restriction about an ahtificial limb to drive a caaah. It's on this license you got from," said another officer, "from where?"

"O-hi-o," said the first officer.

"O-hi-o?" the other repeated.

"Yes," I said. "And that's not a restriction. It just indicates that I drive with my left foot."

"What's wrong wich yah right?"

"I don't have one."

"What about yah left?" asked the first. He pointed to my below-knee leg. I was wearing a skirt with opaque hose that barely covered the screws at my knee.

"It has a knee," I said.

"A knee!" said another, clutching his skull. "Jesus."

"Look," said the first. "They might issue licenses to you folks in O-hi-o, but hee-ah it's different."

"I don't think so," I said, surprising myself. "I have a pedal on the left side. It's made for *folks like me* so we can drive. Legally. I've been driving for seven years. I don't think you're allowed to do this to me. I'll have to get a lawyer. Lucky for me Boston has a very active community for disabled people's rights. You know those people in wheelchairs who picket restaurants and movie theaters? I do. They will sit in your parking lot with protest signs because you can't take someone out of a line who has committed no violation and deny them a license. We do not have people in wheelchairs picketing in O-hi-o, but you are more progressive in Boston."

"We ah, ahn't we?" said one of them, patting his stomach in a satisfied manner.

"That you are," I said, and from there we cut a deal: I could have a license but only if I took handicapped plates. "If I have to," I said. In my license photograph my eyes are leaden, although it's not a bad poker face.

Emboldened by my recent success, I wanted more. My father was seriously ill and might die before his name came up on the kidney donor's list. Anyone could see that he loved us, but he'd never said those words to me. So I wrote a letter and asked him.

For the next month, I raced to my apartment every evening and found no response. Then the day came when I pushed open the door to find an envelope on the telephone table. Dad's Volkswagen logo was on it, my name in his handwriting. Too anxious to take off my coat, I rushed in and opened the letter. My hands shook as I read and reread my father's words, not able to make sense of them. In fact, they were quite plain:

Dear Eileen,

God blessed us with 11 wonderful human beings whom I love beyond anything on earth. My life is you, so please don't doubt my love and devotion . . . You have never done one thing that didn't make me proud and happy to have the privilege to be your father . . . You have an admirable quality in that you want answers for yourself . . . I've never felt I had to have answers . . .

"But do you love me?" I said out loud. Where were those three words written? As I read it at the time, the letter was full of interference from God, my siblings, my mother. Finally I put it back in its envelope and placed it in my dresser drawer.

I tried not to think about why it had taken him a month to write that he loved all of his children. My mind wouldn't let go: he did have kidney failure, maybe he wanted to choose his words carefully, but does every father need a month to choose his words when his daughter asks if he loves her?

I still lacked the assurance that I belonged in my family. Because I had grown up to be so independent, I worried that I might not fit into any family. My desire for a sense of belonging competed constantly with my will to conquer that need. Then Ted showed up at my doorstep, a friend at his back, and my world opened up again.

CHAPTER 22

Orphans and Ophelias

A s a child, I didn't want to associate with Ted. My reputation within the family was bad enough, and Ted, from infancy, was notorious for his bad temper. As a toddler, he terrified nurses during a bout of dehydration by rattling the bars of his crib as if ready to bust out of jail. We siblings mocked him right down to his smelly feet, which were a dead giveaway in every game of hide and seek. "Come outta that closet, Odie," we'd say. "I can smell you from here."

Everyone dumped on Ted, and still his ego was gargantuan. He grew tall, dark, and as entitled as an Ottoman sultan. When he was eight and I was ten, he tied me to the basketball pole with a jump rope and swatted me with a Wiffle-Ball bat. I couldn't understand why he would do that. At the time, I assumed he was showing off in front of Frankie's friends. Later I told Frank, and we hatched a plan for payback.

One day after school, while Ted scarfed down his third peanut butter and jelly sandwich, Frankie and I shoved him into the bathroom and pulled hard on the knob to lock him inside. Ted pounded and threatened to throw himself down the laundry chute. "I'll kill myself!" he screamed. We figured he had about four feet of laundry to pad the fall. "Try it," we said, anxious to see the result. The drop was only one floor. When he stopped pounding we opened the door, but he was gone. Inside the chute, we found Ted jammed between the basement and first floor, his arms wedged against his hips. "I'm stuck," he lisped through the gaps in his teeth. At first we closed the chute and left him there. Then, worried what Mom might do—not to us, but to Ted—we pushed him.

Mom had this thing about Ted. She was forever chasing him out of the house with a broom, slamming the back door when she couldn't catch up to him for a swat, and yelling, "Don't come back until dinner . . . second thought, until bedtime!" Once he tumbled from her unlocked hatchback at a red light. Mom drove several blocks before she realized it. After that, Ted began to announce himself with a howl: "I'm the lone wolf. Aaaaoooooooo!" On the days when Mom kicked him out of the house, Ted ran straight to the window where she washed dishes, his grubby hands on his hips, a half inch of grit under nails he refused to cut, and taunted her: "Don't come back! Ever! Aaaaaoooooo." Sometimes she'd growl back at him or make an ugly face; often she'd laugh.

When Mom was hospitalized for the first time, Ted turned quiet for a while, so quiet he was not even sullen. That summer, the Taylor boys held a carnival in their backyard to raise money for charity. Ted and I decided to collect canned goods for a ring toss. He put me in a Red Flyer and dragged me door to door on steamy summer mornings. The mothers in our neighborhood opened up to find Ted in the tank suit he lived in all summer. His black eyes, fringed by thick lashes, called out to women. Down at the curb I stayed in the wagon, where I dangled my clunky legs over its rim.

"Got any canned food?" Ted would ask in a voice like Phyllis Diller's, but serious. The women stuffed us with cookies and milk, then loaded our wagon with cans.

In the year after Frank died, Ted shot up to six foot three. He grew his hair and bound it gypsy-style with a kerchief, always anxiously twisting a strand at his nape. At St. Xavier High School, he turned a pep rally into a rally for Communism. An irate priest slammed Ted against the bleachers and the incident got Ted elected as class president, although he hadn't run for the office.

The following year, Ted arrived on the Williams College campus in a stocking cap and thrift-store clothes. He introduced himself as "Pip" and led everyone to believe that he and his nine siblings were farm laborers back in Ohio. Perhaps he didn't mislead so much as allow the preconceptions to take over. He, or rather Pip, was given a column on the campus paper.

More recently, Ted had been living his vagabond dreams by hitchhiking through Europe after his junior year in England. When he ran out of money, he came home for the summer to sell cars, but mostly he pinned his poetry to the showroom walls. His poems amused Dad, even though the subtext was always a bash against capitalism. Ted felt bad for people buying cars they couldn't afford.

By the time he turned twenty-one, Ted was about the most ethical person I knew. Based on his morals and his position in the family— more or less orphan status—I decided that he could be trusted. Since the fiasco with my sisters, I'd become paranoid. Groupthink ruled among my siblings. Individuality was tantamount to moral depravity, but Ted derived a sense of wholeness from the contempt family members showed him. He had never expected to be "the one Jesus loved the most." He aspired to be the one whose neck Mom most often threatened to wring. I'd confided to him while he was in England about the rift separating me from the rest of the family. Back home, he promised to help my roommates and me move into a house in Newton before he headed back to Williams for his senior year. Already I felt better.

On a muggy Friday evening before Labor Day, the weekend of the fourth anniversary of Frank's death, I raced through my apartment after work to start boxing things up. Would Ted call to say that he couldn't fit this trip in after all? I reminded myself that Ted was not one to renege on a promise, nor was he one to plan a visit with Bridget and call me to have lunch on his last day in town. This was my status in the rest of the family: the one people squeezed in while visiting Bridget.

Long before Ted was due to arrive, I was cleaning the bathroom when the buzzer sounded. I opened the door and found two men instead of one, which made me self-conscious in my summer night-gown. Ted had not mentioned that he was bringing a friend, but I forgot all about that when he swept me up in a hug. He was thin under the mechanic's outfit that he'd probably lifted from Dad's service department—not that he knew anything about mechanics, but these were free duds. When he set me down, my attention turned to his friend. The guy looked to be about Ted's height, but with broader shoulders and what I would come to learn was a rugby player's physique. His half-smile was hokey in that *Risky Business* way that everyone was affecting in 1984.

"My buddy from X," said Ted, motioning at his friend. "Name's Tom."

"Tom?" I said, amused by my own association with Tom Cruise. His friend's green eyes scolded me, as if he knew what I was thinking. "Tom," I said soberly, before heading off to change out of my nightgown. "There's beer in the fridge," I said on my way to my room.

I came back in jeans and an Indian-print T-shirt. We went out to the balcony, which was more like a rusty fire escape over the alley, and spent about five minutes planning for the next morning. Moving day in Boston deserved at least ten minutes, but I was curious about other things.

"How did you get here so early?" I asked Ted, but it was Tom who explained that the used Microbus Ted had recently bought had engine trouble. "So we didn't stop at all, except for gas, then I push-started the bus."

"You must be hungry," I said.

"Had McDonald's," said Ted.

"But if you didn't stop—"

"Actually, Ted circled the parking lot while I jumped out the back door."

"Really?" I giggled.

"I had to toss the takeouts in the back, then I belly-flopped on the floor to get back in."

Ted squeezed his eyes shut and laughed silently at the thought of it, while Tom's eyes flicked toward me as if to seek my approval. I pressed my lips together and tried very hard not to laugh. Everything was so much more exciting when Ted was involved. His friend wandered inside to use the bathroom.

"I've never met Tom before. Why is he here?"

"He goes to school with me."

"Oh." Before I could ask another question, I saw Tom staring at me from inside the apartment. Embarrassed, I stopped talking and lowered my eyes. Tom's eyes seemed to linger briefly, or maybe I hoped so.

The next night, Tom and I wandered aimlessly along the empty streets of the financial district through a maze of darkened office buildings. We had walked out of a restaurant in Chinatown ahead of Ted and my roommates. Before I knew it, we were lost. I was tired and I'd had too much to drink. I kept asking, "How did we get here? Where's Ted?"

Tom shrugged and kept walking, launching into one of Ted's hitchhiking tales. "Don't worry," the story began, "I'm meeting Chip," to which Mom said, "Chip? Good Lord, Ted!" Chip was a "liberal" from Connecticut, although that detail was tempered by other things for Mom, such as Chip's last name, Lowell. Because of this, Mom would connect Chip with an oil painting: another sour-faced Puritan or a pre-Revolutionary ship with a British flag. Either would put her at ease. ("You really know my mother," I interjected, and Tom nodded before continuing.) Chip was trouble, though, one of those boarding-school types who had ventured out nightly at sixteen to meet girls with names like Ophelia.

"Ophelia?" I interrupted again. "Mom said Ophelia?" That sounded like it was coming from Tom, making me wonder how he fit in with these East Coast "liberals."

Tom ignored my skepticism and mimicked Mom in a humorous falsetto. "But where? Where are you meeting Chip?"

"On the beach."

"Which beach? And when?"

Ted didn't know. Chip had only told him he was taking a charter flight which "should arrive sometime between Wednesday and Friday."

"Now!" said Mom. "That . . . is . . . ridiculous. How will you find each other?"

To this Ted had apparently scrunched up his face as if to say "minor detail," and took off.

Back at home, Mom kept asking Dad, "Which beach?" and Dad kept saying, "Hell if I know." (Tom had that right!) So Mom called information and got the numbers to all the phone booths in Miami. Three days later, Ted made it to the airport just as Chip came down the ramp from the plane.

"No way!" I said to Tom. "Ted got there *exactly* when Chip arrived?"

Tom held up a hand. "And get this: that night Chip and Ted slept on the beach and at, like, six in the morning Chip woke up to the *rrrring ring ring* of a payphone up on the street. Finally he picked it up and screamed, 'It's a payphone, asshole!' Ted woke up just as Chip was saying, 'Oh hey, Mrs. Cronin . . . Sorry, thought you were someone else. Ted's right here.'"

"You mean to tell me that Mom randomly called a payphone somewhere in Miami and Chip picked up."

Tom threw up his hands and shook his head. "I know. I know. But that's the story."

It was all so confusing. We were now hopelessly lost in the shadows of office buildings. "How did we get here?" I asked again. This time Tom stopped and gripped me by the shoulders, hands shaking, face earnest. "What is it?" I asked. I thought we were about to be mugged. Instead, he kissed me.

In the morning, I opened my eyes to find Tom beside me on my bed. I lifted my head to check around. We were in our jeans and T-shirts; both of my legs were attached. I fell back on my pillow, relieved. Then I remembered Ted. What did he think of me vanishing with his friend? I jumped up and found my answer: Ted asleep at the foot of my bed.

Later, after an awkward cup of coffee in my dining room, Ted stood up, twisting his hair. "We gotta get back to school . . . uh . . . We're moving into a house. Who knows what those tomfools have picked out?"

I started to get up, vaguely aware that Tom wasn't budging, which was odd since he would be moving into the house with Ted and his friends, the "tomfools" as Ted called them.

"I'll just hang back," said Tom quietly.

"What?" Ted said. He looked irritated.

"I'm staying another day."

Here? I thought, before turning to face Ted, who looked incredulous. "Looney? Do you *want* him to stay?"

"Um," I said, trying to meet his eyes, "uh," and unable to ignore

Tom's stare from the opposite end of the table, "sure. I mean, it's up to him . . . up to Tom."

Thus began Tom's weekly adventures hitching the Mohawk Trail. Often I'd pull in from work to find him asleep on my doorstep, always shivering in a jean jacket, which he wore even after the leaves had gone from gold to amber to dusty brown. "What are you doing here?" I'd say. "It's only Thursday." He would open his eyes and smile sheepishly.

More than his trips to Boston, I looked forward to my trips to Williamstown. The drive was exquisite, both in terms of its beauty and its treacherous hairpin curve. To manage my fear of that curve I would stop at a store in Deerfield to buy alcohol (not that I recommend it). For me, the hairpin curve, especially in the snow, required two beers. Otherwise I couldn't do it. And yet, the terror of facing that icy, downward spiral only served to heighten my anticipation of the hijinks to follow.

Weekends in Williamstown were as thrilling as camping in the forest with Falstaff, Prince Hal, and their band of merrymakers. Tom lived with Ted and Chip in an antique-red house on Water Street. It looked as if it had been flung onto the edge of a lot, where it teetered over a creek. Inside, a wood stove provided most of the heat, and the place smelled of fire and ash mixed with coffee and dirt. Living on the grounds, which included the red house plus a cottage up front, were six men and a one-eyed dog named Brandy.

We made a film one weekend which qualified as absurd, although we had been aiming for Kafkaesque. Later, with the camera rolling, we drank shots of tequila in Ted's attic bedroom and made our post-film "documentary" with comments from film critics and historians. I played a critic interviewed while lying on the floor with my legs up against the wall. My body formed an L, except that I'd turned one foot backward so that the toes of each leg pointed in opposite directions—a detail about which the interviewer, Ted, made no comment.

After we finished filming, Ted called out to a friend, "Play something on that fiddle, Rich." He tended to order people around as if he were reclining on a bed of goose down, snapping his fingers. In fact, he was sitting campfire-style with Dad's World War II pilot's cap strapped to his chin and circa-1920 glasses on his nose. Wind rattled the eaves around us while Richard, who had studied violin at Juilliard since age eight, played a Bach piece. I watched Ted pick up the antique guitar Mom had given him for Christmas. He stroked its odd, brass body while listening attentively to "Jesu Joy of Man's Desiring." It occurred to me that Ted had a unique kind of love for our mother, that because of Mom he took no hardship personally and had learned to embrace what is strange in this world. He knew that Mom loved him, even if she expressed her love in a contemptuous sort of way. That was enough for Ted. Why couldn't it be enough for me? Why did I always doubt my family's affection?

Richard finished, and we all cheered. Then Ted and Chip launched into their latest ballad, a ditty really, set to a guitar rhythm suspiciously similar to the theme song for *The Beverly Hillbillies*:

Well, it all started at Motel 6,
You ordered hash browns, toast, and grits,
It was there that I knew this feeling was no lie,
For . . . you . . . are . . . the . . . ap–ple dumplin' of my eye

The next night, Tom and I got separated from the others in a cemetery after leaving the Purple Pub, where Ted had bought us all one last pitcher of beer with loose change he scrounged from the floor. Tom and I wandered in circles around headstones instead of office buildings. Our combined navigational skills portended a future of poor planning and missed opportunities, and yet this was the happiest I'd been since before Frank's death. Outside of these weekends, I applied for credit cards, drove a company car, and toted a briefcase. Occasionally I asked myself if I was going backward by dating a college boy. What about Tom's education? He kept leaving campus midweek to visit me in Newton, which was jeopardizing his near-perfect grade point average.

Maybe I was being too hard on myself, but my ambivalence swelled into deeper conflict as I contrasted my life with the lives of Claire and my other friends from Cincinnati. While Claire was having her second baby and moving around the country with her young family, I was going to Ultimate Frisbee matches. Ted seemed to have adjusted to the idea of Tom dating me, but I couldn't bring myself to tell anyone else in my family. I was two years older than Tom. That would be frowned upon. As far as men were concerned, I'd managed to challenge the limits of what my family considered taboo every time. That might not have been such a problem except that I wanted so to get it right this time. My ambivalence grew.

When I couldn't tolerate it anymore, I broke up with Tom. Two days later, he showed up on my doorstep with roses and an excellent short story that he'd stayed up writing the night before. The story was about a rugby match—his metaphor for loss and pain, I assumed. It never occurred to me that I might represent the opposition. Instead, I was humbled by the subtlety of the story's insight. He left for school the next day and after that I couldn't imagine myself without him. I tuned out my reservations about his age. Apparently Ted had learned to do the same, and it helped that we didn't mention any of this to Mom.

"What am I going to tell my friends?" Mom screamed over the telephone. This was in the fall of 1985. Tom and I had recently moved into a basement apartment on Capitol Hill for Tom's first job, and Mom had just found this out through Tom's mother. "That is a sssin," she hissed over the phone.

We had different definitions of sin. To me, a sin occurred when someone intentionally hurt someone else. "We're just minding our own business," I said. "Your friends do not need to know my sleeping arrangements."

"But they already do."

"How?" I asked.

"Whaddaya mean? I had to tell them!"

Well, then you're naive, I wanted to say, because I knew dozens of Catholics who slept with boyfriends and girlfriends before marriage. However, Tom's mother—a newbie to parenting an adult child—had broken the code of silence. She'd asked him if he was living with me. None of the parents we knew actually asked that question. They just pretended that their adult children did not have premarital sex. I was proud of Tom for telling the truth. We would not lie or sneak around, because we had made the choice that was right for us.

We were not prepared for the backlash, though. After his mother called my mother, she stopped talking to Tom. Over several months, Tom's mother's only communication with Tom had come in a package she sent containing the *Confessions of St. Augustine*, no letter included, not even a Post-It. Tom laughed when he opened it, but I could see that he was shaken. Upon settling into our apartment in DC, he read the book. Now he was pressing for marriage.

"Not a good idea," I said. "We have worse problems than our mothers."

"This has nothing to do with our mothers," he said.

"Exactly," I said. "It has to do with the fact that we are not ready." I was referring to our shared history of stubbornness and pride, which had revealed itself after we left Boston and just before we moved to Washington DC.

In between cities, we'd taken the month of August to backpack through Europe, but in the final days of a fabulous and eye-opening trip, I grew tired of lugging forty pounds on my back. I'd taken on too much, and instead of reorganizing our plans, I started griping. Then I got drunk on a train before we arrived in London, which made Tom fume. How could I be so careless? We weren't in Disneyland. There were pickpockets in London. Had I not read Dickens? Of course not! I'd had almost no education in contrast to his, and worst of all, I was foolish. I depended on the kindness of strangers.

To which I reminded Tom that he had no education whatsoever in the school of hard knocks, from which I had a master's degree. As I saw it, he was imperious. All the books in the world could not possibly open the eyes of someone so sheltered.

We were right in front of Westminster Abbey when Tom proved to me that he had earned an honorary doctorate from the school of hard knocks. He'd had his own gaggle of Catholic brothers to brawl with, his mouth washed out with soap, and his head pounded in football and rugby matches since he was in diapers. In front of a constable, he all but beat his chest and yodeled like Tarzan. "Would you like me to take him in?" asked the constable, and for an instant I actually hesitated, but that would have escalated our problem. Besides, it was not as if I hadn't provoked him by getting drunk on the train. We apologized and flew out the next day. But we were not the same couple we'd been in Massachusetts by the time we took up residence in Washington DC.

In September, having committed to living together, having outraged our medieval mothers, and having transferred my job, I realized that there was no going back to Boston for me. Besides, I loved Tom. Yet, by late fall, talk of marriage still seemed premature. As

I saw it, we needed to shirk this penance that our mothers wanted us to make. Until now, I had thought that Tom shared my views on Catholicism, which is to say that we would not be bullied into practicing it. We would pick and choose our own form of worship. I failed to see that the Water Street Tom had been replaced by the Capitol Hill Tom. He was going through his own changes. Hadn't I changed after college? The problem was that Tom's trajectory was the opposite of mine. The new Tom was finding his voice, one that embraced our parents' Catholicism.

I'd hoped that we would find our own brand of Catholicism, one with more wiggle room on certain issues. Tom was talking about law school. "Why law school?" I said. He'd always intended to become an English professor. Next he was saying he would work full-time and go to night school five nights a week and Saturdays. Simultaneously he bemoaned the idea, saying that he should be going to Harvard Law, to which I would say, "Then you should apply to Harvard. You'll probably get in." But he refused. He would stay in his job and go to Georgetown at night.

The only goal that we shared unequivocally was more education. I was applying to graduate programs. I had decided in Boston that I would return to school for a doctoral degree in psychology. I'd imagined us entering graduate programs together, living on stipends and part-time jobs, and being poor for a few years. In Massachusetts, Tom supported that plan; in DC, he supported it only in theory.

Then, on a date that, based on past experiences with my family, I should have deleted from my calendar, Christmas Eve, Tom convinced me to look at engagement rings. At a jewelry counter in Cincinnati, he slipped a ring on my finger, and I said, "Maybe we should put this back. I don't even know which finger to wear it on. This is a claw, not a hand. Let's just wait on this."

"We're past that point."

"We are only starting out." There was so much to sort out: grad school, kids, or not . . .

"Look, if you love me . . ."

Would I have moved to a new city with him, at the risk of losing my family, if I hadn't loved him? But I was beginning to see that Tom's definition of love might be as different from mine as Mom's definition of sin. His idea was to sacrifice what he now considered an irresponsible goal, a doctorate in English, and instead to grit his teeth through work and law school because that was a "responsible goal." As I saw it, that decision made no sense. I didn't need him to support me. If not for the fix I found myself in—our mothers in an uproar, my father suffering from a failed kidney transplant, and the prospect of being banished by my family and by Tom—I would have said no to marriage at this time. Instead, I silently apologized to myself and to Tom for what I was about to do. I accepted.

My father was grinning as he came from the living room, where Tom had just asked for my hand during the Christmas Eve party. Mom's reluctance to show enthusiasm was nothing new as far as weddings went in our family. She'd sulked at Liz's rehearsal dinner. Mom greeted any man who wanted to take a daughter away from her with suspicion.

The enthusiastic parent-of-the-bride role always went to Dad, which was almost comical for a man so taciturn. But he rallied the troops despite his weakened condition to make an animated announcement in the party room, putting a stop to the pinball players, the football watchers, the grandchildren on scooters, and the baby xylophoners. He clapped a hand around Tom's shoulder and told everyone: "Quiet down because Tom's got something to say." A room filled with roughly thirty-five people of all ages went from its customary level of chaos to military decorum. Dad was grinning from ear to ear. I could probably count the times I'd seen him smile that way.

In an equally excited voice, Tom said, "Eileen and I are getting married!" At first there was silence. I thought, "Oh, please," but then Ted and Kevin gave Tom congratulatory slaps on the back. Bridget knew Tom from Massachusetts, and she had liked him from the start. The "babies," now in college, were nice to everybody. On the other hand, I'm not sure some of my siblings even congratulated the groom-to-be. Their stamp of approval would have traveled like a human wave through one of these announcements.

Tom was not used to being snubbed. In fact, he often chided me for my obsequious nature, as he called it. He hated when I stepped aside on a sidewalk or a staircase for strangers to pass, although I thought that was just common sense. Admittedly, though, I would catch myself apologizing to trees or desks after bumping into them. This came from being shoved about, usually unintentionally, but often enough that I was used to getting out of other people's way. As a former rugby player, Tom couldn't grasp my mentality.

We never discussed my siblings' indifference toward his wedding announcement, but I hoped that he would write it off. I was used to it and, while it hurt me, I knew that my siblings would argue that they had a right to uphold their principles. Tom and I had brazenly moved in together and made no attempt to keep it a secret. Aside from that, my siblings were Cincinnatians through and through, which meant that they could be polite but cool with outsiders. They clumped together at social gatherings. They did not intend to be exclusive, but they had an impenetrable bond.

Outsiders bold enough to step into their circle were subject to political and religious scrutiny. Ted and I were outsiders. We knew that about ourselves. When I'd fallen in love with Tom, I'd rejoiced in the idea of a mate who could blend in with my family. He had enough of the Catholic camouflage that he would not be targeted, and yet he was a thinking man who would not dismiss his differences in order to fit in. What I failed to anticipate was that Tom would refuse to be relegated to outsider status. That went against his nature.

Three weeks after Christmas, the phone rang in our bedroom on Capitol Hill. Outside, the sun fought gray clouds; inside, it was a gloomy Sunday afternoon, a day for paperwork. Without thinking, I picked up the ringing phone.

"Have you set the date?" Mom asked.

I was holding in my hands the application to a doctoral program in clinical psychology at Howard University.

"Well?" she said, annoyed.

"I don't know," I said. "Maybe two years from now?"

This was met with a walloping silence before she scolded me in a whisper—I could practically feel her lower jaw jutting out, her chin pushing through the receiver into my ear. "You are killing your father!" Then she hung up on me.

I didn't call back.

A month later, on the eve of Valentine's Day, Dad was giving a speech at a fundraiser for his old high school, accepting an award for George Ratterman, his teammate who had gone on to become a pro football legend. Being there on behalf of his old teammate, Dad was probably the most excited he'd been in years. Before an audience that included Michael, at least one uncle, and a number of Dad's close friends, Dad delivered another one of his "St. Crispin's Day speeches." He began by explaining that the St. Xavier High School football team had once been called the Musketeers, just like the university's team. They had changed their name during World War II, when old teammates were dying by the dozens on the battlefield. What kept hope alive in Cincinnati was George

Ratterman and his blazing passes. Those who had been on the field or in the stands back in the forties would have remembered Dad as the receiver of several passes. Dad paused to describe a few of them. It was because of those passes whizzing over the heads of so many opponents, he said, that Xavier changed its team name. And what did they change it to?

Dad raised his fist in what was supposed to be a cheer: "St. Xavier Bombers!" Instead, he suffered a massive heart attack.

Mom's next phone call to me came at four in the morning. "Your father's dead," she said.

"What?" I could think only of our last conversation.

"He might be dead. I think he's dead. I don't know. I don't know. He's probably dead."

I gasped, and focused on the word "think." She only *thinks* he's dead. In the dark room I saw Tom's face, his eyebrows screwed into a question mark over an open mouth. "What do you mean?" I asked.

"I'm not sure," said Mom. "They said his brain is dead."

"I'm coming home." As I hung up I hoped that Mom was only confused, that she had misunderstood the doctor, that Dad was only ill, not dead.

"What is it?" said Tom, rubbing his eyes.

"I have to get home. Dad is dying. Maybe . . ." A well of tears built up. "I'm buying plane tickets."

Tom shot out of the bed and started a bath for me as I booked two seats on a seven o'clock flight out of National. Sitting in the warm bathwater, smelling the bar of soap in my hands, I realized that a dead brain meant that my father was gone. I rubbed my eyes. The soapy sting made the tears come faster. I would never feel my father's warm hands on my shoulders again; he would not be there to give me away at my wedding. I picked up the soap and squeezed until it squished through my fingers as mush. This was not Dad's fault, I knew, but again he was abandoning me.

Dad's funeral remains even more of a blank in my mind than Frank's, except for the eulogy, which was supposed to be a compilation of all of the siblings' special memories of Dad. The appointed writer would incorporate them into a speech.

"We need a good writer," said Liz.

"That would be Ted," said Kevin.

"How 'bout Rosa?" said Liz, and to my surprise Rosa suggested me, although I was thinking that Rosa would give the best delivery. All this speculation was for naught, though, because as the oldest son Michael would both write and deliver the speech. That was the hierarchy: first Bridget decided it, then Michael agreed, "If no one else wants to," which was followed by silence from the masses, and from there it was a fait accompli.

Michael's eulogy focused on Dad as a man of religious conviction, a man with focus and the determination necessary to get ahead, a man with a sense of humor, and above all a family man who loved his children and grandchildren. In the front pew, Michael's wife and children were arranged like a string of pearls near Mom, each girl with a grosgrain ribbon in her hair and outfits to match their mother's dress. Michael, with his male version of Mom's olive skin and good looks, wore a blinding white shirt and a gray suit. As he neared the conclusion of the eulogy, I thought, "Where is my part? What happened to the bit about Dad being open-minded and encouraging us to be our best no matter what that might be?" For a second my eyes met Rosa's and her expression seemed to be an acknowledgment of my thoughts, but then she turned back to Michael.

Soon after that I remembered the time Dad stayed up all night to fix my leg, which brought on more tears. It also let me know that I would have my own memories of my father. Back in the spring, before I'd left for Europe with Tom, Dad came to Boston for a Volkswagen meeting. His recent kidney transplant was a success, we thought, and he was being inducted into something called the Vanguard Society. We met for dinner with Bridget.

When we came out of the Ritz Carlton, Bridget drove off, and Dad walked with me along Tremont Street. It was a moonlit night with irises in bloom. I'd never taken a walk alone with Dad, never told him what I wanted from life. But there I was telling him that I might move with Tom to DC. Dad didn't ask whether we were moving in together. Instead, he stunned me by saying, "You've done so much here. Do you really want to give that up?" I knew he would not approve of my living with Tom, but I never would have guessed that his biggest concern was my career.

Now Michael was at the deacon's podium summing up a different father's life, a man he and Mom and some of my siblings remembered, but not the man who was my father. It wasn't that Michael's memories were false. His father was as real as mine, but he had cut out my memories of Dad.

It didn't take long for me to start asking myself if I really knew my father at all. Had Dad only been humoring me in those last years of his life? By the end of a eulogy that everyone else would declare uplifting, I was drowning in despair. I was pummeled by memories of those events that Dad missed during my high school years, of that argument we'd had on the phone, and even of him slapping my face once during the time Mom was hospitalized after he left her. He hadn't done that before or since. I tried to block these thoughts and to replace Michael's father with my own, but I wasn't sure I had enough of Dad in me to fight back.

The memorial events culminated in a gathering at Mom's house. Disillusioned and worn out, I introduced my fiancé to scores of acquaintances. When someone asked about a wedding date, I found myself saying, "Next fall. We'll be married by Thanksgiving."

Perhaps I was so distracted by Dad's death, by Mom's recovery, and by stolen dreams, that I failed to see the whole point of this wedding, which was that I was getting married. More importantly, I wasn't ready to get married. On top of that, I believed in my heart that Tom was not ready either. I wanted him to take time to think through his decision, and to stop worrying about what our families wanted us to do.

Then there was Tom's confession. Somewhere along the way, he told me that he and Ted had brawled after Tom returned to school following his first weekend in Newton with me. I'd never known Ted to get into a fight as an adult. As far as I knew, Ted was a pacifist. Now I had to wonder about my role in the brawl between Ted and Tom.

According to Tom, he had won the battle in Williamstown. As for Ted, he had his own way of dealing with this undercurrent of tension. A week before the ceremony, I met him at the airport. He had shaved his head. Only a shadow of his hair remained, black nubs with nothing left for him to twist anxiously at his neck. He was thinner than ever and looked a bit scary. That might not have been a problem except that I'd asked him to stand in for Dad to give me away.

Ted's position on the wedding was driven home through his gift: he had made a painting of Tom and me, in shades of purple, red, and blue, as a medieval couple standing on a stone bridge in England, faces strained and searching in opposite directions, the man saying, "It's time to drop our seeds," and the woman looking as if she were preparing to jump in the river.

CHAPTER 23

Ophelia Gets Her Feet Wet

Our wedding let loose a store of rivalries and grudges, and then gave way to a damn good party. With Chip as best man, Richard on the violin, and Ted taking the place of my father, the "tomfools" managed to bring the occasion together. By the time we came back to Mom's house, we had already lost the videotape that Michael had filmed of the ceremony and reception. The post-reception bash at Mom's house was one for a family album, except that we didn't own a family album. If not for the milestones that required a professional photographer—weddings, graduations, First Communions, class pictures—we would have almost no photographic documentation of our lives. As for home movies, we always relied on the other families on our vacation to do the filming. This was our family's first wedding video, and it got mixed in with the rubble in the party room during the sixth game of the World Series.

That night, the Mets beat the Boston Red Sox in extra innings for an "absolutely bizarre finish," according to an excited Vin Scully. Sporting events of such magnitude trumped even our wedding receptions. Liz had made the mistake of marrying on the same day as the Kentucky Derby. Dad spent most of her reception

270

watching the race on a big screen set up at the far end of the Oak Room.

Now, after eight hours of wedding festivities, I was reluctant to leave for the opulent deco halls of the Netherland Plaza, where Tom and I would spend the first night of our honeymoon before leaving for Zihuatanejo in the morning. In a sense, even our honeymoon would be confiscated by sport, since Tom fancied himself a character in a Hemingway fishing story. Upon our return, he would whip out the photos to anyone we encountered, quickly passing over Mexican sunsets to get to the one of him standing beside a seven-foot sailfish with its glorious fan flapping in the wind.

The crowd at our wedding-gone-baseball party was split. Feverish New Yorkers took on Bostonians hankering to beat the curse of the Bambino. Ted and Richard often teased Chip because he cried over Mets games. Now Chip fought tears while Bridget's husband cheered. Then Chip drank to a comeback while Bridget's husband cursed under his breath. A run here, two there, and the score went back and forth for ten innings. In the end the New Yorkers were jubilant. Right after that, Ted and his friends took all three of the "babies" out on the town. In the middle of the night, Mom woke up and started pacing the halls, worrying herself into a near-manic state over her "babies," which was understandable given that Frank had been out drinking with a friend when he died, and somewhat confusing since Frank's death hadn't stopped most of us from drinking. When Ted returned in the wee hours of the morning, Bridget reminded him that this was not a "flophouse." She never had stopped being the second in command, and when it came to Mom or the "babies," Bridget became the mama bear.

As for the film of the ceremony, two of the "babies," Matthew and Tim, found the unmarked tape the next day, while they nursed hangovers during a run of Clint Eastwood movies. They put it to use. We might have lost my wedding tape, but we gained a copy of *The Good, the Bad and the Ugly*.

For a few months there was peace in my marriage, but everything went haywire in June when I spotted the word "thalidomide" in the *Washington Post*. "A head and a torso" were the words used to describe a thalidomide-affected fetus in a story about how far we'd come in the twenty-five years since *Roe v. Wade*. I clapped a hand over my mouth to stifle an anguished cry. The reporter argued that abortion had spared our nation the burden of babies with deformities. He'd overlooked the basic premise for abortion: a woman's *choice* to end a pregnancy. Not every woman would choose to abort a baby because of deformities, and it was unfair to people with disabilities to confuse the two issues.

Tom and I had recently moved to a third-floor walkup to save money. While Tom attended law school at Georgetown, I took classes at Howard. His tuition was paid with his inheritance and mine was funded by teaching grants and my job in rehab. The apartment had no air conditioning, which, during summer in Washington DC, was maddening on its own. At dusk on the night I read the article in the *Post*, I set up my typewriter in the dining room.

On a task such as this letter, Tom and I shined as a couple. My passion combined with his exceptional editing skills produced a letter not to be ignored. Even so, it yielded no response. At Tom's suggestion, I revised it again and addressed my complaints to the ombudsman. The letter was forwarded to various sections of the paper and caught the attention of David Ignatius, who was the editor of the "Outlook" section.

About a week later, I pulled a letter from our mailbox and read it in the vestibule of our apartment building. Mr. Ignatius was writing to request that I call him to discuss an article. Upstairs, afternoon sun poured through the west-facing picture window. I grabbed the phone. My fingers trembled as I dialed the number, my mouth so dry I could hardly pronounce my name.

"Are you a journalist?" he asked.

I was shocked that he would think so. After reading the article's take on people affected by thalidomide, my old ambitions as a reporter had seemed not only remote but inconceivable. "Um, no," I said, "although I was in a writing program as an undergraduate." Quickly I regretted how sophomoric I must have sounded to such an accomplished writer.

"You wrote a compelling letter," he said.

"Thank you," I said, fanning myself.

"I apologize if this is difficult, but I was wondering if your mother took thalidomide."

If only I knew for sure. I tried to swallow. My throat knotted up. Finally, I said, "My mother says she never took it." He didn't respond. Maybe he wanted more?

"Well, that's what she says," I added.

"And what do you think?"

I thought of all the horror stories I'd read. "I don't know," I finally admitted. "I don't know what to think. If she took it, I can see why she might not want to remember it."

I heard him sigh on the other end. Would he want my story if I couldn't say for sure that my mother had taken thalidomide? I considered what I'd read so far on the subject. "I don't know if my mother took thalidomide but she did go to Germany when she was pregnant with me. Lots of people took the drug in Germany." Then I thought of Mom. He might write an article that proved she had taken the drug, and that would upset her. "Or it could have been a fluke," I said.

"Listen, I'd like you to write an article about all the good that your life has brought. That's what impressed me about your letter."

This invitation far exceeded my hopes. "You want *me* to write it?"

"Why not? It's your life."

Now I had something to worry about. The *Post* would want a resoundingly upbeat article. I'd never been a fan of romanticized articles about people with disabilities. To me, they assumed that readers couldn't digest the reality of life with a disability, which was neither all good nor all bad. Most newspaper stories about someone with a disability took a happy-go-lucky tone. I could not name one that was written by a person with a disability.

"Two thousand words," he said. "Are you up for it?"

"Uh . . . Sure."

"Can you have that in two weeks?"

"Two? Let's see . . . I could do that."

We were just about to get off the phone when he said, "Your family never sued?"

I sighed. No lawsuit. How to explain that? "You'd have to meet my family to understand."

"And what would they say?"

"They'd say . . . Well, they'd say, 'You can't sue God!'"

"Ha! I'll look forward to reading about that."

I hung up, certain that I could not possibly pull off this assignment. Then I set up the typewriter again. Ten days later, as I clacked away at one of my later drafts, Tom came home from a class and peered over my shoulder. "You can't sue God," he read aloud. "You're not going to say that, are you?"

"David Ignatius liked that line."

"And you're going to let him put words in your mouth?"

"They're *my* words!"

Tom was leaning over me at the cheap metal table, the same kind that students everywhere ate meals on, although we almost never ate at ours. Because of our schedules, we'd probably had ten meals together as a married couple. For several days now, I'd had my typewriter parked on it. Through the picture window, I saw the sun's final streaks blood-orange against a blackberry-stained sky.

"I'm hungry," said Tom. He jerked his chin in the direction of a box of crackers on the kitchen counter. "Do you ever eat anything but bird food?" His face glistened with sweat. His near-perfect features had started to trouble me. But he had a point. I lived on cheese and crackers, washing them down with wine. I was pale, had an oily sheen on my face, and I'd become scrawny. Lately I would open a bottle of wine before Tom came home from school. Drinking alone was a scary business, and while I was quick to take some risks, alcoholism was not one I was eager to pursue. Given that I had family members in recovery, I was growing very uncomfortable with my own habits. After all, I had once tried to kill myself under the influence.

Tom squinted as he repeated my typewritten words to himself. "You really cannot say this bit about suing God. That is *so* unprofessional."

I considered the line cheeky, which was my way of communicating what I could not spell out in words. As for Tom, I thought, "What do you consider professional? Only your point of view?" Tom was an extraordinary writer, and I respected his editorial advice. I'd been humbled enough times to know that it is never wise to let pride get in the way of learning from someone who is good at what they do.

On the other hand, our rapidly changing beliefs were taking us in very different directions. Tom was learning civil and constitutional law. With his scholarly mind, I'd imagined that he would put this degree to use in human rights activism or as a law professor, but lately his face would take on a menacing expression while he ranted about *everyone's* civil rights. Of course, everyone should have rights.

Who would argue with that? But he'd say, "Even Nazis and the Ku Klux Klan have the right to stage public marches." All of this was couched in hypothetical situations and mostly for the benefit of our friends, people like Ted and me. I'd glare at Tom and wonder if I should ask what had gotten into him, but worried that would only fuel his antagonistic game. My sense of humor was stretching thin, partly because of my "bull head"—a term that had lately replaced the endearing "pumpkin head"—but also because I was taking classes at the university that had granted Thurgood Marshall a law degree. At Howard I was learning that the "objective" point of view was too often equated with a white, male, college-educated one, and that the world beyond that demographic was characterized as biased. I entertained, although I disagreed with, Tom's argument about Robert Bork's merits as a potential Supreme Court justice. At first, I was fascinated by what I thought was his ability to see all arguments. But I couldn't abide the discussions of Nazis' or Klansmen's rights, not even if they were intended to stretch our imaginations.

Tom was pressing me. "You can't dismiss your family's decision not to sue in that flippant tone."

Dismiss in a flippant tone? I couldn't believe that my husband, a law student, saw my words as dismissive. It seemed to me that I had been dismissed.

I turned to him. "My family has always had my best interests in mind, right? I've spent my life struggling to stay afloat so strangers could slap me on the back and say, 'You must be so grateful to your family.'" Now I was crying. Then, because I never did submit easily to defeat, I unleashed everything that I was trying to contain. "In case you're wondering what I'm feeling, Tom, there are times I want to say to people, 'I am here, not *because* of my family, but *in spite* of them.'"

He flinched, either at what I'd said or at the emotion behind my words. He came as close to my face as he had on the streets of

London when I first saw his temper erupt. Red-faced, he screamed, "Who said your mother took thalidomide?"

"Just about every doctor I know!" I shouted back. "Oh, except for Mom's obstetrician, but then he probably gave her the drug!"

"You can't prove that," he said.

"You don't know half of what I could prove," I said. I stood up and screamed in his face, "And the reason I don't tell anybody, the reason I keep it to myself, Tom, is because of *people like you*." I poked my finger in his face.

As he stepped back and shook his head, I thought, "No, don't back away from me now. Listen to me. Look beyond my anger. I'm dying inside."

Instead he pointed down at me and said, "But *your mother said* she never took the drug."

"Don't twist my intentions around. I'm not blaming Mom for taking the drug. I know she wouldn't have known what it would do. But what about me? What about my future? Our future? Wouldn't you like to know for sure that we won't have a baby with three heads?"

His whole demeanor changed, and he laughed this off as a joke. "If she looks like you, that would be fine with me."

I realized he was only trying to make light of a frightening situation, but I felt that if he respected me at all, he would know that this was no laughing matter to me. Back in Massachusetts, we'd spoken of my concerns about motherhood. He had sympathized with my situation, but since our marriage we'd stopped having those deeper conversations about ourselves. They'd been replaced by erudite diatribes that had little to do with us as a couple.

"Are you really going into law with that naïve attitude?" I said. "When are you going to grow up?"

"Don't," he said, stepping back. His lower lip quivered. I'd gone too far. He jabbed a finger at my typewriter. "Is this all you care about? Does anyone else matter to you, Eileen? You don't even care about family." His eyes narrowed as he glared at my words on the page. "Fuck you!" And he stormed out of the apartment.

After that, my hands shaking, I took out the sentence.

My essay was the feature article in Sunday's "Outlook" section. It came with an above-the-fold photograph of me and the title "I Would Choose My Life." The insets included scenes from my life: a picture of me in my first pair of legs, one of my parents in Germany while Mom was pregnant with me, and one from my wedding day. A story about Oliver North followed. Initially I liked the title because I *would* choose my life, darkness and all.

The response to my article overwhelmed me. Soon the story was sold to the wire service and appeared in papers all over the country. I was invited to appear on television and radio, to cut the ribbon at a Special Olympics event, to testify in a class-action suit, to sell my life story to a screenwriter, and even to go on *Larry King Live.* I couldn't eat or sleep. My weight was down to eighty-eight pounds. Now that I'd published something about my life, people expected more details. I was afraid I'd say the wrong thing and upset my mother or embarrass Tom. More likely, I'd sound stupid.

On the other hand, I saw an opportunity to change the image that most Americans had of people with disabilities, which had become the most pressing goal of my adulthood. Tom was right about this much: for better or worse, I could not divorce myself from that commitment.

Days later, I appeared on a national talk show. The hostess, a clinical psychologist, introduced me as a "thalidomide baby." The phrase sounded patronizing, if not dehumanizing. Who in the media had decided that "thalidomide baby" was an appropriate term to describe an adult in my situation? After a few light questions, the hostess was asking me to describe my "intimate life" with Tom. The question seemed inconceivable on live television. I said, "I'm not sure I heard you. Could you repeat that?" She backed off.

I was drinking two glasses of wine a night or, when I couldn't sleep, as many as four. By the time I was offered three months of free representation by a Hollywood publicist, I was fighting suicidal urges. As a rule I never missed classes or work, but now I called in sick to nurse a hangover. Sprawled on my sofa with a fan blasting me, I could see that alcohol posed the biggest threat to my life, and yet it seemed my only remedy for stress. That day *The 700 Club* invited me to go on their show. When Tom came home from school that night, I told him about the offer. He said, "But you are pro-life. If you're suggesting that even babies with disabilities should be born, then you're pro-life."

At first I was too stunned to respond, then I thought he was joking. On top of that, my mother had delivered my article to our neighbor who ran the National Right to Life campaign. I'd come to see that Mom's actions, at least in matters of religion, were like a nervous tic. She could not stop herself. My convictions about disability often brought me to a similar place, and I felt sorry for her because invariably these convictions isolated us from the people we loved. We didn't give people room to breathe. But now I felt manipulated by my husband. Whereas Mom didn't always think through her actions, Tom was more calculating. I worried that he would use this to bolster a political career—one that I didn't even buy into. Immediately, I dismissed that notion. At the same time, I realized that I had to make changes, and fast.

The next day I met with the director of clinical psychology at Howard. I'd been keeping him apprised of the offers from talk shows and so forth. I worried about the fall, when I would be expected to join the clinical program full-time. My fists were balled as I took a seat in his office. I said, "I can't do these shows and be this person."

"Then don't," he said.

His face was without expression. I knew him well enough to sense that he was trying to decide whether to say something about my appearance—the circles under my eyes, the wrists thin as twigs— or just let it ride, which he apparently chose to do. But he was going to make me work. While I waited for him to tell me what to do he stared back at me without blinking, waiting for me to grow up. Dr. Thompson was a patient man.

"How do I get out of this?" I finally said.

He laughed heartily. "You think those folks don't have anyone else to pick on?"

I smiled to myself. "You mean 'just say no'?"

"Simple as that."

Sometimes I knew the right person to ask for guidance.

At home, I boxed up letters and phone messages along with the copies of my article that friends had sent me from papers around the country. I lingered on a letter from a famous literary agent offering me representation. That one was hard to set aside, but I decided that I would never write about my life again.

I hoped that, having moved past the article, Tom and I would find peace and learn how to reconcile our different views. In an attempt to turn things around, we bought a house with money he'd inherited. Our families were expecting a baby from us. I wanted one very much.

Still, it seemed irresponsible to start a family without having answers about my birth defects. I could seek genetic counseling, but that wouldn't provide definite information until I was already pregnant. I did not want to have to make a decision about whether to keep a baby. One of my first assignments that fall was a psycho-pharmacology paper. I chose to research teratogens, chemicals or environmental factors associated with birth defects.

Teratogens were the last thing I wanted to read about, yet I couldn't stop myself. My evenings and weekends were spent staring up at the mural in the dome of the Library of Congress. There an angelic woman who represents Human Understanding lifts a veil representing Ignorance as she looks toward Progress. At my carrel below, I read that X-rays could cause birth defects which might be transferred to future generations. If X-rays explained my case, that would make for difficult decisions ahead. Although *I* might love a child like me, I wasn't sure I wanted a child to grow up with the obstacles I'd faced. I hated to admit this to myself.

Of course, a person with a disability can have a wonderful life. It was also possible that I might make a great mother to such a child. But how would the rest of the world treat that child? I had lost faith in other people. While my husband was drumming up annoying hypothetical civil rights scenarios, I was engaging in an even less attractive habit: mistrusting every person with two arms and two legs. This put me at odds with almost the entire human race.

The more information I discovered, the more questions arose. Then I sat in on an amputee clinic with the dean of Howard's medical school. A mother came who was born without legs, and next her daughter, who was born without arms. A physical therapist wheeled out a cart with a pile of child-sized prosthetic arms that had been donated to the clinic. The four-year-old girl balked at the sight of them. She knew how to get what she needed, and she wanted no part of those cumbersome arms. I understood her resistance. After all, there had been a time when I prided myself on out-squiddling the neighborhood dogs.

Once the girl and her mother had left, Dr. Epps explained that this family's birth defects were the result of a mutation which began with the mother. The defects could begin in any generation of a family. They could be passed on from there.

"They just appear from out of nowhere?" I asked.

"It can start with anyone."

This was troubling news for me, because it offered validation of my mother's story. If my defects were a fluke, they might well be a mutation beginning with me, and if so my child could be born without arms or legs or both.

Faced with the possibility of a genetic mutation, I was willing to take on thalidomide again. I found all the articles I could drum up on the topic. I learned that limbs develop in the womb during the first trimester. Normally limb buds appear near the end of the first month, and the limbs are formed by the end of the third month. Based on the development of my limbs, my mother would have had to have taken the drug after the first month. One of those anti-abortion posters from the seventies flashed before my eyes: the tiny feet of a ten-week-old fetus. My legs must have stopped developing between four and ten weeks.

I had to rub my eyes and double-check the wording because the authors of one article referred to thalidomide-deformed children as "monsters." This went beyond insensitive. Later I would learn that the Greek word *terato* means "monster," and that thalidomide prompted the creation of the term "teratogen." Eventually I would learn related terms, such as "monster-drug." In the library I tried to see where my family fit into a tragedy that could be studied in tabloids or in peer-reviewed medical journals. I wondered what Mom's initial reaction to those exploitative photographs had been. Putting my own needs aside, I could understand her reasons for distancing herself as far from that tragedy as possible, especially since she had been convinced of the "God's choice" explanation of my defects two years before the truth came out. When I imagined myself in her place, I felt horrible for my younger mother. Then an idea came to me.

I rushed home, pulled out the box where I'd packed the paperwork from my newspaper article, and fished out the photograph of Mom and Dad on their trip to Germany. It was one of the few photos I had of my parents together. Until now I had not fully realized its evidentiary value. I studied it for clues: my parents on a mountaintop with snow sprinkled on distant mountains, Dad wearing only a blazer and Mom not yet in maternity clothes, just a loose-fitting frock and lightweight coat. Since I was born in September, my conception would have been in January. The developmental damage would have likely occurred between late February and early March. Based on the clothing and the snow, it seemed that this picture was taken at about that time of year. Ironically, it was Mom who had chosen this photo for my article.

I tossed the photo along with my notes onto the dining room table. My head ached. I walked to the refrigerator and pulled out a bottle of wine. I'd always suspected that Mom had taken the drug in Germany, but after reading the book my friend Daniel gave me in Boston, I wondered if she had brought the drug from Cincinnati to take on the plane. After filling a tall glass with wine, I grabbed the phone and dialed Mom's number.

"Mom," I said, "it's Eileen."

"Eileen!" she said, as always.

I sat down at the drop-leaf table she had given us. "Guess what? I just ran across that picture of you and Dad in Germany."

"Which one?" she asked.

I could always appeal to Mom's vanity, so I said, "You look like movie stars up there on the mountain, Mom. What is Dad doing in a beret?" I held my breath.

"What was *I* wearing?" she wanted to know.

"A brown car coat. Was it winter?" I needed the season so I could pinpoint exactly where I was in my fetal development.

"Well, let's see, I think it was March."

March covered her second to third month of pregnancy. "Oh," I said, exhaling, "I have to go," and hung up.

I finished off the bottle of wine. Surrounding me were my notes, Xeroxes of journal articles, and that photo. Everything pointed to a pill taken in March. As I alternately tried to digest this news and to numb myself against it, I wanted to convince myself that my mother was telling me the truth, that she hadn't taken thalidomide. But that option left me with the possibility of a mutation. The consequences of a mutation outweighed the problems associated with the idea of my mother lying to me. Mutation versus a lie: which did I prefer?

This circular thinking lasted one full day.

If I had taken a step back years earlier, if I hadn't needed to be spoken to honestly and listened to patiently by my mother, if I had accepted everything Mom told me without question, if I had never questioned my faith, if I had ignored Sister Luke's public announcement, and if I had never educated myself, these years of psychological torture might have been avoided. I could have accepted that everything would work out or that Mom was only telling a "white lie." In fact, my mother had been providing clues to the truth all along. For instance, she'd always made a point of saying that she was pregnant with me on her trip to Germany. She had even selected this picture for my article. Maybe she'd wanted me to figure it out. What she had not wanted was for me to ask her about it or discuss it with anyone.

If I were a different person, I might have realized there in my dining room that I'd made the same mistakes over and over again with my family. I had learned nothing from the alienation after my pathetic attempt to confront Liz that Christmas Eve, nor had I learned not to ask Mom about thalidomide, and I had not learned to make up a female roommate to live with in Washington before marriage. What was I missing that most of my siblings had understood and accepted about our family?

If I were a different person, I might have celebrated right then that I could have ten children with Tom. Instead, I tortured myself over why my mother would lie, which only led me back to whether my own children would be healthy or not. What I did not ask myself was whether I wanted to be married to a man I no longer understood, maybe had never understood, and who did not seem to understand me. Most importantly, I might have asked myself why I drank as much as I did.

The next day, after I awakened with a hangover and showed up at the wrong building to proctor an exam, I came home and put a stop to the drinking cycle. I opened the phone book and called the number for a recovery group. I didn't need a fancy rehab.

"I'm calling to turn myself in," I said to the man on the other end.

"Well, that was easy."

"What happens next?"

"I'll have someone pick you up at five thirty for a six o'clock meeting. Just give me your address. Will you be all right for an hour? Do you need to talk?"

"I don't want to think about this too much or I might change my mind. Maybe I'll take a shower while I wait. I feel so oily."

"That's a good idea. Did you eat anything today?"

"Does Diet Coke count?"

"That makes two things you need to do. Call back if you need anything else."

At the age of twenty-seven, I was finally making a choice that was good for me—one that others might criticize—and I would be okay. Soon a woman came to my door. "I'll drive," I said. She looked at me with concern that quickly softened into a smile. "I'll drive this time, and maybe you can do it another time," she said. This would be my first lesson in handling conflict with subtlety. As I got into her car, I realized that no one in their right mind would take the passenger seat with a driver who had just called a recovery hotline. My second lesson was to accept that I had to earn people's trust, and that my legs were not the only reason that others needed me to prove my competence.

The following summer, I was preparing to celebrate one year of sobriety. My husband had suggested that the meetings I attended might be overkill. That was a sign, I'd decided, that I should keep going to them. These days I felt better, sounded better, looked better, even smelled better.

In July, Tom and I visited Ted and other friends in New York. Ted had recently coached the basketball team of a Catholic school in Harlem to a citywide victory. He was finishing his master's degree in philosophy at Columbia and shared an apartment with Richard above a vegan bakery at 125th and Broadway. The only good thing about his apartment, other than the cheap rent, was the aroma of fresh-baked bread. Realistically, though, Ted could not afford a slice of that bread.

We came out of the apartment drenched in sweat and ready to cool down in Chip's air-conditioned apartment on the Upper East Side. Tom and Richard had gone ahead of us on the subway. Ted and I wanted to ride his bike, a used Schwinn. I climbed onto the book rack, and we got off to a wobbly start.

"Did you pick this bike out of someone's trash?" I asked.

"I paid thirty-five bucks for this thing."

"Dad paid that much for his first car."

Ted snorted. My legs stuck straight out to the sides. Uncomfortable as it felt, I was more concerned about catching an ankle on a street sign.

Humid air swept under my striped cotton pantsuit. It looked like pajamas, though I preferred to see the outfit as hipster chic: cinched at the waist, capri length, with snappy white Keds. We were heading south on Broadway.

Chip was forever scoring great apartments through family connections. He had called the one with the elevator that opened into his living room his "flat." The "loft" we were heading toward was east of Park on a block with an equestrian center. The owners of these sublets were always "abroad."

Ted had taken a lucrative summer job as a waiter in an oyster bar near Wall Street, only to quit because "it wasn't aesthetically pleasing." Since then, he'd spent his summer in his bedroom over the bakery, where he played his brass guitar until its neck split in half. Then he began to paint portraits of it. He tilted it against the radiator and painted it with its neck dangling like a man hanged in a noose, or set the body on his bed so that its curves settled into his cheap bedspread and the sunlight ignited the brass.

We turned onto Morningside. I leaned left and my legs shifted us off-balance. Ted reached back to shove me into place. He started wobbling again.

"How far do we have to go?" I asked.

"Don't know," he yelled back. "Maybe fifty blocks. You should have gone with Tom."

I wanted to tell Ted about the problems in my marriage, but I didn't want to ruin the joy of being with my brother on a bike.

My hair was cut in a bob that lifted in the warm breeze. The pantsuit ballooned at my back. Ted wore cutoffs that had been long jeans when I last saw him, but the holes in the knees had taken over.

He'd grown out his hair, and the wiry black curls behind his ears were back. Neither of us wore a helmet.

Now we were on Amsterdam, and we hit a stretch of crumbled pavement. My teeth rattled, which made me crack up and almost lose my grip.

"What's so funny?" he said. I could tell he wanted to get his mind off the backbreaking task of pumping another forty blocks, so I went with a story from our childhood. One nice thing about my family: no matter what's troubling us, we can pull a story from our past and forget everything else. I've seen it happen during devastating funerals, failing economies, life-threatening illnesses, and the earliest stages of Mom's hospitalizations. Someone would say, "Remember when Michael complained that Odie drew a worm on his freshly painted wall, and Mom said, 'But it *is* a really cute worm, Mike.'"

"Remember the ring toss?" I said.

"Ha!" Ted honked. "The Taylor boys' carnival."

I jiggled with laughter, almost tipping us over. "Remember our can drive?"

"The can drive." Ted's head turned sideways and he licked his lips. "Mrs. A.'s cookies."

"You always got cookies out of her."

"Yeah, but her house smelled like a zoo."

I remembered Mrs. A.'s menagerie of animals. She always gave us Girl Scout cookies, no matter what time of year. "I'll never eat another Thin Mint again," I said.

"I love those things," said Ted.

"Me too."

We were both quiet for a while. Without any distractions, I saw as clear as the road in front of me that it was time to leave Tom. I'd been taking the standard advice not to make any major changes in the first year of recovery. That year was almost up. I had quit my job in an effort to pump more energy into my marriage. Now I had no income.

On Amsterdam, Ted picked up speed. He found a clear stretch on the sidewalk and pulled onto it. Up ahead, a shopkeeper in an apron carried a broom from his store. His buddy followed him to the sidewalk. The shopkeeper swept while his buddy talked. Ted was looking to cross Amsterdam; he didn't see the men ahead of us. I shouted a warning and he slammed on the brakes at the last second. The jerking motion jarred my right leg loose. It spilled from the bottom of my pant leg onto the sidewalk right next to the shopkeeper's broom. His buddy muttered something in Spanish ending in "Dios." The shopkeeper pulled the broomstick to his chest, looked up to the sky, and blessed himself.

Ted reached down, snatched the leg, and tossed it over the handlebar. He started pedaling fast. My empty pantleg flapped in the breeze. "Give me that back," I said. "Everyone can see it."

Ted honked. "I know," he said. "Isn't it great?"

I leaned into his bony shoulder and held on tight. Nothing embarrassed Ted. If I could count on anyone, I could count on Ted.

A few weeks later, I celebrated my first year of sobriety. I spent the evening at the apartment of a friend named Geila, who was in her third year of law school and her fifth year of recovery. We'd bonded because we were both from Cincinnati and both had a connection to Georgetown Law. It helped that her religious upbringing was more confusing than mine. Her mother was Catholic, her father Jewish, and Geila had spent part of her childhood with Mormons. She had known violence from a young age, and she talked like a character from a David Lynch film. Intimidating to some, annoying to others, Geila was also respected because of her nurturing side. She attributed her mental and physical health to swimming.

Geila chatted with people who lived on the streets. She regularly took food and clothing to a man who slept in a doorway. Sometimes she snapped at people, though it was usually in the spirit of a well-intentioned mother who might throw up her hands in a panic and shriek, "Stop!" Her actions were almost invariably helpful and, in some cases, life-changing. At first I was skeptical, but Geila was the opposite of Uriah Heep, and I admired her for that. I started swimming with her and soon I was swimming every day. I became stronger and at the same time more relaxed. Deeper still, I felt a new sense of confidence in myself.

I studied Geila across the table while we ate my anniversary cake. Despite her tiny build, Geila was anything but elfin. She had a lion's mane of black curls and her eyes held "a glint of gypsy," as she would say. I was trying to decide whether to ask her advice on how to leave my marriage. Mounted on the wall above her head was a painting she called *Freudian Dream*, in which a naked seductress lounged next to a staid Victorian couple. It was something two women from the Midwest might understand instinctively. I laid out my problem.

"What are these obstacles you keep mentioning?" Geila prodded, already listening like a lawyer, making careful note, yet occasionally eyeing the paper she needed to finish for school.

"If I leave Tom my family will disown me," I said.

She burst out laughing. "Next?"

"Come on."

"Well, it isn't as if you're alone," she said. She pointed to a number of people who would help me. Topping the list was an older woman in my neighborhood who was also in recovery. She provided the perfect antidote to Geila's sometimes "goon-squad" tactical coaching. For just about any conflict in which Geila perceived the other party to be a bully, she typically advised the threat of a lawsuit, if not a stream of vulgar insults, whereas my older neighbor would say in her soft voice, "Now, if so and so says something insensitive, you might just say, 'That's very interesting,' and 'I'm afraid I have to go now.'"

"Really?" I'd once said to my neighbor on the phone. I couldn't believe this from a woman with a Washington-insider type of job. "That's it? I mean, no offense, but isn't that a bit wimpy?"

Silence on the line.

"Hello?"

"That's very interesting," she said, "but I'm afraid I have to go now."

Ouch, I'd thought, that's rough.

Where would I be without the women who had supported me? What might I have become if not for Claire and Gretchen, or my roommates in Boston, or these women in DC? In my life so far, I'd relied too often on men.

"But I want children," I said to Geila.

She rolled her eyes. Geila had already raised a niece whom she considered a daughter. Her maternal instincts were satisfied, whereas mine had intensified into a near-physical pain. "You can always adopt, if you can't find the right wanker to marry," she said. Having once lived in England, Geila used "wanker" as a staple in her vocabulary.

"Okay," I conceded. We knew single women who had adopted. They seemed happy.

Money was another issue. Or was it? A few days earlier I'd been offered a solution. I was folding laundry with Oprah Winfrey on the television. I hadn't watched daytime television since the days when Colette and I asked each other, "Why is Laura dating Luke after he raped her?" Now Oprah told her audience, "If a man hits you, it means he doesn't like you." The phone rang, and my old boss was calling me to come back to work. "I'll think about it," I'd said.

Now I pointed out to Geila, "I have fifty dollars in my checking account and three more years of graduate school to finance on a part-time job."

"Well," she said, unimpressed, "when you're ready to go, you'll go."

"Ridiculous," I thought. "There is no way I'm trading in my life to live on scraps. I own a house. I could be a mother soon."

After dinner we watched a movie: Meryl Streep lost her baby to a dingo in the Australian outback. Geila threw up her hands and said, "I gotta go finish my paper," and moved to her study. Twenty minutes later she was back. "What's happening now?"

I held up a stuffed animal and said, "The dango got me baby."

That night I slept on Geila's sofa under *Freudian Dream*. I might have had only fifty dollars in my checking account, and the dingo had my baby, but rehab would always hold a job for me. I never went home after that night.

CHAPTER 24

Wings to Fly

The most obvious lessons have always been the hardest for me to learn. The following winter, I went to Cincinnati for the Christmas holidays and managed to embroil myself in a family squabble over a bûche de Noël. I'd brought along a vintage cookbook organized by theme parties from cities around the world, such as "Hungarian Brunch for Six." A new world awaited me as I finally taught myself how to cook. So far I'd made the cream of carrot soup, the veal pâté, and the walnut soufflé. Because I had no children to bring to the Christmas Eve party, I figured at least I could offer this French cake.

On the morning of Christmas Eve, Mom walked into the kitchen, hands on her hips, and said, "You're not messing up my kitchen. Besides, those grandkids won't have anything to do with fancy food. You would know that if you . . . Oh, forget it. Just get out of my kitchen."

If only I had executed my neighbor's plan: "That's very interesting . . ." Instead I told my mother to fuck off. None of us had ever spoken those words to her. Mom and I stood there staring at each other in shock before we escalated to a near-violent screaming match. If we hadn't been so serious, it might have made good material for a screwball comedy. Instead, I realized it was time to go. I packed up and spent Christmas with friends.

Later that week I visited Aunt Gert, who was battling lung cancer for the second time. Because of chemo, she wore a wig, which contrasted oddly with the clown's wig she'd once worn in a variety show.

"Persistent little dickens, you were," she said as we drank coffee at her kitchen table. "Remember that time you stayed with us? You must have been three or four."

"The Michigan trip."

"You kept trying to put Sally's sneakers on your legs."

"Really? I sort of remember that. Were they Keds?" A jolt of pain ran from the tip of my leg, where there had once been something like a toe, to the top of my spine. "Did I try to stand up in that shoe?"

"You tried it this way and that. You tried everything, and I hated to tell you it would never work, but someone had to. You didn't want to hear it, though."

Then she managed to slip this in: "You know, Eileen, marriages are like kits. You have to keep working on them. They don't come together by themselves." After that she shook her head and whistled through her overbite: "You'll figure things out."

I doubted that. But as I drove away, I wondered if she had been talking about something other than my failed marriage.

Before I left town, I spent the night at Ted's house down by the river. He had moved back to Cincinnati to finish his doctorate. On my last morning in town, Ted and I drank coffee in his kitchen. He twirled the hair behind his right ear nervously while I rehashed the argument with Mom. The phone rang. Ted picked it up, and his eyes expanded with horror. Even though I was about ten feet from the phone, I could hear my oldest sister's voice on the line. Bridget was sobbing when Ted handed me the receiver. My voice tentative, I said, "Hello?"

I couldn't make out her words at first because she was shouting through tears. I said, "Bridget?"

She ordered me to stay away from "my mother." Then she repeated her message in every way imaginable.

Why was she calling me now from Mom's house, when it had been several days since Mom and I had argued? I couldn't be certain, but I guessed that Mom had started pacing and complaining of being a nervous wreck. That would have been enough to turn Bridget into the mama bear. While her actions were understandable, Bridget was doing to me what had been done so many times that I needed to consider whether I could have a relationship with this family. No one ever wanted to hear my side of any story.

It was true that Mom and I had complex issues between us. The only thing I imagined might help our relationship would have been an intervention from a therapist, except for this glitch: Mom hated therapy. She chided me for my patronizing psychobabble, and there was truth to her claim. If I'd proposed an intervention, Mom would probably have said, "That's right . . . call in the therapists because they know soooo much more than the rest of us. Just look at how well therapy has helped you." But the main reason I couldn't bring the idea up was that she'd made it clear to me that she had "no guilt whatsoever" about my birth defects. She had nothing to discuss. If I tried to explain that my complaint was about her handling of my birth defects, not that she had *caused* the defects themselves, she would only raise her voice, "No guilt!" Then she would start pacing, and that would send a message to some of my siblings to tighten the defense, keep that Snarleen away from their mother.

As for her own treatment, Mom had seen the same psychiatrist on and off for years for medication alone. She took it until she stabilized. After that, she functioned rather well. Why would she want to upset herself in therapy over this thalidomide conundrum? Even if she might have considered an intervention, my siblings would have advised her not to participate because it would upset her. This was my problem, not hers, not theirs.

Bridget was running out of ways to tell me to stay away from her mother. This was my chance to politely excuse myself from the call, but I screamed back at her, "Okay! I'll stay away from *your* mother." Then I hung up and went straight to my car.

Ted followed close behind. "You shouldn't drive right now. You're too upset."

"I'm fine," I said, fighting tears. We hugged. I peeled out of the alley behind his house, weeping until I met snow flurries out-side of Columbus. There were mountains to the east, and driving through them at night in the snow would be treacherous. I pushed on, even sped up where possible, and miraculously the skies were clear through the Alleghenies. Everything up ahead promised a better day. Bridget was right, I decided. This was her mother, their mother, not mine. Thalidomide had severed the umbilical cord between Mom and me. I realized then that I had done the right thing in moving away. When I left at twenty-one, I didn't know that I was making a choice between self-respect and having my family. If I had realized that my choices had come down to that, I might have stayed in Cincinnati. Within years or even months, I might have swallowed more pills after some drunken mishap. My naïveté had saved me. Finally, with relief, I neared my home in DC.

Four years later, in 1993, there was snow on Christmas in DC. I called it the Winter of Ice. I'd moved uptown only a year before, and already I was looking for my next home. From my apartment on Connecticut Avenue, I watched gray-haired men and women being wheeled around by black women in white uniforms. *Schindler's List* played at the Avalon near Chevy Chase Circle. The Holocaust Museum opened near the National Mall. I'd reached the end of school and of a youth that I was both celebrating and mourning.

My first job was divided into the two most challenging places to work in the mental health system: a twenty-four-hour emergency service and a jail. I was either sitting with a potentially suicidal patient at midnight, driving to the scene of a domestic squabble that could lead to violence, or talking through bars to a detainee, who might have stolen a carton of cigarettes or beaten a child to death with a baseball bat. The work fascinated me, but it also brought me my first silver hairs. In my spare time, I was studying for the national licensing exam in clinical psychology. I lived alone, and I was getting crank calls from a creepy man who was asking for me by name. My insomnia escalated as I worried that he was someone who had been released from the jail.

I was tired and cranky when I unwittingly prompted my Mobile Crisis partner to tell me about the "two camps" that apparently existed within the emergency service. We were driving to the home of a couple in the throes of a violent argument. At first we talked about the time a suicidal man pulled a gun on our mentors, Kenny and Brad, on one of their Mobile Crisis calls. Because of the way Kenny always told the story, we were laughing. He'd say that Brad had grabbed a pillow from the sofa to shield himself from a potential bullet at close range, while he, Kenny, talked the man into putting the gun down. It had ended as well as could be expected. The man gave up his gun and went into a hospital for treatment. What made the story funny to me was that Kenny looked like Kenny Rogers, the Silver Fox, and every time I heard it, I thought of "The Gambler." *Know when to fold 'em . . .*

To survive this kind of work, you had to distance yourself from the violence while at the same time be thinking through a strategy to defuse it. We had two weapons: to not be surprised by our own and each other's failings; and to believe in each other as a team.

At the end of the story I said, "Some people on the staff still treat me as if I were a first-year student. It's kind of hard to do my job under those conditions."

My partner's jaw tightened as he drove. "Eileen," he said, "you don't know the half of it. Before you were hired, there was a battle between two camps. One camp said the job was too dangerous. Another fought to hire you."

"Jesus," I said. "I need this like I need a kick in the teeth." By now I'd been through this game so often that I vacillated between feelings of bitterness and utter defeat. I'd been trying to get hired onto the adolescent team, my favorite population to work with and the age group on which most of my clinical training had been focused, but a colleague from that team had told me, after I was passed over, that the team leader expressed "concern" over a woman without legs working with traumatized children.

As for doing emergency work under the skeptical eyes of a few peers, I was fortunate to have learned to drive with a mother who gripped her door and pumped an invisible brake from the passenger seat. I could teach myself to be a competent professional, if necessary, even if some of my coworkers were convinced I would fail. I had to focus on the coworkers who had a healthy balance of humor and seriousness toward their job, people like Kenny and Brad. They seemed to believe in me and, as far as I knew, they had never been assaulted by a patient.

When I called Ted for advice, he said, "Sometimes you have to slam the door on your way out of a room and not look back. If anyone gets their fingers caught, tough, that's their problem."

Toughness comes in all forms. For me, at times, it would have to be enough just to survive. In fact, my only defense against an addict who threatened to beat me up if I didn't get the psychiatrist to write a prescription for him was to sit still and wait for him to exhaust himself with his own ranting. Maybe this wasn't the most proactive of philosophies, but it kept me from being slugged.

Later that year, after my partner told me about the two camps arguing over my being hired, the man who led the opposition camp was assaulted by an aggressive patient. Apparently, he had first shoved the patient against a wall. From this I learned: a) never doubt myself, especially when someone else is eager to do it for me; and b) when it comes to working with violent patients, I'll take mental stamina over physical brawn any day.

One of the perks of working long hours was that I could take long vacations. Over a couple of years I traveled to Guatemala and Honduras, Greece and Turkey, Mexico, and twice I drove across country.

I also developed a network of friends to replace some of the friends I'd lost contact with after my divorce. By now Claire was living in Atlanta with her husband. Her two kids were in elementary school. I was just beginning to date again, but mostly I slummed with Geila or my other best friend, Jackson, a senior chess master. I'd met him through an old roommate, who played on Jackson's chess team. Because we're the same age, Jackson and I connected on pop hits from the seventies. When he ran out of things to say, he would sing in his nasally voice, "Betcha by Golly Wow," to which I would say, "Sixth grade."

Like me, Jackson had an unusual youth. At sixteen he'd been accepted to Princeton; however, he was so obsessed with chess that he couldn't break away from games to attend classes. Now in his thirties, he spent upward of forty-eight continuous hours playing chess online with masters and grandmasters in Russia. I'd barely heard of the Internet, and Jackson spent half of his life on it. He'd given up a great job for these bonanza chess matches, and it took three years for him to get around to looking for another job. For those three years, outside of his chess games, he was always free to catch a movie or to get a bite to eat, and he never ran out of money. On the floorboard of his one extravagance, a red Ford Fiesta—into which he fit his six-and-a-half-foot body like a Jackson-in-the-box—I'd find paychecks, never deposited, from his previous job. Later, his fiancée collected several thousand dollars in old paychecks just by cleaning his apartment. "And to think," I said, "we could have opened your glove box, cashed a check at a drive-thru, and taken off for Mexico."

Jackson's mother adopted me for holidays. The tradition began with my job on the emergency service. I had to work every holiday in my first year, so Jackson brought his mother's Thanksgiving dinner to me.

Now, on this snowy Christmas, Jackson met me at an all-night diner after I left work at midnight. As soon as we took our booth, I said, "I hate Christmas, and I hate men."

"Hmm," said Jackson, who was never offended by my swipes at men. He was more interested in the songs on the jukebox, and in food. He turned to the menu. On several occasions, I'd watched Jackson consume bushels of food in a single sitting. "Didn't you just eat a huge Christmas dinner?" I said.

He patted his stomach. "Define huge."

"You're lucky you're so tall. I'm just hoping my thyroid holds out. I'm thirty-three!"

"Thirty-three," he said, looking up from the menu, "the age of Jesus at death."

"Thank you, Jackson."

"Things could be worse, you know." Then he did a poor imitation of a Monty Python character singing "Always Look on the Bright Side of Life."

He ordered something from both the breakfast and the lunch menus—because he'd "saved up" that day for Christmas dinner. I watched him eat both meals before he finished off my fries, which was hilarious in light of our last outing, when, after he'd watched me eat a baked potato, he asked, "Should I call in the People for the Ethical Treatment of Potato Skins?"

We left at three in the morning. I drove down an almost desolate Connecticut Avenue and pulled my new white Rabbit into an empty spot next to a snowbank. With no traffic, the only person in sight was a woman in a white uniform shivering at the bus stop across the street from me. I climbed out of my car and was trying to figure out how to get over the two-foot embankment when a sedan raced south on Connecticut, stopped suddenly, then pulled into the side street next to the woman. A car door opened. The light came on inside it, and I saw three men. One man leapt out and dragged the woman toward the car. I stood on my side of the street and watched, helpless. There were no lights coming from the apartment buildings lining either side of the street. This was before cell phones. The woman fought to get into the middle of Connecticut Avenue. Maybe she was hoping for a car to come along. The man reached for her with both hands now. She tried to twist from his grip and reach out at the same time. I realized that she was reaching toward me. I was two lanes away from her, where I waited, waving her to keep coming. Finally, she freed one arm. The man started to reach for something inside his coat. But he looked out to where she was heading, saw me, the unexpected witness, and let go of her. She raced over to me and we hugged. The man climbed back in the car, which zoomed away. This stranger and I were left alone, clinging to each other.

"Was that your husband?" I asked.

"You jokin', right?" She took a minute to gather her breath. "That man was a kidnapper."

I'd become so jaded about marriage. Now the idea of it made me burst out laughing, and she looked at me as if I were creepier than the kidnapper. "I'm sorry," I said. "Just forget it."

She told me that she had just gotten off work and had only seven dollars in her purse. When she had revealed that to a cab driver, he refused to take her down to Southeast, DC, which was why she'd been waiting for a bus. "You saved my life," she said. I think we both understood that because I was white, I had been spared. Those men assumed that no one would look very hard for the kidnapper of a black domestic worker. We went to my apartment. I called a taxi and gave her money for fare. Downstairs we hugged again before she climbed into the cab that took her home.

For a moment I stood at the curb and took in the scene: a pitch-black sky and Connecticut Avenue covered in snow. I went upstairs and climbed into bed. For some reason I slept soundly that night.

Enough drama, I decided. Shortly after the holidays, I took a break from studying for the licensing exam. Now, without a book to study in my spare time, I started ushering for the Shakespeare Theatre, I went to hypnosis workshops, and I hired a tutor to give me Spanish lessons. That spring I went to Mexico City to meet the family of a man who had read my newspaper article while studying at the University of Minnesota. His brother had been born with partial arms because of thalidomide. The three of us had been writing and visiting each other for five years. Now their parents welcomed me into their home and gave me a biography of Frida Kahlo, in Spanish. Then they took me to her home, La Casa Azul, to which

I would return twice more. Frida had expressed herself in words as well as in her paintings. Her diary includes small sketches and paintings, as well as remarkable statements about her life. La Casa Azul seemed to me a painted diary that opened itself to the world. My visit reminded me of what I had lost: my writing. Frida Kahlo's paintings drew me in, but her words described my life:

> *"I never paint dreams or nightmares. I paint my own reality."*

> *"The only thing I know is that I paint because I need to, and I paint whatever passes through my head without any other consideration."*

> *"I paint self-portraits because I am so often alone, because I am the person I know best."*

> *"I tried to drown my sorrows, but the bastards learned how to swim, and now I am overwhelmed by this decent and good feeling."*

> *"My painting carries with it the message of pain."*

> *"Painting completed my life."*

> *"Feet, what do I need you for when I have wings to fly?"*

From Mexico City I traveled alone to Puerto Escondido, where I met two women who had driven from Los Angeles in a Volkswagen camper. We watched the sunset from the beach while the camper's stereo played Astrud Gilberto's "The Girl from Ipanema." The camper and the song brought me back to the days when Frankie and I played for hours in a camper while Mom and Dad listened to "Bittersweet Samba." If I was ever going to be free of mental torment, I would have to recast my childhood memories, sort of like painting the same picture but using different colors, or composing new music to go with old lyrics.

I've long since forgotten the names of the women I met in Puerto Escondido, but now when I hear "The Girl from Ipanema," I see the inside of a Volkswagen camper.

I can easily go back to the brick hearth in our den, where as a child I rummaged through the bookshelves, dreaming of the day I'd become a reader while others became walkers, runners, and bicyclists. At first, I pretended to read the books to Ted, making up the stories as I went along. Finally I became a reader, and those titles gave me a place inside a collective experience, which made me eager to catch up with my older siblings. Every book an older sibling read became something to strive for myself. Our paperback copy of *The Sun Also Rises* was curled at the corner of the cover from so many readers. I worried that corner until it ripped away. *L'Etranger* inspired me to choose French in high school, and once I understood its meaning, the title filled me with ennui. Beckoning from the center of the right-hand bookshelf, Mom's book *The Heart of the Matter* piqued my curiosity: heart of what matter?

The image of my siblings in a full house starts here by the hearth also. In this room after dinner we held "flying contests." Without legs, I was the most sought-after flying partner. The older kids would lie on their backs and propel the middle children with their feet. Because I could balance my abbreviated body on a foot so neatly, Michael and Rosa fought over me. Rosa always lured me to her team by promising to give me a perm. She'd lower me into a "one-foot kiss," or fasten my armpits over her heels and swing me between her legs for the "belle of the ball." Beside us Frankie, with a wad of Mom's stew in his jaw, balanced on Michael's feet while Michael ordered him to swallow and Rosa ordered him to spit it out. Eventually the other middle children grew too big to play, while my short body lasted until well into elementary school. I was still competing when Matthew started as a toddler. It was Tim, the agile acrobat, who forced me off the circuit. Liz wrapped a scarf around his head and secured it with an oval brooch, making it into a turban while he was still in diapers. She called him "Louie, the Great Zambini," cuing him with two claps before he raced into a dazzling flip twist. They were an unbeatable team.

During that window of time when I could still fly but I was old enough to read, I'd focus on the magenta crowns embossed on the binding of *The Little Prince* and imagine that Rosa's musty feet, clad in cable-knit socks and digging into my ribcage, were a magic carpet. Only from above her feet could I spot that strange title sequestered behind the television set: *The Man Without a Country*. The idea behind those words made me contemplate an unknown world, and the distraction might cause me to lose my focus and topple from Rosa's feet with my head aimed at the brick hearth containing a roaring fire, or to soar and twirl in feats of acrobatic finesse.

When I remember who I am and where I come from, I see myself flying in our den beside those books, wearing my Saint Vivian uniform and no legs, my stomach aching from gnarled toes poking into my ribs, my brothers and sisters competing, our parents sharing stories and drinks with our grandparents out on the screened-in porch, and "Bittersweet Samba" on the stereo in the living room.

Brazilian jazz tunes set the beat to my sixties childhood, just as those book titles in our den colored my imagination with their philosophical refrain. All I needed now was to fall in love with a poet in Brazil.

CHAPTER 25

Dancing with Andy

After nearly two years in the jail and the emergency service, I was finally accepted onto the adolescent team. It had taken three tries and a growing camp of supporters, which included the two people who had been hired over me. When I announced I was leaving the emergency service, the director cried and I had to stay another six months because I had become "essential personnel." Before starting my new job, I moved to Arlington, Virginia, having found out that my crank caller was not a released detainee but a man in my apartment building on Connecticut Avenue. By the time I was reunited with adolescents, I was almost a grownup myself. I was thirty-four.

That fall, I met Andy. We were both guests at Geila's fundraiser for a congressional candidate from Cincinnati. Our candidate lost but Andy and I became friends, which we stayed for more than a year. Then we fell in love.

Andy was in DC on a fellowship with the US Information Agency and, after a couple extensions, his time had run out. He would have to return to his job teaching literature at, of all places, Miami University, a school just thirty minutes from Cincinnati. We worried that the odds of finding a tenure-track position in Washington DC for his specialty, American modernist literature, were close to nil. We were only months into our romance when he was invited to teach for a semester in Brazil. He took the job. This would buy him time to apply for permanent positions.

"It's only for a semester," he said at the airport before a convincing kiss. Still, I wondered if I'd ever see him again as I pulled out of National Airport in my blue Miata, a magnificent car that was all wrong for me. I'd crashed it into a pole, and even Andy, who had never so much as dented a car before, bashed it into another pole while backing out of a tight spot in my garage. Then, just before I took him to the airport, he'd accidentally pushed his suitcase through the plastic window in the rear of the convertible top. Driving home on the G. W. Parkway, I tried not to imagine why he'd become the clumsiest man on the planet just as he was leaving town. March winds rattled my diminutive car from inside out, heaving through the fresh hole in my rear window, which now made the dents on either side of my car feel like two black eyes. I had never been so happy and so at peace with a man. Now I had to ask myself, "Why would he come back here?" We both knew that he'd have to go wherever he found a job.

Days passed without any word from Andy. I braced myself for the letter in which he would explain why our relationship could never work out, that we had a good friendship and maybe that's how we should leave it. Was he that kind of man? Trust topped my latest list of values to strive for in a relationship. Still, I had to be honest with myself: trust had nothing whatsoever to do with my initial attraction to Andy.

When I first saw him in his charcoal suit at Geila's party, he had been leaning against the buffet table, the *Freudian Dream* painting at his back. I thought, "This is a man who knows how to position himself well." (Position, I said to myself now as I glanced back at the hole in my window. He'd come to DC to *escape* a dead-end position.)

Maybe it was his dark mustache, or his manner: the way he

crossed one ankle over the other, casually, while folding his arms authoritatively and telling me that I was completely wrong when I quoted a poem by Berryman and attributed it to Eliot. Or maybe I connected his having worked on a farm to earn money for college with my father's youth. Honestly, though, I'd have to say it was his looks. With his thick hair, dark brown streaked with silver, and his mustache, he dominated the room without opening his mouth. "Sublime" was how I saw him; trustworthy wasn't even a consideration.

At the time, though, Andy was more in the market for a job than a girlfriend. In that first year, we swam laps in the basement of my high-rise, went to films—after which we argued their merits—and walked his dog, Polly, a chubby mix of beagle and basset hound. I understood that we were friends, and yet deeper feelings stirred. I had no idea how to bring them out. On a fall evening a year later, while we walked Polly, he mentioned that he'd learned to read tarot cards in Cincinnati.

"Tarot cards," I said. "In Cincinnati?"

"Yes."

"Okay, when will you give me a reading?"

"Did I mention that Polly peed next to James Carville's King Charles spaniel last week over in Lincoln Park?"

"Yes. Maybe three times. How about now? Will you give me a reading tonight?"

"I'm just an amateur," he said, waving it off.

"I'll take my chances," I said.

At this point his fellowship had been extended for an extra six months and his lease was up, so he'd moved into the spare bedroom in Geila's house. We came home and Geila was upstairs. I called up to her bedroom, "Geila, come get your tarot reading."

"Oh, please," she said from behind a closed door. Whatever she said after that we couldn't make out. "I guess that means she'll pass," said Andy, who was already taking his tarot cards from a drawer in the buffet. We sat at the dining room table. He untied the silk scarf that bound the cards. I wondered, "Who gave him this silk scarf?" And he laid out my cards.

I took a frantic look at cards that made no sense and blurted out, "Well, am I ever gonna have a baby?"

Andy had looked at me and blinked, not so much out of shock as out of understanding. He said, "The cards are pregnant with optimism."

Three weeks after Andy left for Brazil and I was still without word from him, my optimism waned. Then I received a postcard. I read it in my high-rise apartment. In teensy print, he explained that the university had put him up in an apartment suite with visiting professors from around the world who rotated through at varying intervals, some for two days, others for a month, still others for a year. Some were there and gone before he met them. The telephone in the rotating suite could not place long-distance calls; a naked electrical wire hovered over his shower; power outages made a sham of the computer lab; and he loved Brazil!

He added a PS with a phone number and asked me to call him. I raced to the phone and dialed the number. Another man answered my call. In an accent I could not pinpoint, he said he'd never heard of anyone named Andy. That seemed to be the extent of this man's English. I hung up, confused and teetering on heartbroken. I dropped the postcard into the basket of mail on my counter and told myself that while it was true that Andy had put himself through college by inspecting tomatoes, it was also true that he'd played in a band. When I put the pieces together it did not look promising: a handsome poet, former band member, now in Brazil. Was this a man ready to make a commitment?

I took that question to my closest advisors. Jackson never held back on his assessment of my relationships' chances of survival. "I'd give it about ten percent," he'd say when feeling optimistic. About a previous boyfriend he'd said, "The odds aren't so good."

"How bad?" I asked.

"Less than zero." Then he added, "You choose guys based on their looks, then you complain that they're conceited."

"Not true. I choose men who are intelligent."

"Hmm," he'd said, closing his eyes as if ready to go to sleep.

Geila shared Jackson's opinion about the men I dated, and neither was enthusiastic about Andy, who was intelligent but suffered from reasonably good looks and a touch of arrogance. Both were quick to admit that he was a fabulous cook. Jackson had even said, with a lick of his lips, "I hope he comes back."

"You're thinking of that African stew," I said. "Aren't you?"

"The peanut sauce was a brilliant move," he'd whispered.

Not long before I met Andy, I'd quit seeing my therapist. She'd been a patient listener but she shied away from challenging me. Because I missed my old therapist in Boston, I started up again and chose a male therapist, but when I told this new therapist that Andy played guitar and sang songs to me that he'd composed himself, the therapist winced and chuckled boyishly.

Eventually I would see that it wasn't my therapists, my friends, or Andy that I didn't trust; it was me. Back when I was contemplating leaving my marriage, I kept asking for everyone else's opinion. Someone would say, "How could you do that?" And someone else would say, "Do you know what you're in for?" Finally I'd complained to my older friend, Queen of Subtlety, who said, "When you start making decisions without the vote of everyone in the room, then you are officially a grownup."

Once again, I was without many votes. There was nothing about

Andy to recommend him as a serious boyfriend. First, he lived in another hemisphere; second, he did not have a permanent job; and third, he'd been divorced as long as I had—a sign that I interpreted to mean that we were both meant to be thrown back in the pond. And wonder of wonders, he was Jewish. How many times had I been down that road?

A couple days passed when a second postcard arrived. Andy gave the same phone number. He's got to be joking, I thought. Then I read the ending, in which he'd squeezed in a sentence about his plane trip to Brazil, confessing that he'd cried over the movie *Babe*. "Please call me," he wrote in even smaller print at the bottom.

"*Babe*?" I could just imagine my therapist's wince.

Once I'd seen a tear fall from Andy's eye. It happened after he met me at the Metro station during a blizzard. By then I had taken and passed the licensing exam and I was in my first year of private practice, which included mostly adult women, a few couples, and enough teenagers to keep me alert. Since our office had closed during the blizzard, I was bored in my high-rise. I called Andy from my apartment in Arlington to ask what was going on in town. "Come down to the Hill," he said.

An hour later, he and Polly greeted me at the top of the Eastern Market escalator. Polly was squeamish. Andy explained that he'd rescued her from the streets of Oxford, Ohio, where fraternities would abandon their dogs for the summer. I remembered Brandy the one-eyed dog and wondered what plans had been made for her after the Water Street boys left Williamstown. I hoped they had found her a home. Had I worried about that back then? It was too long ago to recall.

We started walking back to the house and Polly dragged her heels in snow that was up to her chin. A freezing wind cut through the Seventh Street corridor, sending a tear down Andy's cheek. "My eye leaks in the cold," he explained. Polly hunkered down and refused to budge, so Andy hoisted her over his shoulder and carried her four blocks. She weighed about ninety pounds.

That same afternoon, we cuddled for the first time during a movie. Andy was stiff and awkward. I assumed he had no interest in me romantically. But we met up every day that week while our offices were shut down by the blizzard. One day, after we swam laps in the basement of my apartment building, we went out to lunch and swapped stories about being young and stupid. "Once I jumped from a bridge into a river on a canoe trip with my sorority," I told him. "Actually, I asked Gretchen and Pam to shove me off because I was afraid to let go."

"And they did?"

"Yep. You should have seen the man who was fishing on the riverbank with his son. He looked up and there was this girl without legs getting tossed from a bridge into the Little Miami."

Andy's face turned somber and I thought he was going to tell me that my story was pathetic. Instead he said, "I jumped off a cliff once. But into a lake. I never felt so free. Are you a risk-taker?"

I didn't know how to answer because I thought that was obvious, but his serious face demanded a response, so I said, "Yes. I'm a risk-taker." As soon as I said it, I regretted my answer because I was hopelessly in love with Andy, and I chided myself, "Caretaker, you dope. Men want caretakers, not risk-takers."

Andy looked up and said, "I think we're in dangerous territory." Then he returned to staring solemnly at the table and added, "I think Geila is in love with me."

I burst out laughing. "Geila is not in love with you! She's in love with me. She's always been in love with me."

"What?"

"Oh, yeah," I said. "It's one of those unrequited love stories between friends of the same sex."

"I don't think so," he said, shaking his head. "I know when a woman is in love with me."

"Oh," I said. "You're sure about that?"

That evening we watched *Pride and Prejudice* on the television in my bedroom, and afterward he kissed me. A day later he was back, this time pinning me to the bed, then the dresser, even a counter, anything he could balance me against to gain traction. Once he started, there was no shutting him off.

I might have told Jackson about Andy carrying Polly in a snow-storm, but I knew what he would say: "The old wounded animal act." Then he would have closed his eyes like Yoda. And if I told Geila about the risk-taker question followed by the introduction of sex, she would have said, "And you didn't see that one coming?" I decided not to bother weighing in on the *Pride and Prejudice* kiss with my wincing therapist. It was time to trust myself. I had never felt such a combination of comfort with and attraction to a man.

Now that he was in another country, I missed everything about Andy, including his dog. He'd sent Polly to his father in California for the semester, and I missed the click of her nails on the wood floors as she chased after Andy when he answered the door.

I finished reading the second postcard and ransacked the basket where I'd put Andy's first one. I plucked it out and compared them. The phone number was definitely the same. "Doesn't he know that number is wrong?" I said.

I picked up the phone and dialed again. This time a woman answered in an accent I would come to know as Portuguese. Then Andy came on the line.

"Who was that?" I asked, trying not to sound jealous.

"You called."

"Of course. Didn't you get my message?"

"No, I don't know half the people in this suite, and I don't speak Japanese, Danish, or even Portuguese. I'm so glad you called." The line crackled, and he said, "When are you coming down?" Then he whispered, "I miss you."

"When do you want me?" I asked.

That April, Andy and I sat under an umbrella on Itapuã Beach near the colonial city of Salvador, which was once the capital of Brazil. I was finishing a book that he had handed me on the plane from Brasilia, Jorge Amado's *War of the Saints*. "Read this," he'd said, "if you really want to know Salvador."

Now I tried to imagine my own visit from an *orixá*, which is what African slaves called the spirits they summoned through candomblé. In colonial times, slaves were required to take Catholicism as their religion, so they told their captors they were worshipping saints. These spirits were said to inhabit statues or even people. On my first day at the beach, I carved a mermaid in the sand. "Maybe she'll come to life," I said.

"Look at that," said Andy. "Her tail just wiggled."

That afternoon we visited the market and bought guava, papaya, cashew fruit, and acerola. At night we ordered *mucceca*, a dish made with palm oil and seafood. There was nothing we didn't love about this city: its people, its food, its percussive music, and its dance, samba and capoeira. We visited reliquary shops near the church of Nosso Senhor do Bonfim, where travelers come from hundreds of miles away to leave relics and to pray for a miracle. "I need to buy one of these statues for Ted," I said. Ted was now a father and in his spare time he painted portraits of scowling martyrs, while his family decorated their lawn with bowling balls and saints. For Ted's family, I chose Saint Sebastian tied to a stake with arrows piercing his body.

By nighttime the church of Bonfim was lit up, and even in the dark people waited on the steps to be healed. I told Andy about the time Frankie and I climbed the steps of Mount Adams to ask Jesus for a pair of legs. Andy didn't laugh or write it off as naïve superstition, nor did he believe in miracles. His had been one of the few Jewish families in his small hometown, a place with farmers, prison guards, and schoolteachers. Like his brothers and his parents, he maintained his own beliefs while managing to fit into a Christian community. His father was now serving his fifth term as mayor.

Before leaving Bonfim, someone handed us a few souvenir ribbons. "Make a wish," said Andy as he tied a red ribbon to my left wrist.

I wanted to ask for Andy to come back to DC, but that seemed too self-serving, so I prayed for him to get a job. Then I prayed he'd get a job in DC. I had never figured out whose God I believed in, if any, but I'd stopped worrying about it. Now I just believed in the universe, in the joy of life, and I was beginning to believe that the energy driving all of nature was love.

"Is it a prayer or a wish?"

"Wish, prayer, whatever," said Andy. He handed me a yellow and green ribbon. "If you tie this on my wrist, I'll never take it off."

"Why not?" I asked.

"Because that's the rule. You tie the ribbon on and make a wish. Or a prayer. Then you can never take it off. It has to disintegrate in the shower or something."

"That could be a while," I said, fingering my ribbon.

"I'm prepared to deal with that."

From Bonfim we were ready to take on the African spiritual roots, and we started to search for a candomblé. This took us a few days. Authentic ceremonies are hidden, as they were when slaves had to practice their religion in secret. The ceremony has to take place on soil. Since so much of Salvador is covered in concrete, it's only in the ramshackle hills of a favela that one can find enough bare earth for a candomblé. We came in a cab. The driver parked and walked us up a steep hill on a broken staircase. We arrived just before the ceremony started. Andy joined the men on one side of an otherwise barren courtyard, and I joined the women on the opposite side. Our jeans and white skin made us obvious outsiders. No one embraced us, but no one questioned our sincerity either. They even gave us each a seat among the few chairs lined up on either side.

Soon a woman entered, wearing a white colonial dress with a turbaned headdress. Ruffled from waist to shin, she carried a plate of food to set at a distance from the crowd. Andy and I looked at each other from across the room. *For the orixás?*

The drummers pounded an African beat, and the center of the room filled with a stream of dancers whose full white skirts lifted and swirled as they brushed past us in circle upon circle. With her hooped skirt, the leader wore pink slippers with pom-poms. She might have picked them up at K-Mart, except that we were in Salvador. Andy's eyebrows shot up at the sight of those slippers, and just as quickly his subdued expression returned. I had to cover my mouth so I wouldn't laugh.

The woman shuffled her slippers in a dance based on an African beat with percussive instruments. In a commanding alto, she led the song. A string of dancers followed her into a circular dance, each twirling circles into a larger circle. Just watching the movement was hypnotic. For two hours the women danced without resting. Then one woman dropped to the floor, her body rigid then spasmodic as the spirit entered her. I looked to Andy, who was looking to me. We both turned back to the woman on the floor, whose fits and jerks continued as the woman in pink slippers crouched beside her. An invisible force wrestled with both of them until they surrendered. From the silence came a barely audible sigh. We sank back into our seats, exhausted.

After we left the ceremony, having been permitted to come so close to the secret of another culture, we were silent. That night there was no critiquing, no debating. We just felt closer, safer in each other's arms.

On our last night, Andy and I drank coffee outdoors in a square surrounded by colonial buildings painted turquoise, pink, and yellow. We faced the gold and white façade of São Francisco Church. I was trying to quit but I still smoked a cigarette or two every night, which Andy tolerated even though he was adamantly against smoking. His home had burned down when he was a boy, possibly due to a cigarette; now he tapped strangers in public to point out the "No Smoking" sign. On this last night in Bahia, we tried to break free of our fears.

"Try one," I said, joking, as I slid a cigarette his way. "It's a clove cigarette."

"Okay," he said, lighting up. Soon he stamped it out. "That is sickening."

I stood up. "Okay. I'm going to get you drunk. Come on, I'll be the designated walker." I grabbed his hand. "Everyone's going to that church." I pointed to São Francisco. People jammed into the space beneath the arches so that the vestibule and the square blended into one. Organ music played inside. Every chandelier was lit; it gleamed like a palace.

A priest in silver robes doused the frenetic mob with holy water from an ornate aspergillum, which reminded me of a scepter. We joined the masses.

"This is wild," said Andy.

"Church was never this much fun back in the States," I said.

Drenched in holy water, we wandered out onto a cobblestone street leading to the *pelourinho*, the pillory. In front of another church were iron shackles where slaves had been flogged if they refused Catholicism.

"Let's find some capoeira," said Andy.

"I agree," I said, taking one last look at the iron shackles. Capoeira is a martial arts dance that was developed by slaves in secrecy, since they were not allowed weapons. Young men and women perform it on the streets to the accompaniment of the berimbau, an instrument made from a gourd and a reed shaped into a bow. We found the stage where some of the best dancers performed. A woman in a muscle shirt with rippled biceps oiled to shine like mahogany kicked a leg over her partner's ropy shoulder. He crouched before springing from his toes into a back flip.

When they finished the dance, we made our way back to the main square again. "I thought you were going to get me drunk," said Andy.

"I know, but everywhere we turn is a church."

We heard drums pounding to a samba rhythm and Andy walked toward the sound, stopping in front of a building with a sign that read "Grupo Filhos de Gandhi."

"What does that mean?" I asked.

Andy had been studying Portuguese since his arrival in Brazil. He explained how Carnaval is organized. "This is like a fraternity," he said.

"A fraternity?" I rolled my eyes and started to leave.

"Not like fraternities in Ohio," said Andy, catching my arm. "This is a fraternity for Carnaval. This group is called the Sons of Gandhi."

From inside an otherwise empty lobby, two skinny boys in droopy jeans and soccer shirts beckoned us to join them. We shook our heads because we were both thinking they might rob us. It had been risky enough to go to the favela. Maybe this was pushing it. As we turned away the boys called us back, laughing and raising their thumbs. *"Todo legal!"*

Andy lit up at the expression. *"Todo?"* he asked, stopping.

"Todo!"

"What are they saying?"

He told me that his students used this phrase to mean "It's all cool." The boys said something else to Andy, who strained to comprehend their Portuguese before he threw up his hands in surrender. Waving us in, the boys pretended to pound drums, their feet moving to a samba beat.

"It's a nightclub," said Andy. "You want to try it?"

"I guess it's safe. They are the Sons of Gandhi," I said.

Soon the boys were ushering us down an ominous hallway. We paused before entering a dark staircase, but the music grew louder from below and promised festivities ahead. We took the stairs, then an alley, and came to a courtyard by following the high-pitched voices and thundering drums. On the stage, four bony boys in soccer shirts and sagging jeans played homemade percussive instruments. They couldn't have been more than fourteen years old. The singer's voice hadn't quite changed yet. Pounding instruments made from metal, animal-skin, or gourd, the boys sang to an audience of about five people sitting at cheap plastic tables. They included a woman who might have been one hundred years old. She rose up every so often to dance until she collapsed into another plastic chair. The place was too empty to leave.

"You want to stay?" asked Andy.

"I love it," I said. "These guys are great."

He gave me his dreamy stare with his heartthrob smile, probably a remnant of his days in a band. I wondered if he knew how cute he looked. He'd shaved off his mustache before we ever kissed, but I couldn't remember when it had disappeared.

Andy ordered a caipirinha, and I drank Guarana, a Brazilian soda with the same effect as Jolt. The place was filling up. By the time a new band came on, the place was packed. This band was led by boys who were maybe sixteen. They set a long-necked beer bottle on the stage and started to hiss and cackle. The audience let out a collective sigh just as the drumming began. Andy and I looked at each other. What was so funny about an empty bottle? Then someone said, *"Boquinha da garrafa."*

"What's that?" I asked.

"The mouth of the bottle," Andy explained awkwardly. "It's a euphemism."

"For what?"

"A penis."

"What?"

"You'll see."

Two girls were coaxed onto the stage: one with cornrows, compact in her tube top and stretch pants, the other a sultry girl with kinky auburn hair and mocha-colored skin, in a backless sundress. The girls in the crowd rattled their hands then squeezed them over their eyes as if to say, "I can't watch."

I worried for those girls onstage. What was about to happen up there?

The compact girl stepped forward easily. Without much ado she danced over the bottle, lowering herself into a crouch over it, and gyrating athletic hips to a raucous cheer from the crowd.

"Oh. I see," I said.

"Mm hmm," said Andy.

The sultry woman in the backless dress took her place. Before long we witnessed girls of all ages and shapes, in all manner of dress—miniskirts, hot pants, bikinis—lining up to crouch over the beer bottle, shimmying down on it. Even the old woman gave it a shot. She tipped and swayed from age abetted by alcohol until two young men gently led her back to another plastic chair on the sidelines.

Sweat, toil, and sex permeated the air. We were deep in the swell of the crowd, dancing and cheering for the latest contender when two boys whisked me away from Andy. With drumbeats pounding, girls gyrating over bottles, and other girls latching onto the newly freed Andy, I was lifted from my place and sandwiched between boys who ground into me, front and back. I grew frantic until I saw Andy's face pop out from a tangle of female limbs. He was searching the crowd for me. Our eyes met. We reached our hands through the crowd, but our captors squeezed tighter and edged us apart.

Lost between the boys, frightened but now laughing nervously, I wrestled against their playful rocking to get back to Andy. I shoved into the chest of one boy and elbowed the other in the gut. This only freed me enough to keep my head above the fray. The rush of aggression mixed with my fear of losing Andy, and was topped off by the heart-pounding effects of Guarana. Drums throbbed and echoed so that I couldn't tell whether the swirl of madness was inside me or had engulfed me. Finally I spotted Andy inside the confusion of girls, ecstasy shadowed by hysteria on his face. Our eyes met again; his body slackened with relief. Then he wiped a tear from his cheek, which made me laugh so hard that I cried.

When his semester ended in July, Andy and I began our life together by catching a charter flight from Miami to the Dominican Republic along with about one hundred people, most of them my family. We were on our way to a wedding; Tim, my youngest brother, was getting married.

It had been seven years since Bridget warned me to stay away from her mother. Shortly after her phone call, she sent me a note that included the exact words Mom had once said to me: "Eileen, you sow what you reap." That only stiffened my resolve.

A few years later, in the spirit of reconciliation, I went home to visit every sibling in Cincinnati and take photos of their children. I was most eager to see Ted's baby boy, who would grow into a gentler, downright angelic, version of Ted. If there was one unifying feature among all my siblings, it was that we loved children. It amazed me to see how much of my parents were alive in each of my siblings, even in my nieces and nephews. I saw fragments of my parents in every laugh, every smile, every wince, and that meant that there were fragments inside me: pieces of my parents, my siblings, my grandparents.

No one had changed, really. The insider siblings still clustered to talk about the stuff they'd always talked about, only now their stories included condos in the south and summer homes in New England. I'd hear them and think, "I didn't even know so-and-so owned a summer house." Bridget and Mom's garbled prophecies had come true. I'd become the woman without a country.

During those years, I had faced another of my battles with an insurance company over a pair of legs. Out of a sense of frustration, I called Mom and asked her why she and Dad had never sued the pharmaceutical company. She told me that back in the sixties she'd been approached by our old neighbor Charlie Keating about a lawsuit.

"You can't be serious! Why didn't you do it?" I asked.

"Because I never took that pill!" she said.

Sometime during that period, Mom had Michael call me. He gave me a forty-five-minute lecture on taking responsibility for ourselves and our families, mentioning that it was a shame I hadn't wanted any children. Children were the whole point, he said. Then he asked me why I'd wasted so much time in school. Did I not value family? Before I could answer, he said he would take out a modest life insurance policy for Mom and list me as the beneficiary. I appreciated the gesture, but it wouldn't solve my problem, which was that I hated asking Mom for help and lived in fear that I would have to ask her for it one day. What if she said no? My worrying made me resent my mother. Worse, it kept my relationships with my siblings strained.

In recent years, the "babies" had been getting married. I attended each wedding. Tim's was the last. He was marrying Isabela, a spirited Montessori teacher from Santo Domingo.

I was pleased to have Andy accompanying me. The ceremony took place in an old church in Puerto Plata. Isabela made a striking bride in startling white, her black hair styled into a perfect bun.

That evening, the DJ mixed salsa with popular wedding tunes such as "YMCA" and "Shout." Liz rallied folks for our traditional circle dance, starting us off with a go-go step to a Beach Boys number, then Ted did his drunken uncle routine—Tom Waits meets Dick Van Dyke—and right after my cousin's husband cartwheeled through the Circle of Doom, Andy jumped into its core.

Musicality is what I love most about Andy. His tastes range from Bossa Cubana to Appalachian strings. He plays guitar and piano, writes lyrics and melodies, but it's his dancing I love most. Andy's light step turns an ordinary bounce into a spring. He drops his torso and his knees alternate up and down, fingers snapping at his sides. Whether he's shimmying to "Hava Nagila," clapping to flamenco, or doing the do-si-do, the dance is uniquely Andy's.

And here's the best part: even when he's taking up a good chunk of space, he's inviting me in and is not too concerned about where I'll fit. Leave it to him: Andy always makes it work.

From the rim of the Circle of Doom I watched him dance and couldn't help but notice his dreamy smile, even as my older siblings eyed him suspiciously. The younger ones cheered him on: Ted, Nina, and then Isabela, who already adored Andy because he could carry on a respectable conversation with her mother in Spanish. The simplicity with which Andy fit in overwhelmed me. Who would have thought that love could be this easy?

I had to consider that Mom's absence played some role in the success of Andy's introduction to my family. She had stopped flying after her trip to Las Vegas when Frank died. I felt sad for Tim and Isabela that Mom couldn't be here; for myself, I was relieved.

I was wearing a black silk dress that dipped into a V in back accompanied by a sheer scarf with a red-and-black leopard print. The saleslady in a boutique in Georgetown showed me how to drape it over my shoulders. "See, it draws attention to your back and shoulders and those sculpted arms of yours." *Sculpted?* Until then I'd seen them as more along the lines of Popeye's sister.

I lifted my slinky skirt and stepped into the Circle of Doom with Andy. I raised the leopard-print scarf over my head and slid it across my shoulders, which raised goose bumps all over my body. I looped it around Andy's neck, pulling him to me. His arms steadied me, and his breath was on my cheek. When I looked up at him, we kissed.

I had told Andy very little about my family. How could I explain our complex relationships? None of that mattered to him. He enjoyed those who reached out. If others snubbed him, he ignored them. From Andy I was learning how to create a neutral space with my family.

That night in bed, I reminded myself how lucky I was to have met this man. I'd been drawn to his mustache, and yet when it disappeared I hadn't even noticed. I sat up and asked, "When did you shave off your mustache?"

"That thing," he murmured sleepily. "Long time ago."

"Why did you shave it off?" I shook his shoulder. "I loved it."

"Are you joking?" he asked, opening his eyes. "That mustache made me look like a car salesman."

"Hey," I said, poking him in the chest. "My family is full of car salesmen."

"And your point is?"

I bit the inside of my mouth so he wouldn't see me laughing at his comment. Still, I had to admire his poker face.

On the eleventh anniversary of my father's death, Valentine's Day, I came home from one of my first days in private practice to find Andy boiling a lobster. He had turned down offers at universities in Brazil and Singapore so that he could move in with me in Arlington. He would open the employment pages of the *Chronicles of Higher Education* only to remember that he had a curry dish he needed to make. Recently he'd planted a magnet on the refrigerator with a picture of James Dean that said "Rebel without a Job."

This period of unemployment might have taken a toll on both of us except that we were having so much fun. We loved the same things: travel, music, art, swimming, films, books, and cooking, especially cooking for other people. In the fall, we'd rented a tandem to bike around the neighborhood. Then we tried rollerblades.

Occasionally a friend at the State Department would give Andy work as a contractor. Andy helped open libraries in Latvia and Kazakhstan. In Almaty, he was awarded an honorary doctorate and brought home a hand-woven carpet. The migraines he'd endured throughout his teaching career were gone, and I was sleeping better than ever. If Andy was troubled about his career during the day, by sundown he was boiling black beans to Afro-Cuban music.

I'd never met anyone so handy. He patched flat tires and unclogged drains. At this rate, I told myself, he might turn out to be the kind of man who would stay up all night to fix my broken leg.

There had to be a catch. We were two people who had previously and separately jammed ourselves into lives that required too much planning; together, we were now careering toward a place called Slapdash, only we were doing it with contented stomachs.

Along with a lobster dinner on that Valentine's Day, Andy presented me with a ring. He had already given me a garnet ring from Brazil, and now he slipped a sapphire onto my left hand. We had agreed that we wouldn't get married until he had a job, but he was letting me know that he was working toward a wedding band.

At two in the morning he shook me awake. "Let's go see Hale–Bopp," he said.

"Take a picture," I said. "I'm sleeping."

Soon we were gliding onto the G. W. Parkway, following the Potomac south in the Mazda 626 for which I'd traded my Miata. This sedan suited us better. When you are hurling toward Slapdash, it's best to have four doors and a few safety features.

Andy pulled into a parking lot by a monument to soldiers lost at sea. The nearest light came from across the river, the Jefferson Memorial. Above us was clear sky, stars visible. "This is the perfect spot," he said, climbing out of the car.

I opened the door and my nostrils burned from the cold air. "I'm freezing," I said. "I'll just watch from the car." Then I shut the door and fell asleep.

Andy scanned the heavens with binoculars. When he spotted the comet he tapped at the window, waking me up. "There it is!" he shouted.

"Where?"

He opened the door and pointed up at the sky.

"I don't see it," I said, climbing out.

After steadying my shoulders, he placed the binoculars in my hands. "Follow my finger," he said. Eventually I found a two-tailed fireball swimming across a navy sky speckled with starlight.

He tucked his arms around my waist and we took turns with the binoculars.

Back at the apartment, we threw off our coats and climbed into bed. I hadn't bothered to change from my pink and white flannel pajamas to go out, and I was ready for sleep. Andy had another idea.

"But it's that time of month," I said.

"Perfect. We won't need the diaphragm."

I can still feel myself there, in that moment, on my lopsided, antique bed. That I can remember this one-in-a-zillion of the times we've made love is no coincidence. I will never forget these four things: it all started on Valentine's Day; we were going to get married; we had just seen Hale–Bopp; and it was the only time in my life that I'd agreed to unprotected sex. Ever.

Six weeks after Hale–Bopp, I struggled to take it in: that a woman could get pregnant while in the middle of her period. Mom wasn't lying. Maybe we both ovulated twice a month. Why was it that the most absurd of her warnings often came true? She'd tell me on a September morning when I was already sweating in my Saint Vivian blazer, "You better put on a coat." And I'd say, "No way," as I pushed through the screen door to leave. Halfway to school, I'd be shivering.

When I told Mom my news about the baby, she said, "We Fanger gals have the heftiest uteruses in the world. Count on it! When are you getting married?"

We "eloped" to the Homestead in Warm Springs, Virginia, on Andy's birthday, a clear spring day in April. Redbuds bloomed in a forest of bare tree limbs with air sweetened by honeysuckle. I wore a twenties-style dress and walked a tulip-lined path to meet Andy and the local justice of the peace. We stood under an arbor of wisteria not yet in bloom.

For two days we celebrated in bliss. We had our first argument as a married couple while we walked the trails around a golf course and bantered over names for the baby. Here I discovered the curse of marrying a man with tastes nearly identical to mine. He is every bit the contrarian that I am: if I said Iris, he said Lily.

That night, we watched the Masters tournament at Sam Snead's Tavern. An older man came in and took the booth next to ours. "That's him," whispered Andy.

"Who?"

"Sam Snead."

We started a conversation with the golfer, who said he'd just flown in from Augusta. Our argument over Iris versus Lily was forgotten as we stared open-mouthed while Sam Snead watched Tiger Woods win his first Masters. Our food arrived, and we looked at our dinners as if we'd forgotten why we came. Then Andy said something that I would think back on again and again over the years, reminding myself of why I fell in love with him. As long as I've known him, he would look into the future and see a happy ending. He leaned toward me as we watched history unfolding on the television and said, "Can you believe it? We're witnessing the birth of a new era."

By May, each day greener than the last, we faced the genetics clinic at the George Washington University Hospital. In an exam room lit only by the flurry of white jackets and a sonogram screen, a physician made his way through about ten interns and medical students. My bladder swollen from the water I had to drink for the sonogram, I lay on my back, belly exposed to the crowd. I was less self-conscious than I was nervous about the results. What would we do if this baby had no legs or arms? What if Mom was telling the truth?

The doctor took my right hand to shake it, and just as quickly picked up my claw hand to study it. "This is very nice work on the plastic surgery," he said.

"I was a baby when most of it was done." My hand shook from the freezing temperature in the room, but the doctor squeezed it gently in his warm palm.

"Eileen, I trained in Germany and saw a lot of babies affected by thalidomide. Your hand is convincing, especially here, where there were once webs." He opened his palm and pointed to the spaces between my fingers, where thin braids of scar tissue remained as evidence of them. "I think you're going to finally have an answer. We'll send the results from the CVS soon. In the meantime, let's see what the sonogram shows us."

He nodded to the technician, who dabbed cold gel on my stomach before moving the wand over it. Andy stepped closer to rub my shoulder, and I leaned into him. There was a lot that I couldn't make out onscreen.

"I don't see it, do you?" I said, nudging Andy. "What are we supposed to see? Is there a baby in there?"

"Right here," said the technician, pointing to a fishlike form swimming back and forth, flipping and kicking.

"What was that?" I asked. "A foot?"

Andy wasn't talking. I looked up at his face. He was already in love with that baby goldfish. I could tell by his silence. This is where we are totally different. When falling in love, I tend to babble and quiver, whereas Andy freezes.

The technician zoomed in on the legs and arms, then hands. She counted the fingers. "All ten are there," she said. "And look at that," she pointed. "It's a foot. And that's the other." She wrote "FEET" on the screen and took a snapshot. "Your souvenir from the genetics clinic."

"I knew this would go well," said Andy in a hoarse whisper, while I swallowed my tears and silently thanked the universe.

As Andy faced fatherhood, he decided to abandon his search for a university teaching position. He cashed in his pride for a paycheck from a temp agency and was given a data entry job. I arrived home one evening ahead of him and found the letter from the genetics clinic in our mailbox. Despite every intention of waiting for Andy to come home, I stepped out of the elevator and ripped into the envelope, scrolling down the page in the hallway. It said there was no sign of any defective-genetic blah blah blah in our . . . baby girl. Girl? In my hand I held the news for which I'd been waiting more than thirty years. The torment was over. My baby would be fine. I was cheering out loud in the hallway.

By the time I made it into the apartment she already had a name: Ania Sophia. Andy was thrilled to hear the good news, and he quickly agreed to this name. From then on, the pregnancy became a humbling experience. We were supposed to go to Cincinnati to have a small party to celebrate our wedding. Mom put Liz in charge and Liz hired Colette to cater a dinner party. But the baby lodged herself right on my sciatic nerve. Pain riveted down my spine into my hip and leg. I had to crawl to the bathroom. The doctor said I couldn't fly or tolerate a long car ride. We had to miss our own party.

The situation resolved itself, and next my cervix began to dilate. Now the doctor ordered total bed rest. By then we'd bought a house. Andy had found a full-time technology job, his launching point for what would become a successful career in financial exchange.

Ania came two weeks early, at six pounds. She had an inch of black hair, monkey down all over her body, the strongest legs of any baby I'd ever held, and Frankie's almond eyes. "Caramela," she would be called by a Guatemalan boy from our neighborhood. I had just breastfed Ania for the first time when Andy fell asleep. Exhausted, I closed my eyes and started to sleep until I remembered the baby. She might fall out of the bed, or I might smother her. I tried to call for the nurse, but I couldn't find the button. When I sat up I found my bed drenched in blood. I screamed for Andy.

In seconds, a nurse was hooking me up to a monitor while Andy, holding Ania, backed away from an expanding crowd, his skin ashen. Ania peered down at me from his arms, attentive as a grandmother in a baby blanket. Already she seemed to know who we were and how we fit together. Above me a monitor read 73 over 37. I thought my eyes were inverting numbers. "Is that my blood pressure?" I asked the nurse to my right. "Am I going to die?" The nurse didn't answer. I closed my eyes.

I might have remembered that I'd once visited Heaven. I was about four when Rosa and Bridget blindfolded me and twirled me around before lifting me to Heaven. Actually, they took me through an opening from Rosa's closet to the attic. When they lifted my blindfold I faced Mary and Joseph, baby Jesus, and a few wise men, all of whom looked similar to my older sisters and cousins enrobed in blankets. The Virgin Mary, who looked like Bridget, held a baby who looked like Ted.

"Eileen, you are in Heaven," said a wise man in a voice similar to Rosa's.

Now I opened my eyes and watched a group of men and women in scrubs staring down at me, hands working, lips moving, and Ania's little face peeking down from over their shoulders. Andy swayed back and forth while he held her, already comfortable with the baby. One of the nurses called out for a drug. Someone else took off running, and seconds later the first one injected me. Everyone grew silent. My contractions slowed down, which brought the hemorrhaging to a stop. My blood pressure picked up. Frazzled energy gave way to relief. Someone rubbed my arm, assurance that I was still there. When I looked up, I found my family smiling down at me.

Epilogue

We take our seats near the orchestra to the right of the stage. Andy and I are at the Kennedy Center's annual presentation of *The Nutcracker*. Our twelve-year-old Ania is playing two roles as an extra with the Joffrey Ballet: a mouse and one of the boys in the party scene. She's less thrilled with her parts than she is with the idea of being in a production with her favorite male dancer, a principal who used to be with the Paris Opéra Ballet. She knows him from watching hours of dance online while practicing poses in her playroom, an attic-like space upstairs. That space is the heart of the house just as my parents' old screened-in porch was, except that Ania and I used it for tea parties rather than cocktail hour for priests. She always dressed in a pink cape, giving me the red velvet one. During those tea parties, I often wondered if she felt alone as our only child. If so, she has at least thirty cousins to make up for the lack. She is never happier than on a visit with her cousins. From my family alone she has six girls in her age range, and three cousins close in age on Andy's side.

As the lights dim, Andy and I reach for each other's hand. He's got that somber look on his face. Is he fighting tears? It's Thanksgiving weekend. Andy's father has recently died, and Andy has been missing him.

In my family situation, one critical change will soon come to pass: after tears and a painful argument, Mom will explain that a stewardess on a Scandinavian airline gave her a thalidomide pill on her flight to Germany. Finally we have a sense of calm in our relationship. We speak in softer voices. When my mother says my name I hear "Eileen," the name Mom chose before I was born because it was a good Irish name and it flowed so naturally from "Mary."

Here in the Kennedy Center, I'm fighting joyful tears as I think back to my dreams of being a ballerina. Sitting in the audience, watching my daughter dance, is even better than my childhood dream.

The orchestra begins the opening music, which leads to a family happily rushing to a Christmas party. Andy and I tighten our grip on each other's hand. At moments like these, it feels as though we are about to jump together from a high cliff into a pool of water. My stomach drops. Is Ania ready to be onstage, our shy daughter who has to be coaxed and prodded even to make a phone call? The first dancer steps onto the stage, and to our surprise it is Ania. She's tossing a gift box, playful and confident in an eighteenth-century boy's suit with a fez-shaped hat. This trickster character reveals a side of my daughter I have never seen before, and yet it makes perfect sense. There she is, our Ania, leading her family into the party.

Acknowledgments

This book could not have benefited more than from the open-minded, objective, and reflective editorial skills of Amy Cherry. Similarly, I am deeply grateful to Wendy Weil, the agent who put me in touch with Amy. Wendy's unexpected death is an enormous loss. Thank you to Paul Bresnick for helping to ease that transition and to my new agent, Emma Patterson, whose grace and wisdom made the completion of the book run smoothly; to Allegra Huston, for superior copyediting; and to Anna Mageras, for managing a million details. As always I am grateful to Andrew Lakritz for sharing his brilliant literary talents, among so many other gifts, and to Ania Lakritz for her patience. Thanks to Danielle Ofri, MD, for early instruction in the art of writing memoir and for the support from the *Bellevue Literary Review*. Thanks to Benee Knauer for her careful read and especially her insight into the families of children with disabilities. Many thanks to all of my writing group members over several years: Deborah Forbes, Sara Hov, Beatrice Edwards, Frank Morring, Sean Carman, and Anne Levy-Lavigne. Thank you also to my memoir workshop leaders at Bread Loaf and Squaw Valley, Jane Brox and Lynne Freed respectively. I am grateful to the Carlisle family's scholarship to the Squaw Valley Writers' Conference, to the Hall family for their dedication to the Squaw Valley

Community of Writers, to Wheels for Wheels for their scholarship to the Vermont Studio Center, and to the Vermont Studio Center for a fabulous retreat. Thank you to Alan Cheuse, in whose class I wrote the first scenes for this book. I thank Dr. Joshua Ellenhorn for his assistance with medical information. Thank you to Nell Favret Boyle for always being there. Thank you to my mother, and a thousand thanks to all of my siblings.

I am grateful to the following magazines for publishing versions of several chapters of this book: *Bellevue Literary Review*, *The Literary Review*, *Third Coast*, *Slice,* and *Narrative.*